The Archaeological Site at Easton Lane, Winchester

Hampshire Field Club and Archaeological Society: Monograph 6
General Editor: Kenneth E Qualmann

The Archaeological Site at Easton Lane, Winchester

by P J Fasham, D E Farwell and R J B Whinney
with a Preface by Dr G J Wainwright

contributions by

M J Allen, A Cameron, W J Carruthers, S M Davies, A B Ellison, P F Fisher,
C J Gingell, P A Harding, J W Hawkes, J D Henderson, J M Maltby, S Olsen
R Seager-Smith, S J Shennan and P Wilthew

illustrations by

D J Flower, S C Garrett, K Holt, S E James, G D March, K M Nichols and R C Read

cover illustration by

K M Nichols

Published by the Hampshire Field Club
in co-operation with the Trust for Wessex Archaeology

HAMPSHIRE FIELD CLUB MONOGRAPH 6
Published by the Hampshire Field Club and Archaeological Society.

This monograph is published with the aid of grants from the Historic Buildings and Monuments Commission (England), Hampshire County Council and Winchester City Council, which bodies deserve the grateful thanks of the authors and publishers. Crown copyright is reserved in respect of material in the volume resulting from central government expenditure.

Publication by the Hampshire Field Club does not imply that this body endorses the views expressed; the factual content and the opinions presented herein remain the responsibility of their authors.

ISBN 0–907473–06–7

Produced for the Society by
Alan Sutton Publishing, Gloucester
Printed in Great Britain

CONTENTS

LIST OF ILLUSTRATIONS
All photographs, Trust for Wessex Archaeology, except where otherwise indicated.

LIST OF TABLES

Preface

by Dr G J Wainwright

Archaeological investigation is a research activity and as such requires policies for the best use of archaeological resources, employing correctly identified academic priorities which are implemented within an appropriate methodological framework. Where the unavoidable destruction of archaeological sites is concerned, the objective is to preserve them through a record which ensures that the data is preserved for future generations as well as analysed and disseminated for scholars of today and the general public.

The extension of the M3 motorway south towards Winchester has been an example of publicly financed destruction of the man-made heritage along its route and the response to this challenge has been orchestrated by Pete Fasham and his colleagues for over a decade.

The results of their investigations have been published as a series of articles and monographs, as well as popular publications for the general public and the subject of this monograph is the investigation of the great interchange of roads which is sited north of Winchester at Easton Lane. The problem facing Mr Fasham and his team was how best to investigate an apparently empty tract of 15 hectares or more of featureless chalk downland which was then in arable cultivation and surrounded by archaeological sites and find-spots. The elegant solution was to devise a sampling strategy for 15 hectares which was based on a 10% sample by transect. This was followed by additional excavation where the sample trenches indicated that this was necessary. The value of this approach was amply demonstrated in the unsuspected chronological depth that was revealed – from the prehistoric to the historic periods.

Further the M3 project in general and Easton Lane in particular has provided a rare opportunity to investigate a large area of chalk landscape and to observe the development of human settlement through some 4000 years. This opportunity has been grasped firmly and with imagination by Mr Fasham. The Easton Lane excavation and his report on it vividly portrays the ebb and flow of the settlement and whets the appetite for the integrative account of the M3 project that is to follow.

Author's Note

I had always hoped that this report would be totally complete when published and that there would be no need for an author's note. However circumstances beyond our control mean that certain information has not yet reached us.

The nature of the archaeological evidence ensured that the internal site chronology could be established only by reliance on datable parallels for objects and feature types from external sources. This was supplemented by the use of distribution plans for broadly dated items – mainly pottery – across the site, whereby specific areas could be dated by reference to the dominant period find. The approach is discussed in the section on post-excavation methodology. It was intended to supplement these broad chronological suppositions with a series of radiocarbon dates from specific contexts. In August 1983 a request for fifteen radiocarbon determinations was submitted to the Ancient Monuments Laboratory of which, for reasons of economy, nine were approved. The nine were sent to Harwell in October 1983 and a tenth submitted via the Ancient Monuments Laboratory in March 1985. These dates were highly relevant to the report but so far only four certificates and two provisional results have been received. One sample is waiting for the small counter.

It proved impossible to receive guarantees of when the results would be available and the changes in personal circumstances of those involved in the production of this report, which was completed in 1987, led to the decision to publish without the complete list of radiocarbon dates. In order to maintain the momentum of the work and to ensure a reasonably rapid publication this decision, although regrettable, became unavoidable.

Two of the four samples for which certificates have been received have produced results at odds with the perceived chronologies. The most obvious is HAR 6122 of 2740±70bp from a Bronze Age inhumation with an amber necklace. In a Wessex context this determination is perhaps 500 years too late. A second sample from that inhumation is being measured. Similarly the associations we perceived for the date of HAR 6123 were about half a millennium earlier than the results. It is difficult to fully assess how many of the samples are producing or will produce later than expected dates.

All three authors felt the necessity to make a statement of their reasons for publishing their report without the full list of radiocarbon dates. Interestingly, if the man-months spent on post-excavation and writing had been continuous from the end of the excavation then the report would have been completed before any radiocarbon determinations were received. I take the opportunity at the foot of this page to publish a further radiocarbon date from Winnall Down. A full list of the radiocarbon dates from the entire M3 project will be published in the review of the project which will be published as another monograph in this series.

The excavation, starting as a genuine sampling procedure, was a very invigorating exercise for all involved although the area of the site investigated produced problems in post-excavation. Therefore, on a happier note, Richard Whinney and I would like to express our gratitude to Dave Farwell for his patient and painstaking contribution to the post-excavation process and this report.

P J Fasham
June 1988
Bangor

Winnall Down
Further radiocarbon date.

HAR 2651, 2440±100bp, 490±100bc, was on animal bone from the primary silt of the main enclosure ditch and associated with haematite coated pottery.
This date should be compared with HAR 2653, 2560±80bp and HAR 2251, 2540±90bp from the same ditch (Fasham 1985, 18).

Acknowledgements

The Easton Lane project was a complex exercise and the results published in this volume have been achieved only by a considerable effort by many people and organisations.

In the first instance, the assistance of the Department of Transport through its consulting engineers Mott, Hay and Anderson, led to the purchase and fencing of the site some nine months before the road was built. This contribution to the entire operation is greatly appreciated.

The faith of the Department of the Environment's Directorate of Ancient Monuments and Historic Buildings through its staff, especially Dr G J Wainwright, Mr S Dunmore and Mr P Gosling in the initial project design, its funding of the sampling programme and its rapid support at the crucial time when the scheme needed to be enlarged are warmly acknowledged. Winchester City Council through its Archaeology section, provided both office and living accommodation for the project team in addition to one of the co-directors, and a handsome contribution to the enlarged scheme. Hampshire County Council also supported the larger scheme.

The excavation was directed by Peter Fasham and Richard Whinney, assisted by John Hawkes, and post-excavation by Peter Fasham with David Farwell. Excavation supervision was by Wayne Cocroft, Chris Hudson and Royston Clarke, aided by various members of the hard-working excavation team.

We thank all specialists for their contributions. The illustrations and photographs were prepared by staff of the Trust for Wessex Archaeology.

We are grateful for the comments, observations and advice about various aspects of the project to Richard Bradley, David Hinton, Ian Kinnes, Arthur ApSimon, Tim Champion, Ann Ellison and Geoff Wainwright. Richard Bradley, Geoff Wainwright and Andrew Lawson have all commented on the text, but the authors remain responsible for any errors and omissions.

Mr Allen wishes to thank Dr M G Bell for checking the identification of the Helicellids and Mr G J Oulton for extracting the Mollusca from pit 1017. Mr P Harding wishes to express his thanks to Richard Bradley and Claire Halpin for providing useful information, much of it in advance of publication.

Abstract

Archaeological evaluation and large-scale excavation at Easton Lane in 1982 and 1983, adjacent to the previously excavated site of Winnall Down, uncovered a wealth of material with dates ranging from the middle of the fourth millennium BC up to the early Medieval period. Traces of dispersed settlements and land divisions, more commonly met as isolated features, were followed in plan.

The remains included a Neolithic structure, a burial with grave goods and conical pits, Early Bronze Age cemeteries, a substantial Middle Bronze Age settlement and ditch system, an Early Middle Iron Age open settlement which complements the Early Iron Age and Middle Iron Age occupation phases recorded at Winnall Down, Romano-British burials and enclosures and an enigmatic Saxon ditched enclosure.

The archive is housed at the Hampshire County Museum Service.

Chapter 1

Introduction

The Background

In 1976/77 the excavation of a prehistoric occupation site took place at Winnall Down on the east side of Winchester (Fasham 1985). The area excavated was located to the east of the Easton Lane Interchange, now Junction 9 on the M3 motorway (Biddle and Emery 1973). The results of the excavation at Winnall Down can be summarised as follows:

1. Neolithic circular feature of the fourth millennium BC;
2. Later Bronze Age occupation with post-built circular and other structures;
3. Early Iron Age enclosed settlement of sixth and fifth century BC date. Internal zoning for different activities was suggested;
4. An open settlement with separation of circular buildings from areas of pits;
5. An arrangement of conjoined enclosures linked with a ditched track of Late Iron Age origin and lasting into the second century AD;
6. Traces of Medieval field ditches.

Problems raised by the 1976/77 excavations included whether the western limits of the Late Bronze Age and the unenclosed Middle Iron Age settlements had been discovered and how far to the south the Roman enclosures extended.

By 1981 it was certain that the motorway was going to be built and that construction of Junction 9 would involve the excavation and redistribution of at least 50,000 tonnes of chalk over an area of about 15 hectares (37 acres). The area of the Interchange had been walked as part of the preliminary survey of the route of the motorway and a few casual finds, mainly of Medieval date, were collected in 1974. A geophysical scan of the area had revealed no significant anomalies. The lack of magnetic response is not too surprising when the slightness of the archaeological remains is taken into consideration. The farmer was reluctant to allow fieldwalking to take place and thus the amount of pre-excavation investigation was limited. Aerial photography provided the most information about the field in revealing the enclosures of Winnall Down. The only crop or soil mark between Winnall Down and the then Winchester By-Pass, the A33, was a single linear ditch running north-south along the long axis of the Interchange (Fig 1, site 5). Twenty-five archaeological sites and features of most periods surrounded the site (Fig 1).

A costed project design for a sequential excavation strategy based on a sampling programme was submitted to and approved by the Directorate of Ancient Monuments and Historic Buildings of the Department of the Environment. The land was purchased by the Department of Transport approximately nine months before construction work began, so as to enable the archaeological investigation to take place. Fieldwork commenced in July 1982 and was directed by Peter Fasham of the Trust for Wessex Archaeology and Richard Whinney of Winchester City Council, who were assisted initially by John Hawkes of the Trust for Wessex Archaeology. Most of the post-excavation work has been compiled by David Farwell under the supervision of Peter Fasham. The illustrations have been prepared by the Trust for Wessex Archaeology.

The Project Design

The broad but brief project design as submitted to the Department of the Environment is in microfiche; the precise details of the excavation design were formulated after approval was given for the project. The following section is an expanded version of the design which helps to place the site in a broader context.

The main problem for the project design was how best to tackle an apparently empty tract of chalkland which was surrounded by archaeological sites. The area of the Easton Lane Interchange stood as an island with almost no known archaeology in a sea of archaeological sites and findspots. The 25 locations shown on Fig 1 are all within 1300m of the site, the majority being much closer. This excludes sites of all periods from within the Roman, Saxon and Medieval walls of Winchester.

Of all the sites shown on Fig 1, Winnall Down (sites 1 and 2) with its long sequence of activity primarily in the last millennium BC is the most relevant (Fasham 1985). The linear ditch (site 5) running north-south along the site has already been mentioned. Immediately to the east are another 'D'-shaped enclosure (site 3) similar to Winnall Down and an arrangement of one hexagonal enclosure within another (site 4). A scatter of Medieval

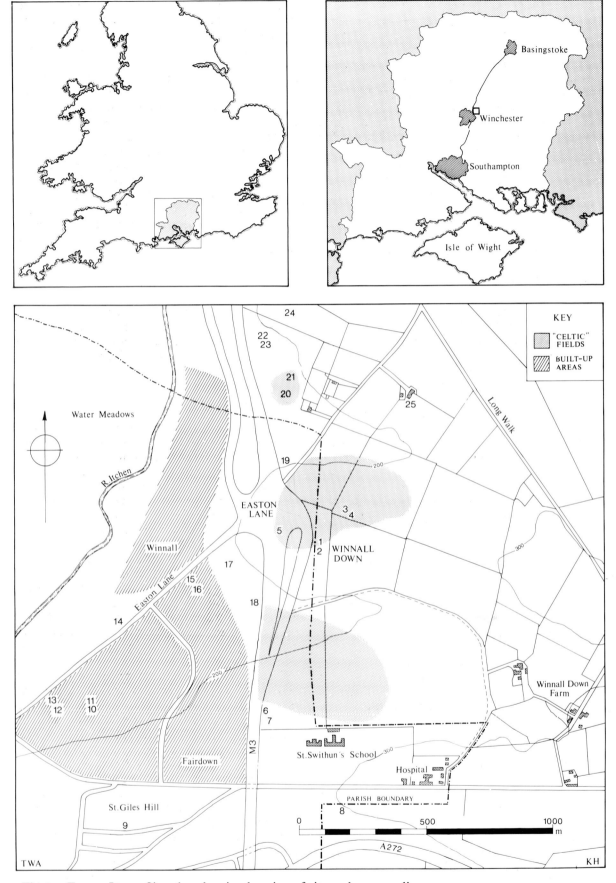

Fig 1.   Easton Lane. Site plan showing location of site and surrounding area.

pottery has been recorded about 100m south of the Interchange (site 18). Adjacent to St Swithun's School, to the south, aerial photographs revealed a ring ditch (site 6), and a possible linear ditch (site 7). These were examined as part of the subsequent watching brief when the motorway was constructed. There was no burial within the ring ditch but a few sherds of pottery of a fabric similar to local Bronze Age pottery were found in the ditch (Fasham and Whinney forthcoming). Less than half a kilometre to the southeast are three surviving round barrows (site 8). A number of Iron Age and Roman features and enclosures (sites 10–13) were recorded from 1955 onwards as the Winnall housing estate was being built (Collis 1978).

Until recently the best known parts of the archaeology of the Winnall area were two Anglo-Saxon cemeteries: Winnall I (site 14), a pagan cemetery of the sixth century; and Winnall II (site 15), interpreted as of later date and Christian (Meaney and Hawkes 1970). At least one Anglo-Saxon burial is known from St Giles' Hill (site 9). During the excavation of the Winnall II cemetery, pits were discovered containing sherds of Bronze Age globular urns, more mundane Bronze Age pots and fragments of quernstones (site 16, Hawkes 1969). Between the Bronze Age pits and the Interchange, on the east of the By-Pass, a possible ring-ditch had been identified on aerial photographs (site 17). No trace of this feature was discovered during the watching brief so it must have been contained within the topsoil (Bowen 1975). Careful examination of topsoil was not possible in the pressing circumstances of access to the site where immediate subsoil disturbance occurred. The area concerned had been used for various activities in the recent past and it is quite possible that the mark seen on the aerial photographs was not of archaeological origin.

North of the site was a ploughed-out round barrow (site 22), almost certainly a Bell barrow, with a Wessex style cremation in the centre (Fasham 1982) and several pits containing very early Iron Age pottery (site 23). Iron Age pottery is recorded as having been found about 100m northeast of the ring-ditch (site 24). Between the ring-ditch and the Interchange a geophysical anomaly (site 20) had been recorded by Mr Clarke of the Ancient Monuments Laboratory (Clarke 1975) and one sherd of possible Iron Age pottery had been discovered from almost the same location (site 21). In the northeast sector, a track of uncertain date was visible on aerial photographs (site 19). An oval mark has been seen (by PJF) from the air about 500m northeast of the Interchange (site 25).

The Interchange therefore was an area of 15 hectares of more or less featureless arable land with sites and findspots all around. It seemed unlikely that such a large area could be devoid of all archaeology apart from the linear ditch. The surrounding archaeology suggested several different elements that might be examined:

1. The presence of any further Neolithic features;

2. The western extent of both the later Bronze Age and the Middle Iron Age features excavated at Winnall Down;
3. The southern extent of the Roman enclosures recorded at Winnall Down;
4. Traces of the Celtic field system in the area;
5. The Interchange seemed to possess the right topographic qualities to be the location of an Anglo-Saxon settlement, which might have been related to the two Anglo-Saxon cemeteries of Winnall. The sites at Chalton (Addyman and Leigh 1973) and Cowdrey's Down (Millet 1980) were on the crest of ridges. In 1986 two rectangular post-built structures of Middle Saxon date were discovered at St Martin's Close in Winchester, about 1.2km away from the site. These were either part of a suburb of Winchester or, more likely, a seperate rural settlement (Morris 1986).

The Excavation Design

The excavation design incorporated three successive stages of response, each dependent on the preceeding stage, with an initial programme designed to last for eight weeks and exhaust the available budget.

Stage One

In the absence of a corpus of practical sampling experiences of settlement sites on the chalk of England, it was decided that a 10% sample was the minimum area that could be investigated to determine whether a second stage of work was necessary. The project design and associated costings were therefore based on an initial 10% sample. Practical reasons dictated the use of transects. A 10% sample involved the removal of the topsoil from 1.5 hectares ($3\frac{3}{4}$ acres), a large operation in its own right. This would have to be done by machine and the most cost effective machine for cleaning an area of that size is the Box Scraper. Thus it was decided to use transects rather than quadrants, as this provided the maximum exposure of the chalk surface within the confines of both the original estimate and the final budget.

The transects were to be cut across the main north-south axis of the Interchange. The area of the road junction included slip roads, a roundabout and major carriageways of varying widths and thus the area was divided into five zones, I-V, of comparable widths and the transects selected from each zone, Fig 2. The transects were 2.–2.5m wide and were selected within each zone on a random number basis. The slip road to the east of the Interchange, zone II (Area H), was not available when the rest of the land was acquired. Although it had been included in the initial sampling design and transect selection, it proved easier to completely strip it in one single operation when it became available.

The excavation commenced on 2nd August 1982 and the machine clearance of the thirty transects took about one and a half weeks.

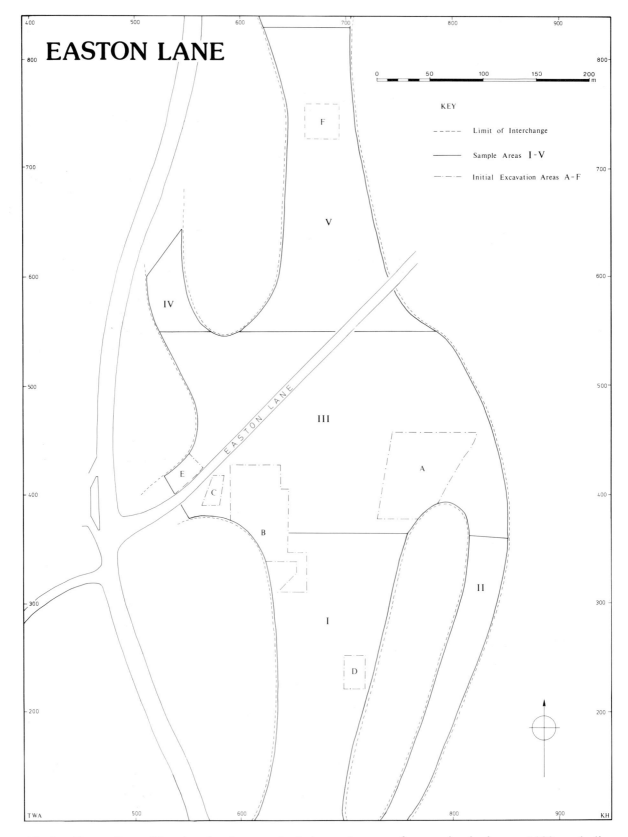

Fig 2.   Easton Lane. Site plan showing sample design and extent of excavation in August 1982, excluding the transects.

Fig 3. Easton Lane. Area D from the south; initial machine strip as in August 1982 (see Fig 4).

Stage Two

Where archaeological features were identified in Stage One, they were quickly evaluated in terms of their date, nature and, by implication, their significance. Decisions were then taken to clear Areas A and B with the D6 and Box before it went off hire. This clearance was completed within two weeks of the start of the excavation. The decision to open Areas A and B immediately was based on the extent and number of Iron Age features revealed in Area A and their relationship to the established aims of the project, and in Area B, evidence of Early Bronze Age activity. From week two to week four, excavation of Areas A and B proceeded alongside continuing assessment of other transects. In week five, a Hymac cleared further areas including more of the Bronze Age area at B and the adjoining area at C. An area where there appeared to be a concentration of postholes of uncertain date was also opened, Area D. Two small areas north of Easton Lane were cleared: Area E to see how far west the Bronze Age features in Areas B and C extended; and Area F to investigate the context of a Bronze Age cremation. By the beginning of week six, with 9,200m² (2¼ acres) open, it was possible to state that there was Iron Age activity in Area A, that houses, ditches and pits of probable Bronze Age date had been revealed (but not excavated) in Areas B, C and E, that a Bronze Age cemetery associated with post-hole structures existed in Area D and that Bronze Age features existed in Area F. It was possible to suggest, erroneously as it proved, that there might be a substantial structure of prehistoric date in the south of Area B. The site was clearly of some importance and it was obvious that not all the features revealed could be excavated

within the remaining two weeks and budget. This led to the submission of a report to the Department of Environment outlining the need for Stage Three.

Stage Three

The report that was submitted to the Department of the Environment contained the following proposals:

The maximum response to adequately investigate and record this important archaeological site is to strip the 2 hectares of field between Areas A, B and D and also, to a certain extent, to the south of D. This would take about an extra 12 weeks and cost £20,252.

The minimum response to fully excavate and record what is now exposed and to uncover and excavate all the complex timber structures adjacent to the Early/Middle Bronze Age mixed cemetery would cost £6,854 and take an extra five weeks of excavation. Details of costing for both options are appended.

Motorway construction is now scheduled to start in the New Year and the site will be totally destroyed by the construction of the Interchange. The archaeological remains are slight and it would be impossible to record them during construction. The maximum response suggested is the only way in which the academic importance of the site can be properly fulfilled. The minimum response, while achieving a basic record, does represent a compromise of academic and archaeological principles in relation to what may be one of the most important Bronze Age sites ever excavated under modern conditions in England.

These proposals were prepared on 6th September and submitted to the Department of Environment on 9th September. The excavation was scheduled to stop on 24th September if no further funds were forthcoming. As volunteer recruitment had not been quite as high as planned, there was a small balance of money that enabled the team to be kept in the field beyond 24th September 1982.

By the 28th of September a package had been

verbally agreed with the Department of the Environment that would enable the maximum response to be pursued. The agreement was as follows, in addition to the original grant of £14,746.

Wessex Archaeological Committee savings on other current projects	£6,550
Wessex Archaeological Committee interest on DoE funds	£1,853
Additional DoE grant	£8,500
Total	£16,903

In addition Hampshire County Council responded immediately with a grant of £500 later followed by a further £1,750. Winchester District Council approved a £2,000 grant. Great credit is due to all those who were able to respond so positively and quickly and raise the £21,153. Later in the financial year Winchester District generously granted another £2,000 towards the cost of the project.

Following the confirmation of funding, it was intended to complete the topsoil strip and the excavation by Christmas 1982. The topsoil strip was to include the zone between Areas A and C and south of the linear ditch which joined them to about 50m south of Area D. The sample transects north of this ditch had revealed no archaeological features of significance. Area F was to be enlarged and Area H, which had not been available at the start, was to be stripped. A geophysical survey was to be carried out around Area G to see if there were further archaeological features. A self-elevating motorised scraper was the only machine available on the market at the time, but wet conditions, after a small amount had been stripped, meant that it would not function properly. It was replaced by a Hymac dumping into a combination of Shawnee-pull and Volvo dump truck, but this was clearly not cost-effective. Area H had still not been made available. It was decided therefore to close the excavation down at the end of November and to restart in mid-February when it was possible to proceed with the topsoil strip. Including the transects, an area of 5 hectares (12½ acres) was excavated. The site was handed over to the Department of Transport on the agreed date of 1st April 1983.

The Watching Brief

The small triangle of land immediately south of Area B was not available during the main excavation and nor were the areas between the Interchange and the A33, on both sides of Easton Lane, as they were in private ownership. Access to these two areas was acquired by the contractor and various sub-contractors for offices and temporary accomodation. Arrangements were made by the consulting enginers, Mott, Hay and Anderson, for archaeological work following a contractor's clearance of overburden. In parts of these areas a sufficient period of time accrued between clearance and the start of groundworks for a controlled watching brief to take place. In effect this meant that all visible features could be planned and partly excavated. Elsewhere the clearance was of limited value or there was no time available for archaeological interpretation. These areas are indicated in Fig 4 as salvage work. The area south of Easton Lane was designated Mowlems Compound (Mc) and that to the north as Blackwell's Compound (Bc). This work involved the observation and recording of five hectares (12½ acres) in a 3–4 week period in May 1983 by a team of five.

Excavation Method and Recording

The development of the excavation, watching brief and salvage work has been presented in some detail as it demonstrates the logical outcome of the sampling strategy and gives an opportunity to assess the approaches adopted and by implication the quality of the total record from the different forms of work.

The method of excavation following topsoil clearance was straightforward. The surface of the chalk was usually cleaned and all visible features planned at 1:50. Most features were half-sectioned (at least) and the sections were recorded at 1:10. A higher priority was given to features of Neolithic and Bronze Age date to those of the Iron Age. All post-holes and pits of the earlier periods were completely excavated, often sieved and extensively sampled for flotation. In the Iron Age area it was decided to only half-section pits and to half-section no more than 50% of the post-holes. The additional data likely to be retrieved by complete excavation of all post-holes was not thought substantial enough to aid interpretation of the site. In Area B a large number of natural features (? tree-holes) were planned and partly excavated. It was decided at the outset that 10% was the minimum sample to be excavated from ditches, but in many areas of archaeological sensitivity the minimum was greatly exceeded. Indeed in Area D, 50% of one ditch was excavated. In all, a length of 1,330m of ditch was recorded in plan, of which an average of 13.68% was excavated. This included 450m, of ditch in the watching briefs where only a minimal sample was possible (lowest recorded 2.86%)

Of the 5,195 context numbers allocated, 261 were used to record the ditches. There were 216 pits, of which 144 were unphased and many of which may have been natural, 1,415 post-holes, 186 other features and at least 200 natural features.

It is not possible to produce figures for totals of records and samples by features compatible with those produced in Table 1 of the Winnall Down report (Fasham 1985), as the same level of access to computer facilities was no longer possible. It is quite interesting to note that 11,278 contexts were recorded from the 1.26 hectares (3¼ acres) of Winnall Down, compared to 5,195 contexts from 10 hectares (25 acres) on the Interchange.

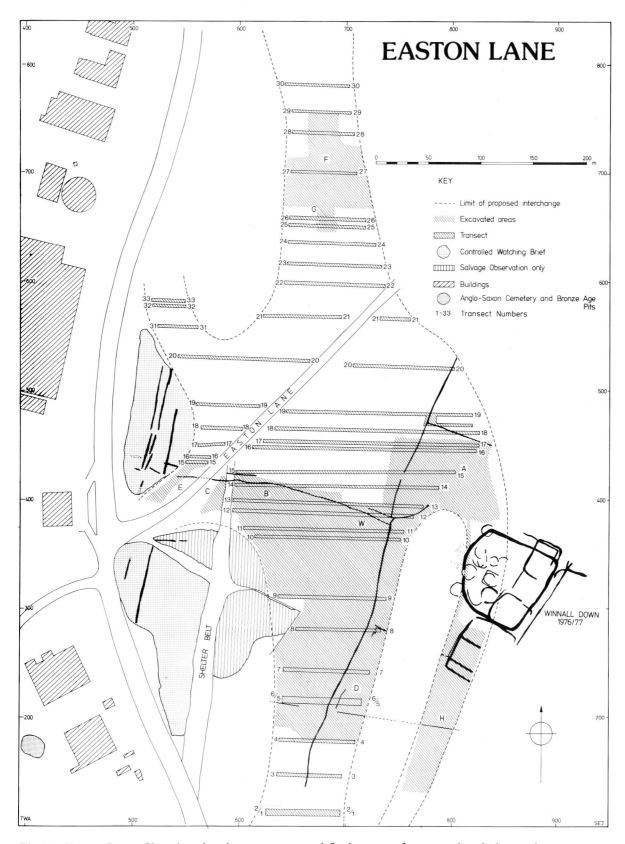

Fig 4. Easton Lane. Site plan showing transects, and final extent of excavated and observed areas.

Fig 5. Easton Lane. Aerial view of the site with Winnall Trading Estate. Winchester City Council.

Post-Excavation Methods

In accordance with Prof Cunliffe's report on publication (DoE 1975), a research design for post-excavation recommending only a basic level of work was prepared in March 1984 and submitted to the Department of the Environment/English Heritage. Although the first two sections are summaries of material included elsewhere in this report, the full statement is included below.

1.   Introduction
    a)   Extensive excavation of about 5 hectares (12½ acres) followed a successful sample excavation. Burial and settlement remains, ditch systems *etc* were found dating to the Late Neolithic, the Bronze Age, Iron Age, Roman and Medieval periods.
    b)   Subsequent work during the M3 Watching Brief revealed further prehistoric and Roman features over an additional 4.75ha (12 acres) of site known as Blackwell's Compound and Mowlem's Compound. This material is to be incorporated into the project.
    c)   The site is adjacent to the Winnall Down excavations of 1976–7, a report on which was completed in early 1980 by P J Fasham. The Hampshire Field Club have now agreed to publish that report. It will not be amended in light of the recent excavations, therefore the Easton Lane project and publication will have to include pertinent revisions of parts of Winnall Down.

2.   Report Digest
    The site involved the excavation of a number of unusual features relating to prehistoric funerary and settlement remains, which included a proportion of Iron Age material not covered by the Winnall Down excavation. The artefacts associated with the later Neolithic and Bronze Age remains do not constitute a great volume although the features covered a large area. It is thus proposed that these elements be published in full, that the Iron Age data be treated summarily, allowing for integration with Winnall Down, and that the Roman and Medieval components be similarly treated.

3.   Primary Processing and Research
    All classes of data will be incorporated into the Winchester City Council computer facility into which data base the field records have already been translated.
    a)   Produce on computer full context catalogues of all related finds and environmental attributes.

    b)   Produce from a) phased context catalogues and relevant mapping.
    c)   Analysis of flint artefacts for cultural affinities and explanation of unusual relationships with other artefact types; input to computer.
    d)   Detailed fabric and form analysis of all ceramics to be related to previous records from Winnall Down; input to computer.
    e)   Analysis of non-ceramic material remains and input to computer.
    f)   Organisation of faunal remains programme once phasing attributes are finally determined.
    g)   Organisation and distribution to specialists of floral samples and further radio-carbon, molluscan and pedological samples as relevant.
    h)   Intra-site analysis of structural forms both contemporary and diachronic.
    i)   Intra-site analysis of all artefact types to determine criteria for establishing variable functional activity areas across the entire 15 hectare site. Both contemporary and diachronic aspects will have to be considered.

4.   Archive
    Items 3a-3i should create the full archive for the site.

5.   Secondary Research
    In parallel with 3c–3e, re-evaluate by same methods the prehistoric finds from the Winnall II Anglo-Saxon cemetery and other finds in the area of the Winnall trading and housing estates which adjoin the western limits of the excavated zone.

6.   Ancillary Research
    At this stage, it is not believed that further detailed ancillary research is needed apart from the obvious consideration, within both the archive and the level 4 texts, of sites of similar date and nature.

7.   Publication
    It is too early to make firm recommendations for publication, but a monograph in the Hants Field Club series to supplement Winnall Down seems the logical choice once detailed proposals can be formulated.

The deviation of the actual post-excavation programme from the stated objectives needs to be noted. The most obvious and critical component was the absence of the computer facility. Although a partially-cleaned field record data-base was established on the Winchester City Council Archaeology section microcomputer, it was never developed as had been hoped. The main problems were access to the heavily-subscribed yet still developing Winchester system and the physical separation of the computer facility in Winchester from the workbase in Salisbury. Had the Winchester software been fully developed it would probably have been worth making suitable arrangements for data capture in Salisbury and moving it to Winchester. There was no suitable computing facility available in Salisbury and thus, at an early stage, it was decided to do the work manually. This decision was taken with considerable reluctance after experiences of writing up M3 sites with computer assistance (Fasham and Hawkes 1980). In fact, the manual integration of the finds and structural evidence was not the onerous task it might have been, although the analysis and distribution of the ceramics would have been aided by machine-based procedures.

The intra-site analyses of structure and artefacts (points 3h and 3i in the post-excavation design) were completed on 1:200 scale plans. The distribution of diagnostic artefacts became crucial in the arguments and debates about the internal site chronology and phasing. An abbreviated context record was compiled on a word processor basis, post-hole structures were planned on separate sheets, and plots produced of the dimensions of post-hole diameters and depths, which occasionally helped to resolve the allocation of specific post-holes to structures. One of the main thrusts of the initial post-excavation programme was consideration of the graphic presentation of widely-dispersed data from a large area while staying within both the traditional bounds of 'archaeological style' and the likely restrictions, for financial reasons, of the number of pull-outs or large drawings in the volume. It is hoped that the attempt to standardise published plan scales facilitates the reader's orientation. In general, large area plans are at a scale of c 1:500, details of the Neolithic and/or Bronze Age structures are at 1:100 and, in accordance with the post-excavation research design, the Iron Age structures are dealt with at a scale of 1:200. It was a futile exercise with the Iron Age post-holes to attempt to define structures, because there already seemed to be discrete clusterings of post-holes. These were assumed to indicate considerable rebuilding of structure upon structure. Individual patterns within these clusters were not readily detectable, unlike Winnall Down. In both text and illustration the context numbers assigned during the excavation to features and structures are retained, in the case of structures a prefix has been added, eg CS, LS, MS or RS to distinguish circular, linear, miscellaneous and rectangular structures respectively. The matters outlined above were the main areas of concern tackled in dealing with the Primary Processing and Research. The steps taken obviously led to the creation of a paper archive.

On a stratified site, the phasing sequence is constructed by establishing the relationship between structures, floors and other stratigraphically associated contexts. Residual and intrusive sherds of pottery or other artefacts can be discerned and evaluated on the basis of wear, relative proportions and stratigraphic security. This involves certain subjective processes. The associated context groups are then dated by their related artefact groups.

At Easton Lane there was no stratigraphic sequence and most of the features contained few, if any, finds. The artefactual dating evidence has therefore been considered in terms of distribution patterns, and the phased sequence owes more to the excavation and post-excavation interpretation of feature types and groups related to a broad artefactual pattern.

Iron Age and Roman pottery had a restricted distribution and the negative evidence of its absence is of importance in considering the distribution of earlier material. Quite often groups of features and post-holes are dated by the absence of later material and by the presence of sometimes just a very few sherds. Large areas of the site have been phased in this manner, the assumption being that it is more useful and reasonable to place undated features in phase groups covered by the pottery distribution. Most of the Bronze Age areas of the site are dated in this manner. The pottery distributions are shown on the relevant phase plans where the discrete nature of the prehistoric distributions is manifest. There is a wider spread of Medieval pottery, which is presumed to be intrusive from the spreading of night soils from Winchester. A sherd of Medieval pottery and fragments of slate were intrusive in pit 1700 which contained an inurned Bronze Age cremation. The evidence for the Medieval period may be understated.

In view of the observations relating to Medieval ceramics it was decided to assess the relative effect of interpretation on feature type, phase and area. As this was to be a working guide to the internal security of the phasing, based on the preliminary pottery data and for use during the post-excavation process, a swift comparative method which lent itself to simple graphic representation was preferred to a more rigorous, statistically valid test.

The data was ordered in two ways. In the first, occurrence of phase (1–10) was checked against the main Areas (A-H). Phase occurrence was gauged firstly by the incidence of contexts with datable pottery (Table 1) and then by the incidence of features sorted to phase by reference to that pottery (Table 2). Any significant changes could then be noted when considering the security of specific areas and/or phases (see also Fig 6).

The second way involved cross-checking the main

Table 1. Context incidence of datable pottery by Area.

Area Phase	A No	%	B No	%	C No	%	D No	%	E No	%	F No	%	G No	%	H No	%	Bc No	%	Mc No	%
1	3	1.78	5	7.58	0	–	1	1.72	0	–	0	–	3	7.50	0	–	0	–	0	–
2	3	1.78	10	15.15	0	–	1	1.72	0	–	0	–	6	15.00	0	–	0	–	3	30.00
3	4	2.37	9	13.64	0	–	4	6.90	0	–	3	12.50	2	5.00	0	–	0	–	1	10.00
4	18	10.65	20	30.30	0	–	22	37.93	1	25.00	0	–	3	7.50	1	3.03	1	33.33	1	10.00
5	12	7.10	4	6.06	0	–	1	1.72	0	–	0	–	6	15.00	0	–	0	–	2	20.00
6	37	21.89	2	3.03	0	–	4	6.90	1	25.00	0	–	0	–	1	3.03	0	–	0	–
7	45	26.63	0	–	0	–	0	–	0	–	0	–	0	–	0	–	0	–	0	–
8	37	21.89	1	1.52	0	–	1	1.72	0	–	0	–	0	–	3	9.09	0	–	0	–
9	1	0.59	0	–	0	–	0	–	0	–	2	8.33	0	–	19	57.58	0	–	0	–
10	9	5.33	15	22.73	2	100	24	41.38	2	50.00	19	79.17	20	50.00	9	27.27	2	66.66	3	30.00
	169		66		2		58		4		24		40		33		3		10	

EASTON LANE

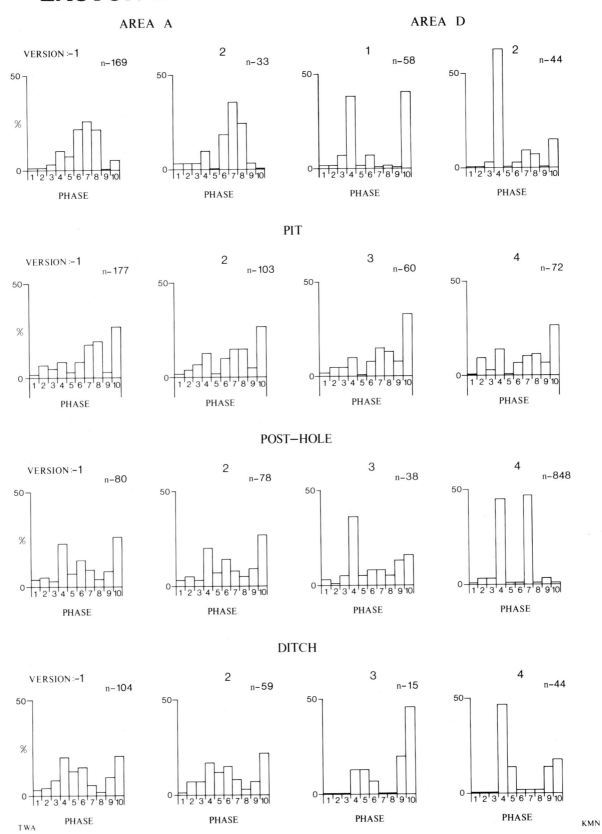

Fig 6.   Easton Lane. Post excavation phasing bar charts, showing the evolution of fully-phased features from the occurrence of datable pottery in Areas A and D, and for feature types – pits, post-holes and ditches.

Table 2. Feature incidence of datable pottery by Area.

Area Phase	A No	%	B No	%	C No	%	D No	%	E No	%	F No	%	G No	%	H No	%	Bc No	%	Mc No	%
1	1	3.03	0	–	0	–	0	–	0	–	0	–	0	–	0	–	0	–	0	–
2	1	3.03	3	15.79	0	–	0	–	0	–	0	–	?	?	0	–	0	–	0	–
3	1	3.03	1	5.26	0	–	1	2.27	0	–	2	16.67	0	–	0	–	0	–	1	14.29
4	3	9.09	7	36.82	0	–	28	63.64	0	–	0	–	0	–	3	11.11	2	66.66	1	14.29
5	0	–	1	5.26	0	–	0	–	1	33.33	0	–	0	–	0	–	1	33.33	2	28.57
6	6	18.18	1	5.26	0	–	1	2.27	1	33.33	0	–	0	–	0	–	0	–	0	–
7	12	36.36	0	–	0	–	4	9.09	0	–	0	–	0	–	0	–	0	–	0	–
8	8	24.24	0	–	0	–	3	6.82	0	–	0	–	0	–	1	3.70	0	–	0	–
9	1	3.03	0	–	0	–	0	–	0	–	0	–	0	–	17	62.96	0	–	0	–
10	0	–	6	31.58	2	100	7	15.91	1	33.33	10	83.33	?	?	6	22.22	0	–	3	49.86
	33		19		2		44		3		12		?		27		3		7	

Table 3. Incidence of contexts with datable pottery by feature type. Ph = post-hole.

Phase	Ph No	%	Pit No	%	Ditch No	%	Gully No	%
1	3	3.75	4	2.26	3	2.88	1	5.26
2	4	5.00	12	6.78	4	3.85	0	–
3	2	2.50	10	5.65	8	7.69	0	–
4	18	22.50	15	8.17	21	20.19	2	10.53
5	5	6.25	5	2.82	13	12.50	2	10.53
6	11	13.75	14	7.91	15	14.42	6	31.58
7	7	8.75	30	16.95	6	5.77	4	21.05
8	3	3.75	34	19.21	2	1.92	1	5.26
9	6	7.50	5	2.82	10	9.62	1	5.26
10	21	26.25	48	27.12	22	21.15	2	10.53
	80		177		104		19	

Table 4. Incidence of features with datable pottery by feature type. Ph = post-hole.

Phase	Ph No	%	Pit No	%	Ditch No	%	Gully No	%
1	2	2.56	2	1.94	1	1.70	0	–
2	4	5.13	4	3.88	4	6.78	0	–
3	2	2.56	7	6.80	4	6.78	0	–
4	16	20.51	13	12.62	10	16.95	2	18.18
5	5	6.41	2	1.94	7	11.86	1	9.09
6	11	14.10	10	9.71	9	15.25	4	36.36
7	6	7.69	16	15.53	5	8.47	2	18.18
8	4	5.13	16	15.53	2	3.39	1	9.09
9	7	8.97	5	4.85	4	6.78	0	–
10	21	26.92	28	27.18	13	22.03	1	9.09
	78		103		59		11	

Table 5. Incidence of features directly phased by pottery by feature type. Ph = post-hole.

Phase	Ph No	%	Pit No	%	Ditch No	%	Gully No	%
1	1	2.63	1	1.66	0	–	0	–
2	0	–	3	5.00	0	–	0	–
3	2	5.26	3	5.00	0	–	0	–
4	14	36.84	6	10.00	2	13.33	1	50.00
5	2	5.26	0	–	2	13.33	0	–
6	3	7.89	5	8.33	1	6.66	0	–
7	3	7.89	9	15.00	0	–	1	50.00
8	2	5.26	8	13.33	0	–	0	–
9	5	13.16	5	8.33	3	2.00	0	–
10	6	15.79	20	33.33	7	46.66	0	–
	38		60		15		2	

Table 6. Incidence of features directly phased and phased by association by feature type. Ph = post-hole.

Phase	Ph No	%	Pit No	%	Ditch No	%	Gully No	%
1	2	0.24	0	–	0	–	0	–
2	16	1.89	7	9.72	0	–	0	–
3	16	1.89	2	2.77	0	–	0	–
4	380	44.81	10	13.89	21	47.73	0	–
5	1	0.12	0	–	6	13.64	0	–
6	1	0.12	5	6.94	1	2.27	0	–
7	401	47.29	8	11.11	1	2.27	22	100
8	1	0.12	16	22.22	1	2.27	0	–
9	28	2.36	5	6.94	6	13.64	0	–
10	2	0.24	19	26.39	8	18.18	0	–
	848		72		44		22	

feature types – post-hole, pit and ditch – against the phases (1–10) and comparing their relative frequency. The incidence of phased material was tabulated in four ways: 1) number of contexts per feature type which included datable pottery; 2) number of features per type which included datable pottery; 3) number of features per type which were then phased by reference to that pottery; and 4) total number of features per type which were assigned to phase by pottery and by association (Tables 3–6 and Fig 6).

From this it can be seen that interpretation has muted the occurrence of Medieval pottery both in Area D and in post-holes in general. To a lesser extent Early Bronze Age pottery in Areas B and D has been played down, whereas the Middle Bronze Age component has been increased in those areas. Phase 4 Middle Bronze Age ditches and post-holes and Phase 7 Early Middle Iron Age post-holes show a marked increase after interpretation. Obvious changes such as these could then be checked against the site records to see if the underlying interpretive assumptions were realistic.

Most of the post-excavation work was done with reference to preliminary pottery reports and phase sequences, which were periodically refined and enlarged, *eg* an initial Bronze Age component was subdivided into Middle and Late Bronze Age and a Middle Iron Age component into Early Middle and Middle Iron Age. In some cases material submitted for specialist consideration was ordered according to these earlier phase sequences, *eg* slag and seeds, and the reports still reflect this. However, in some cases, especially the animal bone, an effort was made to submit the material with limited subjective data and use, where possible, direct pottery associations, even when this involved giving samples combined phase estimates. In this way the specialist had a clearer view of the relative reliability of the samples and in some cases the specialist's evidence was used to confirm or deny initial phase allocation; *eg* pits 537 and 5103 contained animal bones of a size which accorded with a Medieval date, while pit 6083 was included in Phase 2 Late Neolithic by reference to its flintwork.

No secondary research was undertaken on the prehistoric material from the Winnall II Anglo-Saxon cemetery and the obvious corollary is that no auxillary research was done. In 1986 the preliminary statements on phasing, the validity of the assumptions inherent within those statements, and general hypotheses about the site development were discussed in Salisbury at a seminar attended by members of the team working in various ways on the project and by an invited group of specialists in later prehistory. Nevertheless, the statements in this publication remain the responsibility of their authors.

Chapter 2

The Development of the Site

Phase 1. Neolithic (Fig 7)

Pottery of Early or Middle Neolithic type was recovered from fifteen contexts. Pottery generally regarded as Neolithic is also included within this category. Most sherds are small residual fragments in later features or otherwise disturbed contexts. A number of Neolithic or Late Neolithic sherds in the north of Area B hint at a period of activity earlier than the Phase 2 pits.

In Area B, post-hole or shallow pit 1587 contained three sherds of Peterborough ware and four other Neolithic sherds including a plain rim from a bowl. This post-hole was paired with post-hole 1589. A sherd of Neolithic pottery was found in close proximity in post-hole 1509 which may have formed the northwest corner of a possible four-post structure within CS 2341, a Middle or Late Bronze Age post-ring, and so could be a disturbed context.

In Area E ditch 1054, a Middle to Late Bronze Age feature, contained a quantity of Neolithic pottery which included a rimsherd (Fig 86.2). It is probable that the ditch cut or ran close to a Neolithic feature.

A very small Neolithic rimsherd was found in Phase 4 feature 6039 in Area Mc and further sherds of Neolithic pottery were discovered in later features in Areas A and H and in transect 20.

Phase 2. Late Neolithic (Fig 8)

Late Neolithic pottery was recovered from sixteen features. It is possible to allocate six of these features to this phase with a reasonable degree of confidence. The Late Neolithic pottery in the remaining ten features is assumed to be residual.

The six features are a post-built circular structure, an amorphous feature and four pits, two of which contained human remains. Three other pits contained sherds of Beaker or indistinguishable Late Neolithic or Early Bronze Age pottery. In addition, one containing contemporary flintwork will be considered in this phase, and five features in Area B will be discussed, although only two contained dating material.

Circular structure 3918 in feature group 653 (Figs 9 and 10)

Feature group 653 in Area G was a depression, 0.3m deep, with gently sloping sides covering an area of about 135m². It was discovered during the routine cleaning of transect 26 when sherds of Peterborough ware and Beaker were found. The topsoil was stripped as part of Stage 3 and the whole feature was excavated in 0.10m deep spits and by 1m squares (Fig 11) so that all finds could be relocated to within 0.1m³. Within the group of features a circular structure, 3918, was represented by a circle of sixteen post-holes forming a diameter of 4.75m, although at the base of the depression the diameter was only 3m. Post-holes 3889 and 3891 could have formed a splayed entrance facing southeast and, if the walls were founded on the top edge of the depression and extended from the entrance posts, the diameter of the structure would have been about 7m.

In this way, the group of four small pits, 3919, pit 3802 and a pit, 3831, with burnt material (possibly a hearth) would have been within the hut. The vertical distribution of the pottery (Fig 10) within the main area of the structure suggests that the feature could have been of Late Neolithic date, because three of the four sherds in the bottom spit were of Neolithic type, the fourth being a sherd from a Late Bronze Age jar (Fig 88.61). A sherd from a Neolithic bowl was on the southern lip of the structure (Fig 86.3). There is clearly an admixture of later ceramics, both Bronze Age and Medieval, in the upper fills of this complex and, while a date later than the Neolithic cannot be ruled out for at least some of the features, it seems reasonable to assume that all the features in group 653 are broadly contemporary. The only significant animal bones were the remains of an adult steer from the partially excavated pit 537. Samples of animal bone from two base layers within structure 3918 were submitted for radiocarbon determinations. Preliminary dates of 2490±100bp (HAR 6120) and 3090±90bp (HAR 6121) were received. Unfortunately these would seem more likely to reflect later contamination than secure dates for the structure's period of use.

Pit 5456

Pit 5456, cut by the Late Saxon ditched enclosure 5635, was 50m north of feature group 653. The pit was circular, 1.10m in diameter and 0.34m deep (Figs 13 and 14). The acidic nature of the soil in this area, where there was considerable decalcification, led to the erosion of the surfaces of the fourteen

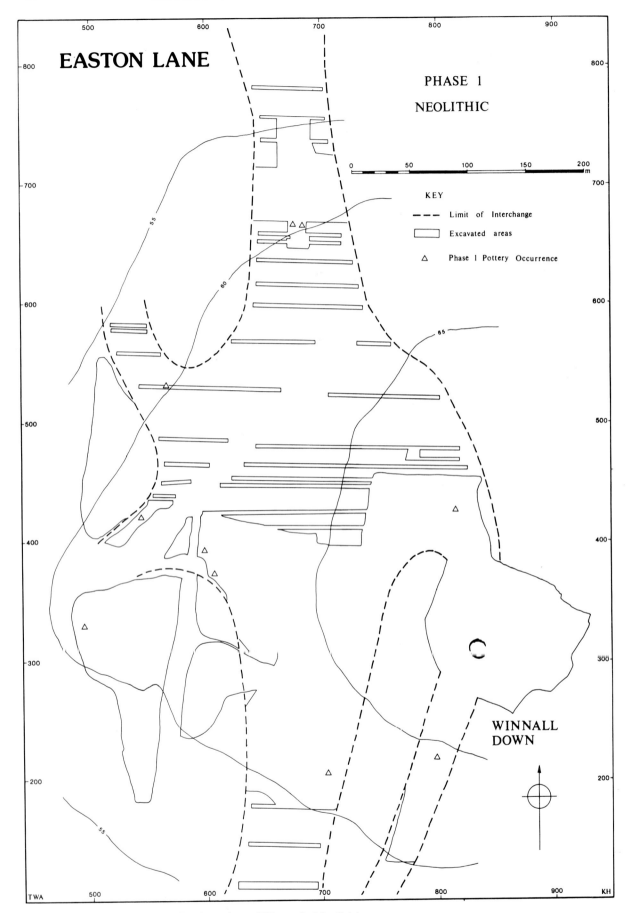

Fig 7.   Easton Lane. Distribution plan of Phase 1, Neolithic, pottery.

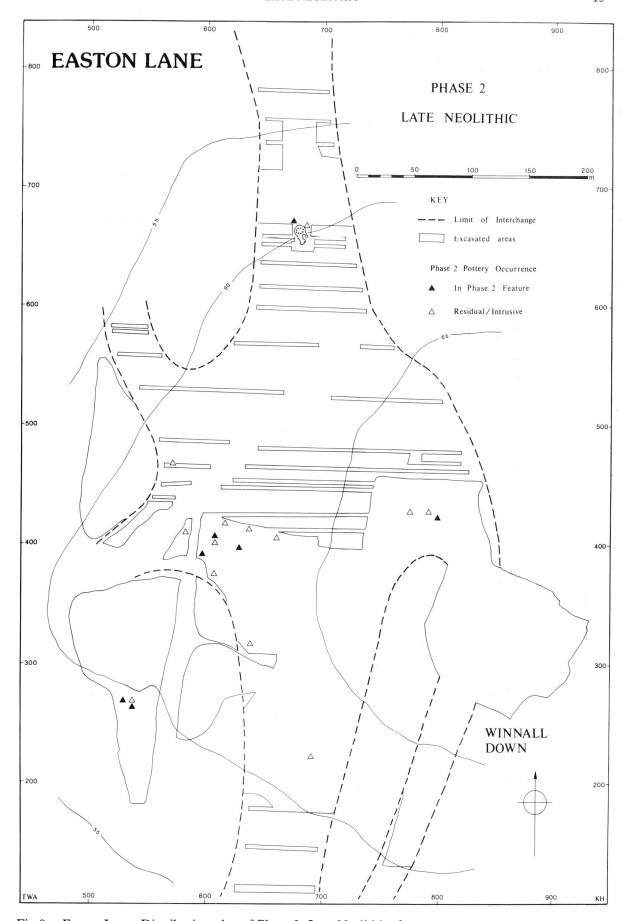

Fig 8.   Easton Lane. Distribution plan of Phase 2, Late Neolithic, features and pottery.

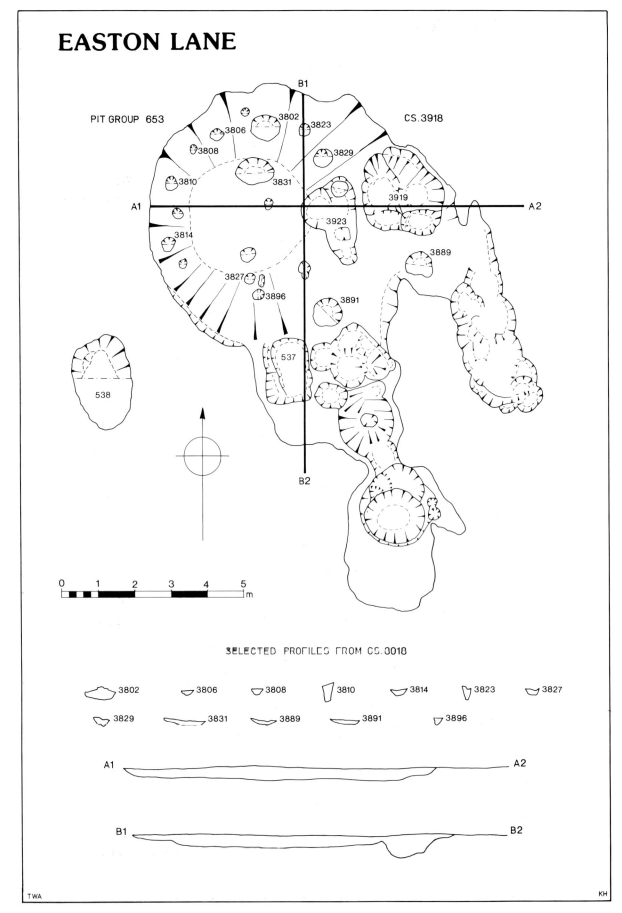

Fig 9.   Easton Lane. Phase 2, Late Neolithic, Area G: detailed plan and profiles of feature group 653, and CS 3918.

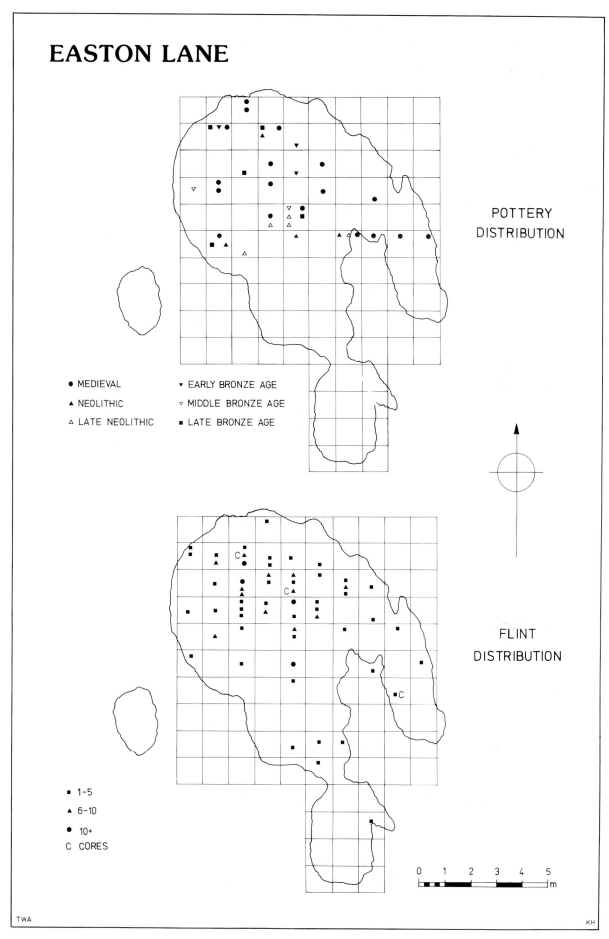

Fig 10. Easton Lane. Phase 2, Late Neolithic, Area G: feature group 653, pottery and flint distribution within CS 3918.

Fig 11.   Easton Lane. Phase 2, Late Neolithic, Area G: feature group 653 with one-metre boxes
half-excavated, and the entrance visible to the left. View from the north, scale 2m.

Fig 12.   Easton Lane. Phase 2, Late Neolithic, Area G: CS 3918 in feature group 653, looking through
entrance; lack of relief due to overcast November conditions. View from the southeast, scale 2m.

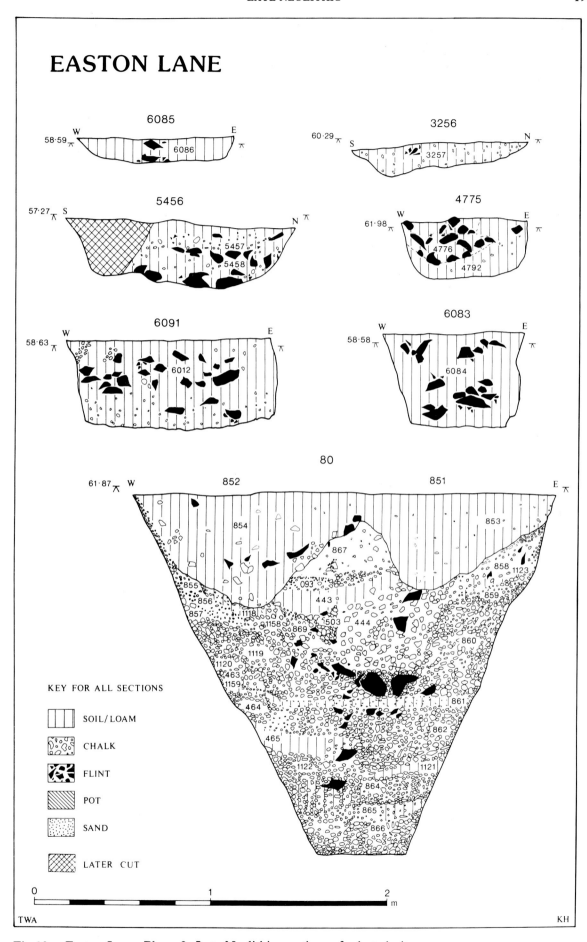

Fig 13.   Easton Lane. Phase 2, Late Neolithic: sections of selected pits.

Fig 14.   Easton Lane. Phase 2, Late Neolithic,
Area F: pit 5456 showing bone and antler.
View from the east, scales 0.5m vertical
and 0.25m horizontal.

sherds of Grooved ware found within it. The 317 pieces of dumped waste flint in this pit were probably derived from an adjacent knapping floor and included refitting flakes (Fig 99.31). The pit contained a considerable amount of animal bone which included a tibia of an auroch and five fragments of unworked red deer antler. A piece of the antler has been submitted for radiocarbon determination (HAR 8882) and a date of 3800±70 bp received. After calibration to two levels of confidence a date of 2470–2040 BC results (Pearson and Stuiver 1986).

Pits in Area B

Pit 80 (Figs 13 and 15) was conical with a surface diameter of 2.4m and a basal diameter of 0.5m. It was 2.4m deep and had a volume of 4.04m³; in the lower fills there were no artefacts. There were two possible shallow features, 851 and 852, cut into the top of pit 80 which were distinguishable only in section and thus there is no separation of finds between them. From these features came a small coral or fossil sponge bead (Fig 104.1) and 53 sherds of pottery from at least seven vessels which included an Early-Middle Neolithic plain bowl (Fig 86.1), a plain Peterborough ware rim (Fig 86.4), a Beaker handle (Fig 86.26), a rim of an Enlarged Food Vessel urn (Fig 87.36) and a rim and a collar from two Collared urns (Fig 87.37,38). Also at this level there was a small greensand fragment possibly from a quernstone. All the pottery was in the top, intrusive, deposits from features 851 and 852 and would seem to post-date the digging and use of pit 80 which in

Fig 15.   Easton Lane. Phase 2, Late Neolithic, Area B: section of pit 80 from the south after removal of
Enlarged Food Vessel urn (Fig 87.36). Scale 2m.

size and profile was directly comparable to pit 1017. Antler from layer 869, which was below the disturbance in pit 80, was submitted in 1983 for radiocarbon determination (HAR 6115) but results have not yet been received.

Pit 1017 was also conical with surface and basal diameter of 2.90m and 0.60m respectively and with a depth of 2.08m, and had a volume of 6.50m^3 (Fig 16). A human burial and the amount of pottery are the main areas of interest in this pit. Burial 2752 (Fig 17), of a 35–45 year old male, was inserted into the pit when it was more than half full. The burial was observed as being in the cut represented by layer 1049. The remains were only partially preserved but it was clear that this had been a crouched inhumation with the head on the south edge of the pit and the feet extending halfway across the pit. The arms had been tucked up in front of the chest but only the hands survived *in situ*. In the area of the groin were five barbed and tanged arrowheads (Fig 95.1–5) and four fragmentary antler spatulae (Fig 96.1–2, Fig 97.3–4). These nine objects had perhaps been in a bag. Just above the groin was a bone awl (Fig 97.5) with a sixth barbed and tanged arrowhead (Fig 95.6) lying on it. A nest of struck flakes was close to the hands.

Differential disintegration may provide a prosaic answer for the absence of some bones without the need to invoke excarnation or scavenging, and of course there are examples of disarticulated Beaker burials, such as Barrow Hills, Oxfordshire (Bradley pers com). However, the looseness of the fill may be indicated by the displacement of some vertebrae to a location between the feet and the hands and thus there exists the likelihood of preferential disturbance of the top of the pit by burrowing animals. Also discovered among the remains was a molar tooth from a second individual, though no other indications of a second burial were present.

The burial seems to have been infilled reasonably rapidly. Ninety-six sherds of pottery were found in and above 1049, indeed there were no artefacts discovered below 1049. The earlier prehistoric pottery was recovered as follows: two sherds from 1049, one of which was a Grooved ware sherd (Fig 86.10) which fitted with the single sherd from 1040; two sherds from 1044; three from 1042; 26 from 1019; and 37 from 1018. From the latter context were 16 sherds of Iron Age, Roman and Medieval date. There were two sherds of Fengate ware (Fig 86.7–8), but the majority of the earlier prehistoric pottery was Grooved ware (Fig 86.9–17,19–22,24,25). Unlike pit 80, where there were clearly intrusive cuts into the top, the upper fills of 1017, layers 1018 and 1019, were broad thick layers slumping into the top of the pit and incorporating material which was either contemporary with the pit or residual and lying around on adjacent areas.

Pit 4775 (Fig 13) was 18m southeast of pit 1017. It was a shallow circular pit with vertical sides, 0.35m deep and 0.75m in diameter. In the upper fill, 4776, which was possibly a secondary feature cut into the top of 4775, were two fragments of human bone and 21 sherds of Late Neolithic pottery including sherds

of possible Fengate and possible Peterborough ware. One further sherd was in the lower fill, 4792.

Immediately east of a straight line joining pits 80 and 1017, an arc of pits or post-holes extended for a length of about 15m (Fig 34). Four of the features, 365, 367, 372 and 374, were circular with mainly decalcified soil fills and were between 0.90m and 1.10m in diameter and 0.26m and 0.40m deep (Fig 19). An antler from 372 was submitted for a radiocarbon determination (HAR 6119) but a result has not yet been received. A fifth feature, 368, the eastern part of a natural feature, may relate to this arc, and contained one sherd each of Beaker or Early Bronze Age and Medieval pottery.

The other features

Pit 3256 (Fig 13) in transect 18, north of Area A, was a shallow, 0.15m deep, circular feature with an irregular base. It contained 13 sherds of Grooved ware including Fig 86.18, 1.1kg of burnt flint and some animal bone.

Feature 23 in Area A was a rather amorphous, shallow, irregular feature only partially excavated but which contained a sherd of a decorated Mortlake Bowl (Fig 86.5).

The three pits containing Beaker or indistinguishable Late Neolithic pottery were 3768, 6085 and 6091. Pit 3768 in Area D was oval and measured 1.90m by 1m and was 0.27m deep. It contained two sherds of Peterborough bowl (Fig 86.6). The profile of the feature suggests that it may have been two pits. In Area Mc pits 6085 and 6091 contained sherds of undiagnostic Late Neolithic pottery and Beaker (respectively Fig 86.27 and Fig 86.28–32). Pits 6085 and 6091 formed a small discrete group with pit 6083, which occupied an area less than 4m^3. Pit 6083 contained worked flint of Late Neolithic form (Fig 98.16–19). The three pits were oval with either sloping or belled sides and measured 0.85m by 0.77m and 0.13m deep (6085), 1.14m by 1.10m and 0.47m deep (6091) and 0.85m by 0.75m and 0.55m deep (6083).

Phase 3. Early Bronze Age (Fig 20)

Early Bronze Age finds and features showed an increased dispersal across the site when compared with the preceding phases. Phased features and feature groups included a post-hole group in Area Mc, MS 5651, a mixed cremation and inhumation burial group in Area F, and a second mixed burial group in Area D which has been included with this phase.

The post-hole group, MS 5651 (Fig 21)

An irregular group of fifteen post-holes in Area Mc occurred in an area measuring 19m east-west by 9m north-south. Pit 6053 (Fig 19) towards the west of the post-holes was circular with a diameter of 0.70m and a depth of 0.25m. Among the finds in this feature were sherds of Beaker (Fig 86.33–34) and of

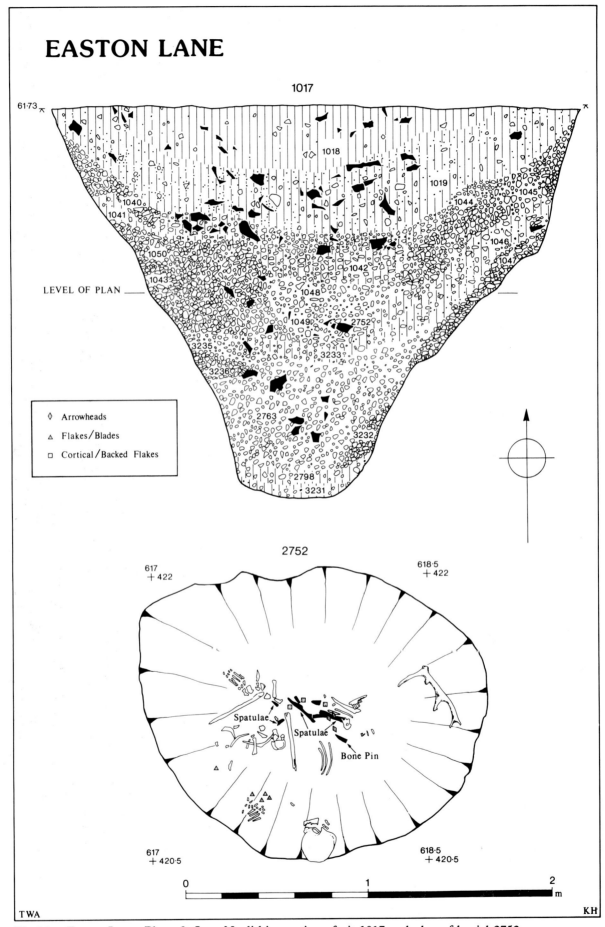

Fig 16.   Easton Lane. Phase 2, Late Neolithic: section of pit 1017 and plan of burial 2752.

Fig 17.   Easton Lane. Phase 2, Late Neolithic, Area B: inhumation 2752 in pit 1017. View from the north, scale 0.5m.

Fig 18.   Easton Lane. Phase 2, Late Neolithic, Area B: inhumation 2752, detail of barbed and tanged arrowhead against bone awl. View from the south.

Collared urns, a bone gouge (Fig 105.1), a bone awl (Fig 105.2) and a contemporary flint assemblage. It seems reasonable to assume that this Early Bronze Age assemblage in pit 6053 should provide a date, by loose association, for the eleven post-holes and for the other small pit 6055, 0.80m diameter and 0.63m deep (Fig 21), located 1m to the northeast.

Cemetery in Area F (Fig 22)

In Area F there were two cremations, an inhumation and a find of disarticulated bone in a Medieval pit. The cremations and inhumations were in features that only just penetrated the chalk surface; inhumation 595 was the deepest at 0.25m while cremation 507 was more or less resting on the surface of the chalk (see Fig 23). This shallowness suggests that they were contemporary, although only cremation 507 was associated with diagnostic artefacts. Cremation 507 (Fig 23) was in an inverted Collared urn (Fig 87.35) and associated with a copper-alloy awl. The cremated human remains in cremations 507 and 598 weighed only 81g and 33g respectively and could not be aged or sexed. Cremation 598 was loose. Inhumation 595 was the badly preserved skeleton of an elderly woman which had been buried in a shallow subcircular pit, 1m in diameter (Fig 24). A limb bone was submitted for radiocarbon determination and a date of 2960±80bp has been received (HAR 6123). This Middle Bronze Age date is not supported by other artefacts or by association. Pit 596 contained disarticulated human bone which

represented almost half of one adult skeleton. This was probably a Medieval pit which had disturbed an Early Bronze Age burial.

There were a number of Medieval pits in the area, in one of which, 600, were sherds of a Collared urn (Fig 87.41) possibly from a disturbed cremation. The sherds were not from the same vessel as that associated with cremation 507.

Cemetery in Area D (Fig 25)

This cemetery consisted of five cremations and two inhumations whose area described a right-angled triangle with a base measurement of 6m and a perpendicular of 13m. It is referred to as burial group 4022. No other man-made features occurred within this cemetery area.

Cremation 1700 (Fig 26), in an oval pit 0.70m by 0.55m and 0.25m deep, was in an urn (Fig 87.45) which only partly survived. The 149g of cremated remains could be identified as from an adult human. The urn had been placed upright in the pit and packed around with large flints for stability. Two kilograms of flint nodules were removed from within the pit. This urn was stabilised in the field and lifted by Hampshire County Museum Service so that its contents could be excavated under laboratory conditions.

Cremation 1705 (Figs 27 and 28), of a young adult male, was in a circular pit of 1m diameter and about 0.35m deep. The cremated remains, 3129g, had been placed in an upright, Wessex biconical urn (Fig

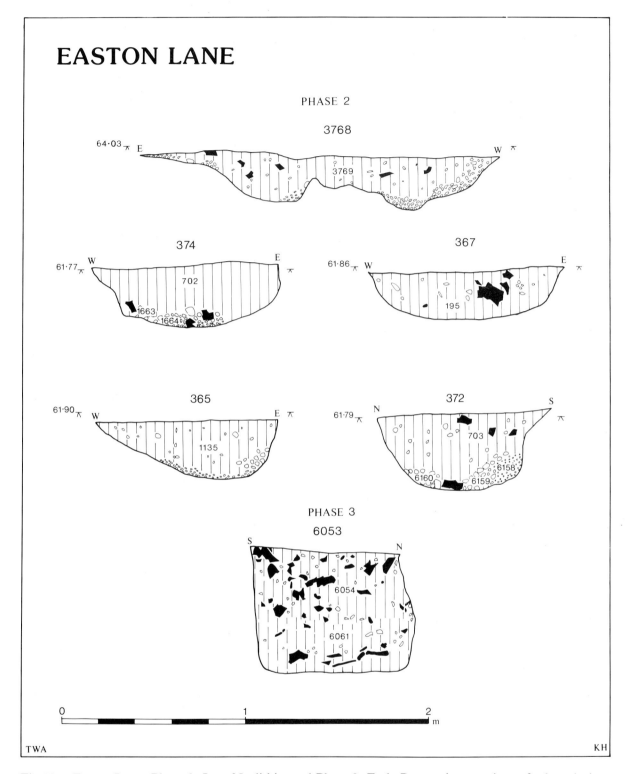

EASTON LANE

PHASE 2

3768

64·03 ⊼ E — W ⊼

3769

374

61·77 ⊼ W — E ⊼

702

1663
1664

367

61·86 ⊼ W — E ⊼

195

365

61·90 ⊼ W — E ⊼

1135

372

61·79 ⊼ N — S ⊼

703

6158
6160   6159

PHASE 3

6053

S — N

6054

6061

0   1   2
                m

TWA   KH

Fig 19.   Easton Lane. Phase 2, Late Neolithic, and Phase 3, Early Bronze Age: sections of selected pits.

87.44) which was in the southwest quadrant of the pit. The urn had been surrounded by 'slabs' obtained (? cut) from a second Wessex biconical urn which is reconstructed as 46 on Fig 87. The slabs from the outer urn had been placed in a triangular arrangement around the base of the upright urn. The slabs seem to have been cut from rim to base.

Slab 1, on the west, had been laid vertically on edge with the rim to the north and adjacent to the chevron on the west side of the upright urn. This slab was 315mm long and the detatched base was located 150mm to the southeast. Slab 2 again was laid vertically on edge on the north side of the upright urn. Its rim was adjacent to the chevron on the west of the upright urn and almost touched the rim of Slab 1. Slab 2 was intact from rim to base, some 372mm. The basal angle lay north of the upright vessel. A second sherd, extending from

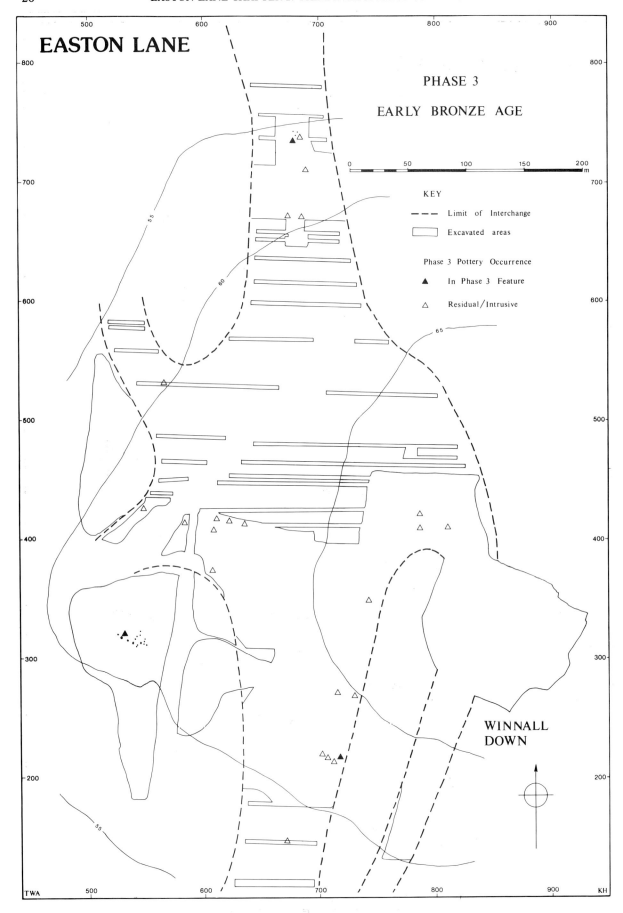

Fig 20.   Easton Lane. Distribution plan of Phase 3, Early Bronze Age, features and pottery.

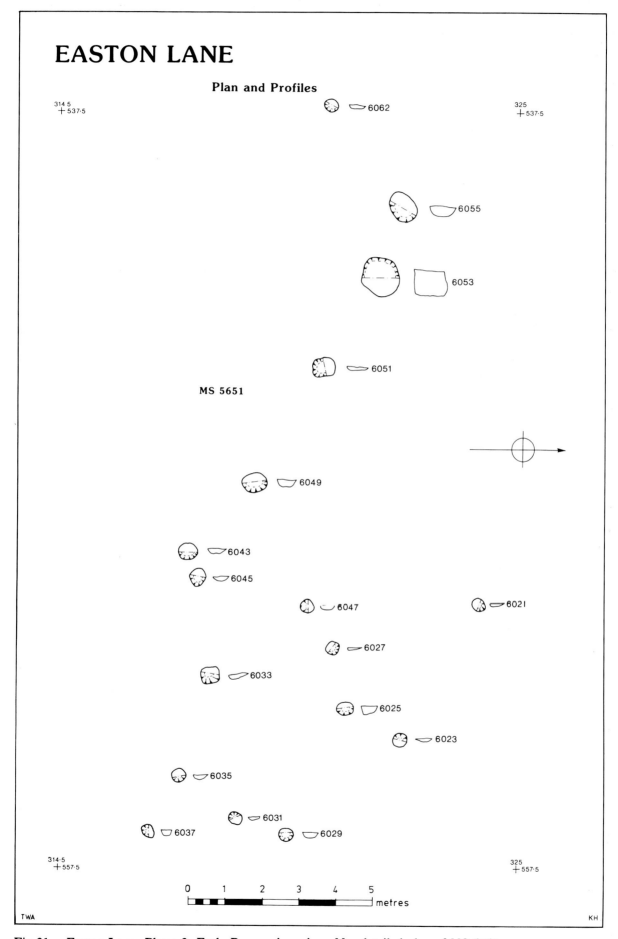

EASTON LANE

Plan and Profiles

Fig 21.   Easton Lane. Phase 3, Early Bronze Age, Area Mc: detailed plan of MS 5651.

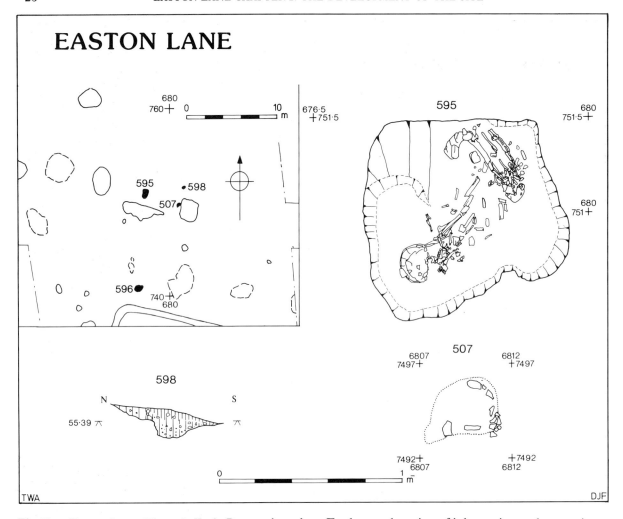

Fig 22.   Easton Lane. Phase 3, Early Bronze Age, Area F: plans and section of inhumation and cremation.

cordon to base, was outside of but touching Slab 2. Slabs 1 and 2 were reasonably intact and placed with their insides towards the primary vessel. A third slab is indicated by the presence on the east side of a series of sherds.

Sherds from the outer vessel were placed inside the upright urn on top of the cremated remains. Once again the urn and its contents were removed intact by Hampshire County Museum Service for excavation in the laboratory, where the fill was excavated and planned in 5cm spits and all material was sieved.

Inhumation 1708 was the contracted skeleton of a young adult with its head to the northeast. The torso was supine with the forearms folded over the base of the chest; the legs were contracted to the left of the body. The grave pit was oval measuring 0.90m by 0.70m and 0.20m deep.

Cremation 1729 contained 34g of burnt human bone in a circular pit, 0.47–.52m diameter, with a flat bottom and almost vertical sides. It was only 0.11m deep, but contained 2 kg of burnt flint.

Cremation 1735, in a circular pit of 0.72m diameter and 0.30m deep, contained 55g of burnt human bone and 19 kg of burnt flint.

Cremation 1744 of a young adult (determined on a skull fragment) was in an oval pit, 0.80m by 0.65m and 0.19m deep. Apart from the 88g of cremated bone, the fill contained a large number of flints, 8kg of nodules, 7.5kg of burnt and 8.1kg of blackened flints.

Inhumation 3058 (Fig 29) was the skeleton of a 35–45 year old female buried in an oval grave which measured 1.6m by 1m and 0.40m deep. The body was crouched and laid out on its left side with the right arm across the chest and upper left arm. She had been buried with a necklace of amber, jet and lignite beads (Fig 103). There were 22 complete and five fragmentary cylindrical amber beads, two biconical jet beads and one biconical lignite bead. A radiocarbon measurement from a limb bone produced a date of 2740±70 bp (HAR 6122), but even when calibrated to two levels of confidence the date of 1090–800 BC (Pearson and Stuiver 1986) seems too late for the artefacts. This sample has been resubmitted and a further determination is awaited.

Other occurrences of Phase 3 pottery

Residual fragments of pottery occurred in Iron Age pits 17, 317 and 4567, in Area A. In pit 317 there was

Fig 23. Easton Lane. Phase 3, Early Bronze Age, Area F: cremation 507 from the west, scale 0.20m.

Fig 24. Easton Lane. Phase 3, Early Bronze Age, Area F: inhumation 595 from northwest, scale 0.5m.

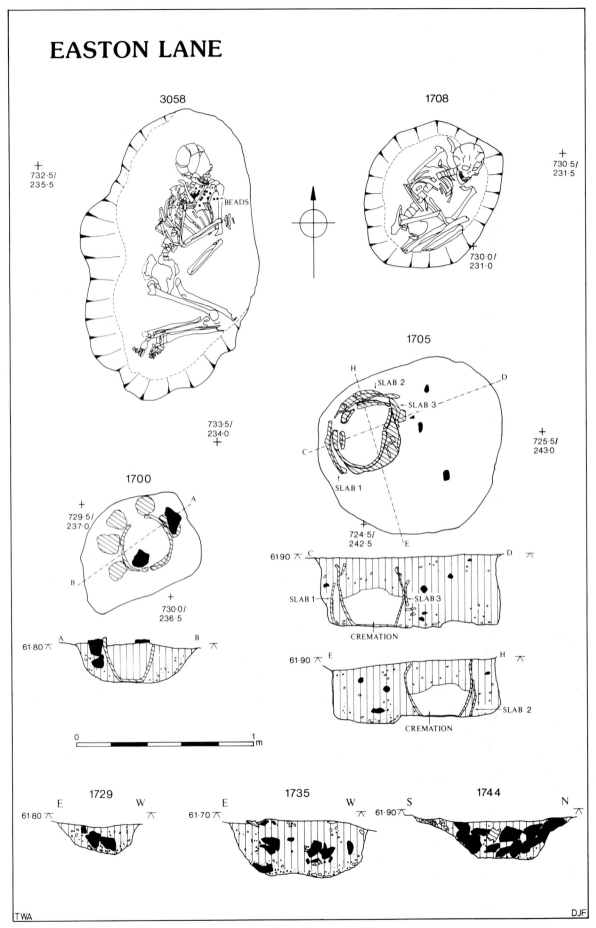

Fig 25. Easton Lane, Phase 3, Early Bronze Age, Area D: plans and sections of inhumations and cremations.

Fig 26.   Easton Lane. Phase 3, Early Bronze Age, Area D: cremation 1700 from the west, scale 0.20m.

Fig 27.   Easton Lane. Phase 3, Early Bronze Age, Area D: cremation 1705 from the east. Scale 0.5m horizontal, 0.20m vertical.

Fig 28.   Easton Lane. Phase 3, Early Bronze Age, Area D: cremation 1705, detail. Scale 0.20m.

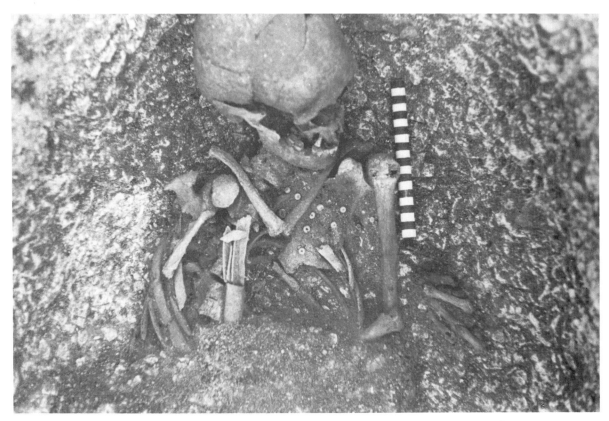

Fig 29.   Easton Lane. Phase 3, Early Bronze Age, Area D: inhumation 3058, detail of head and beads. Scale 0.20m.

a sherd of Biconical urn (Fig 87.42). In Area B, Phase 3 pottery was recovered from Phase 4/5 ditch 1054, which included a decorated sherd of Collared urn (Fig 87.40), and from disturbances in the upper layers of Phase 2 pits 80 and 1017. To the north of Area D, a post-hole, 3721, was assigned to this phase. In Area G, sherds of Early Bronze Age pottery from pit group 653 were interpreted as intrusive. In transect 3, Early Bronze Age pottery was recovered from Middle to Late Bronze Age ditch 3634, and in transect 20 from Late Bronze Age ditch 3274.

Phase 4. Middle Bronze Age (Fig 30)

Post-built circular and other structures are the main features of this phase. They were spaced in clusters between the 60m and 65m contours of the slope from Area H in the southeast through to Areas C and E in the northwest. Ten circular, eight miscellaneous, three rectangular and a range of structures from Area D have been assigned to this phase. Many had no direct dating evidence, *eg* CS 2782, CS 3290 or MS 5658, or only a limited number of associated sherds, *eg* CS 2159, MS 2789 or CS 5636. Others, like CS 2341, contained pottery of both Middle and Later Bronze Age type. In general, structures have been assigned to the phase which predominated in their immediate area and it is therefore likely, especially in Areas B and C, that some structures have been included which should have been considered as part of Phase 5. It is also possible that Bronze Age structural evidence from Area A has been masked by the concentration of Iron Age material. A limited number of associated pits and burials were discovered. A double-ditched boundary system, which enclosed a minimum area of five hectares, appeared during this phase. The ditches and structures were not obviously related and may have represented changes in land use and social structure within this period.

The structures are described by area.

Area A

Miscellaneous structures 2159 and 5658 were discovered in this Area. Both were some distance away from the areas where most contemporary structures were recorded. MS 2159 had associated sherds of both Late Bronze Age and Early Iron Age pottery. MS 5658 was close to and west of Middle Bronze Age ditch 1810.

MS 2159, an oval or subrectangular structure of sixteen closely spaced post-holes, range 0.80m-0.05m apart, mean 0.34m (Figs 31 and 32). An entrance 0.70m wide on the west was formed by the two shallowest post-holes, 960 and 961, with an opposed pair, 970 and 955, 0.80m apart to form an entrance on the east. Dimensions of the structure are, if oval 4.10m by 3.90m, if subrectangular 4.00m by 3.70m. Sherds of Late Bronze Age and Early Iron Age pottery were found in post-hole 955. A sample of animal bone from post-hole 965 gave a preliminary radiocarbon determination of 2220±100 bp (HAR 6118). However the structure was situated within a corner of the Middle Bronze Age ditch

system and, on that basis, has been allocated to the Middle Bronze Age.

MS 5658 (Fig 33), a discrete group of seven post-holes which formed a rough semi-circle with an open side facing west, and maximum width of 7.00m. One of these post-holes, 3756, contained a sherd of Bucket urn (Fig 88.54). It was close to and west of Bronze Age ditch 1810 and 60m south of MS 2159.

Area B

Four circular and three miscellaneous structures in Area B were assigned to the Middle Bronze Age, Phase 4. CS 2373 and 2375 were not strictly contemporary as their ground plans were superimposed.

CS 2341 has been extracted from a cluster of post-holes from which a series of structural interpretations are possible (Figs 35 and 36). The interpretation illustrated is based on the coincidence of size and depth of the post-holes. It provides a post-ring of 8m diameter with a porch, 1.25m long and 3.25m wide, facing southwest. Within the post-ring were four pairs of slight post-holes. If the structure is interpreted as having walls extending in a circle from the outside edge of the entrance (Guilbert 1983) then three other pairs of post-holes would be within the structure. A four-post structure 2.50m square, constructed from post-holes 1509, 1548, 1558 and 2325 (RS 5660), was coincident with the entrance. Two pairs of features lay outside even the largest conceivable structure. Post-holes 1210 and 1524 were of proportions comparable with the four internal pairs of post-holes. Features 1587 and 1589 are best regarded as discrete features, possibly the bases of shallow pits and need not necessarily be contemporary. Three sherds of Peterborough ware and five other Neolithic sherds were in feature 1587 and a sherd of probable Late Bronze Age pottery in feature 1589. A sherd of Neolithic pottery (Fabric C4) was in post-hole 1509 and sherds of Middle and Late Bronze Age pottery were in post-holes 1149, 2087, 2325 and feature 2090 which was described as natural. Feature 2090 may be the base of a shallow pit similar to features 1587 and 1589.

CS 2373 (Figs 37 and 38), an oval or subrectangular building, consisted of an arc of twelve post-holes and two centrally placed internal post-holes. The ground plan was not fully recovered since it extended beyond the edge of the main excavation and it was not possible to observe its full extent during the watching brief. Diameter or width was 5.00m.

CS 2375 (Figs 37 and 38) was a small oval structure, 5.00m north-south by 5.20m east-west, with an elongated porch to the south, 2.80m long by 1.40m wide, possibly entered from the east to give a right-angled approach, and similar to House C on Winnall Down (Fasham 1985 Fig 8). The post-holes were often double or replaced. Natural feature 364 contained Early and Middle Bronze Age pottery (Fig 87.43, Fig 88.48–49), presumably derived from this building.

CS 2723 (Fig 39) was an oval structure of twenty-two post- and stake-holes which measured 7.30m east-west by 6.70m north-south. A possible entrance, 1.25m wide, on the northwest was formed by post-holes 2387, 2050 and 2053, together with secondary or replacement post-holes 2389, 2397 and 2390. An alternative entrance in the southeast could be represented by post-holes 2385, 2395, 2509 and 2544. In the former case only three post-holes, 2385, 2391 and 2509, occurred within the post circle. Medieval pottery was recovered from multiple feature 2540/1/2.

MS 2789 (Fig 40), a discrete cluster of twenty-four post-holes in an area of natural features, was probably a circular structure. It consisted of a porch 4.60m long by *c* 2.00m wide which faced south, with an irregular body of post-holes to the north. One sherd of Grooved ware (Fig 86.23) and one sherd of Middle Bronze Age fabric A9 were found in post-hole 2704.

MS 5654 was a small group of seven post-holes in the southeast of Area B, 6.50m long and 2.25m wide (Fig 41). The post-holes may represent three two-post structures with an outlying single post.

MS 5657, a discrete group of nine post-holes, formed an irregular, two-sided arrangement open to the west with a maximum width of 6.00m (Fig 42). A group of three post-holes were in the southern corner. Northeast of CS 2341.

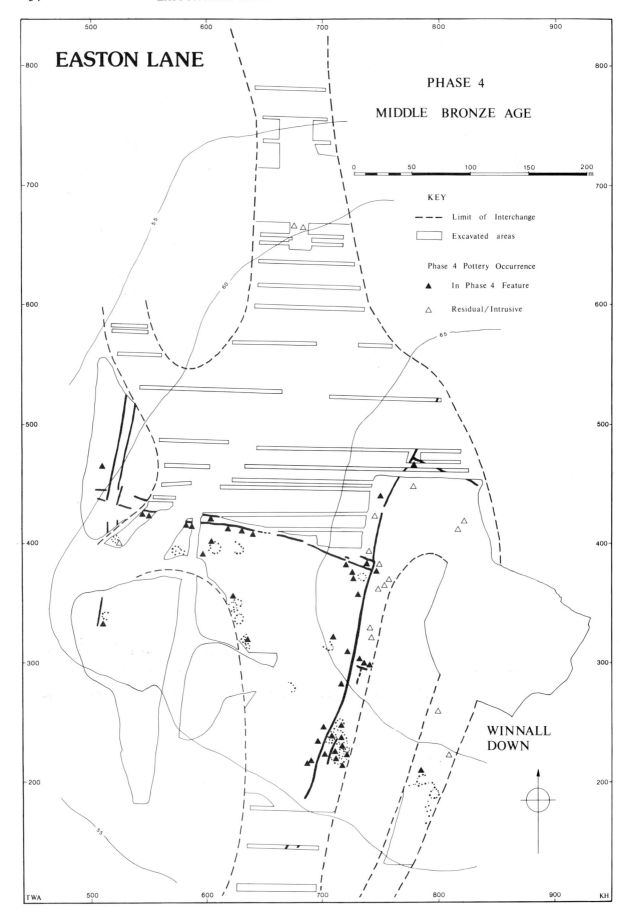

Fig 30.   Easton Lane. Distribution plan of Phase 4, Middle Bronze Age, features and pottery.

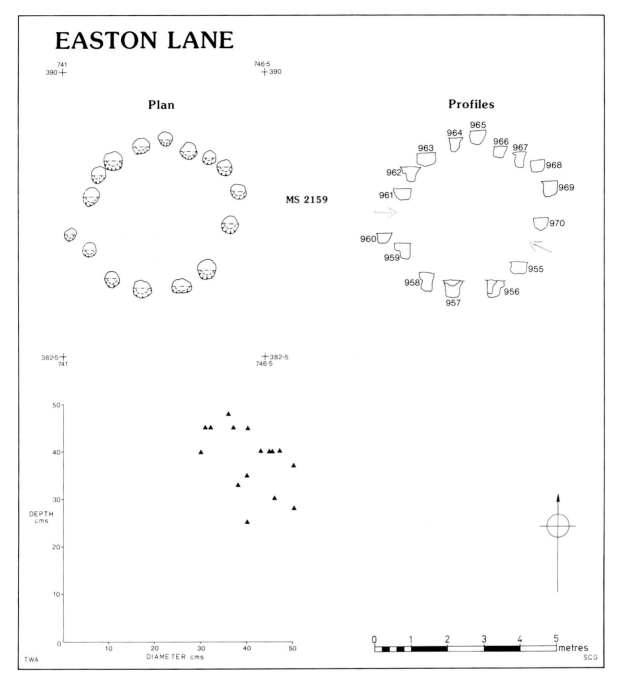

Fig 31.   Easton Lane. Phase 4, Middle Bronze Age, Area A: detailed plan of MS 2159, and post-hole dimension diagram.

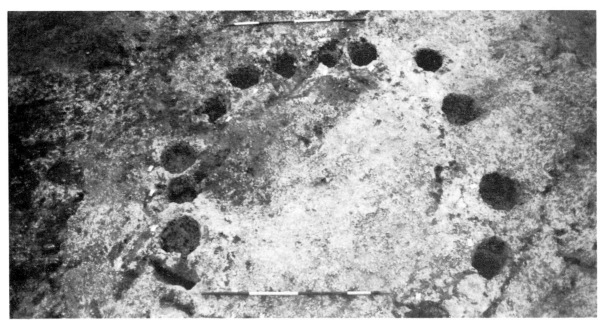

Fig 32.   Easton Lane. Phase 4, Middle Bronze Age, Area A: MS 2159 from the south, scale 2m.

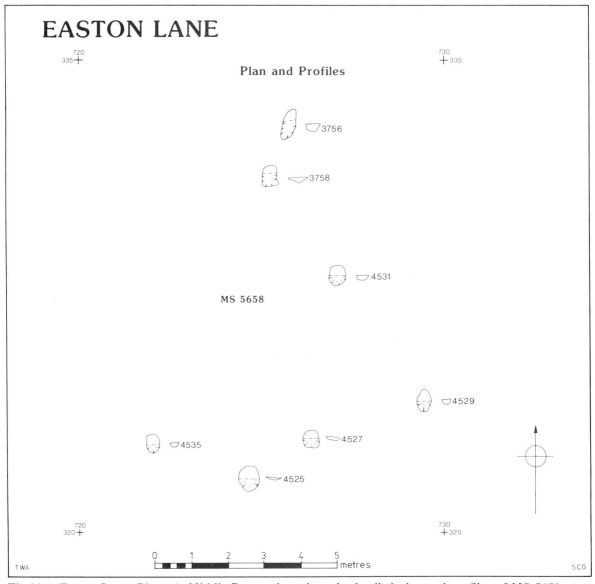

Fig 33.   Easton Lane. Phase 4, Middle Bronze Age, Area A: detailed plan and profiles of MS 5658.

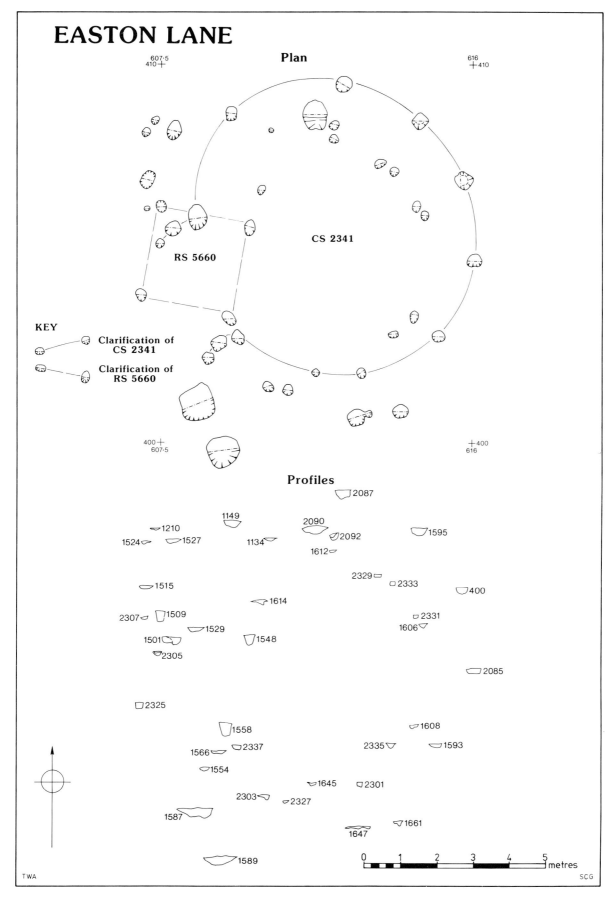

Fig 35.   Easton Lane. Phase 4, Middle Bronze Age, Area B: detailed plan and profiles of CS 2341.

Fig 36.   Easton Lane. Phase 4, Middle Bronze Age, Area B: CS 2341 from the south, scale 2m.

Also within Area B but some 40m east of the main group of structures was RS 5609 (Fig 43), a small four-poster 1.60m square. No pottery was recovered from this structure but it was similar to the four-post structure within CS 2341.

Area C

CS 2782 was the only structure in Area C.

CS 2782 was a 5.15m diameter, circular ring of nine equidistant post-holes about one central post-hole, with two porch post-holes forming an entrance, 1.90m wide and 1.60m long, which faced southeast (Figs 44 and 45). The porch and entrance post-holes were larger and deeper than those which formed the ring, while the central post was shallower. Medieval pottery was recovered from post-hole 2750.

Area D

About 300 features, mainly post- and stake-holes, were clustered in a small area approximately 40m square (Figs 46 and 47). Twenty-two of these features contained Middle Bronze Age pottery, of which two are illustrated, a sherd of decorated Bucket urn (Fig 88.56) from 1748, an isolated post-hole to the east of burial group 4022, and a perforated lug from a Globular urn (Fig 88.52) from post-hole 3423 which was immediately adjacent to the southern entrance to MS 4010. The area was defined on the south side by a lynchet and a fence, LS 4011, and on the west by ditch 1810. There were no obvious limits to the north and east, although the latter may have been outside the area of the exca-vations. Discrete groups of features are identifiable, including burial group 4022, circular structures

4008, 4009 and 5653, miscellaneous structure 4010 and several other possible structure groups. Three white coral or fossil sponge beads were found in Area D and have been included in Phase 4, Middle Bronze Age: one from CS 4009 post-hole 2992, one from MS 4010 post-hole 1768, and one from a post-hole to the north of the area, 1770. The burial group 4022 has been dealt with in the section on the Early Bronze Age, Phase 3. One structure, MS 5631, was west of ditch 1810.

CS 4008 was a circular post-ring of 18 post-holes, diameter 4.75m (Fig 48). The two largest post-holes, 1721 and 1725, formed a 0.75m wide entrance facing southeast. A second possible entrance was formed by post-holes 1718 and 1863. It was 1.25m wide, and faced west.

CS 4009 (Fig 48) was a circular cluster of 21 post-holes with a diameter of 5.50m. The northwest quadrant intersected ditch 1810 and, despite extensive cleaning of the surface of the ditch fill, there was no suggestion of post-holes being cut into the ditch. It is likely therefore that the ditch cut away post-holes from the northwest of CS 4009. Two large post-pits, 1723 and 1807, formed an entrance to the southeast with a small porch 1.50m long and 1.00m wide.

CS 5653 was a small post-built structure of fifteen post-holes, 4.00m diameter (Fig 49). There were two central post-holes, 3071 and 3073, and post-holes 3035, 3037, 3039 and 3042 formed a porch 1.50m long by 0.65m wide which faced south.

MS 4010 was a round-ended rectangular structure which occurred within an area of tightly packed post-holes, the focus of a number of fence lines (see below, combination 3). Thirty-one post-holes have been extracted to form a ground plan of sym-metrical proportions about the short axis, which measured 11.50m long north-south by 4.50m wide east-west (Figs 50 and 51). The west side consisted of roughly equidistant post-holes, 1.75m-2.00m apart, mean 1.90m, while the east side was appar-ently less regular with some double or replaced posts. Internal

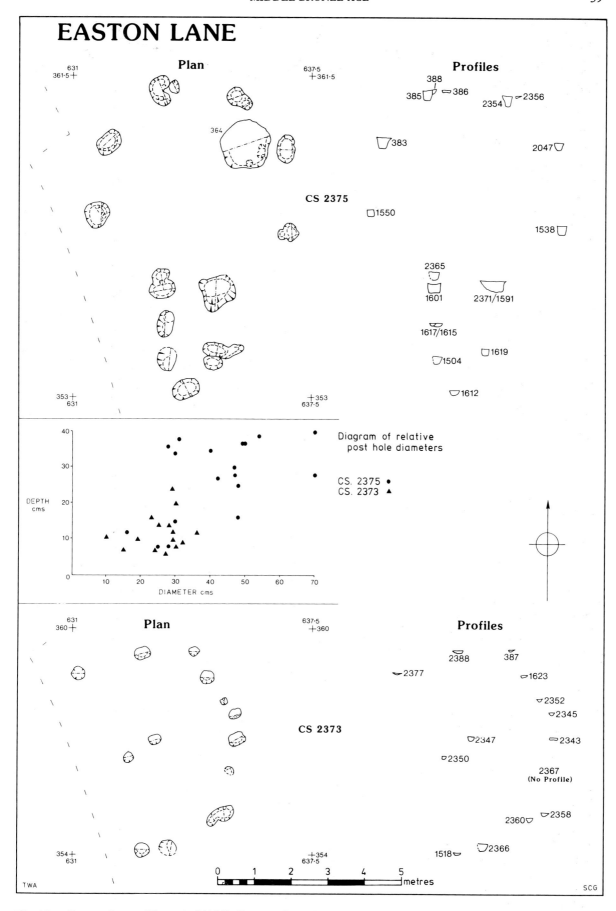

Fig 37.   Easton Lane. Phase 4, Middle Bronze Age, Area B: detailed plans and profiles of CS 2373 and CS 2375; and diagram of post-hole diameters.

Fig 38.   Easton Lane. Phase 4, Middle Bronze Age, Area B: superimposed structures 2373 and 2375 from the north, scale 2m.

arcs of three post-holes each at the north and south ends have been interpreted as inturned entrances. The symmetry of the structure about the central east-west partition argues strongly for this being a single building rather than two juxtaposed circular structures.

MS 5631 was an oval of thirteen post-holes, 6.50m north-south by 4.00m east-west with a 2.40m gap on the west side, possibly an entrance (Fig 52). It was to the southwest of the main group of structures in Area D and 32m west of ditch 3581.

LS 4011 was twenty-one post-holes in a linear arrangement 15m long running east-west (Fig 53). The group comprised three almost parallel lines of post-holes presumably the result of fence replacement. The line was established at its east end by the two largest post-holes, 3605 and 3467. LS 4011 was parallel to, but south of, LS 4014. LS 4011 straddled the preserved line of the lynchet.

LS 4014 was eleven post-holes which formed a straight fence line 16.25m long which ran east-west (Fig 53). Posts were set 1.00m-2.80m apart, mean 1.48m. All the post-holes were of similar depth and diameter except for 3131 and 2882 which formed a larger central pair 1.50m apart. The fence line ran from ditch 1810 in the west to MS 4010 in the east.

LS 4015 comprised fifteen post-holes in an arc running roughly north-south for 21.75m (Fig 53). The post-holes were similar in depth and diameter and were 1.30m-4.15m apart, mean 2.24m. Three pairs of post-holes, 2886/2888, 2928/2954 and 2926/3552 formed a possible double entrance with 3.35m and 2.75m wide openings respectively.

LS 4016 was an arc of twenty-two post-holes which ran west from ditch 1810 to LS 4011 at the south (Fig 53). It was interrupted by two short sections of converging lines of posts which formed a funnel entrance narrowing to the east. The whole structure was 26.50m from west to south. The funnel was 6.75m long east-west, 10.25m wide at the west, 1.35m wide at the east.

LS 4017, of twenty-four post-holes, formed an arc 31.25m long which ran parallel to LS 4016. The post-holes, which were spread 0.90m to 4.20m apart, mean 1.75m, showed a wide variation in depths and diameters (Fig 53).

For ease of reference these various structural elements have been arranged into three main combinations (Fig 53). These combinations are not mutually exclusive and different elements can be integrated in different ways. Indeed, very different interpretations can be proposed. There is no chronological significance in the ordering of the elements within these different combinations.

Combination 1 sees the three roughly parallel arcs of fences LS 4015, 4016 and 4017 extending from ditch 1810 on the west clockwise to LS 4011 on the south. The arcs were not part of an arrangement of concentric rings but were integral entities in their own right. The central fence, 4016, was interrupted by a funnel-shaped formation which extended east as far as a gap in the outer arc, LS 4017. This construction may have been reflected in the adjacent paired post-holes in the otherwise regular line of LS 4015, from which a through passage, east-west, could be postulated.

Combination 2 involves the rectangular structure MS 4010 with a roughly rectangular area to the west. This was enclosed by LS 4014 extending at right angles from the north of MS 4010 to ditch 1810 on the west. The southern side of the area was delimited by LS 4011 which also ran east-west, parallel to LS 4014. A 2.50m gap separated it from MS 4010 and a short section of connecting fence can be postulated. LS 4011 was 15m long and LS 4014 16.25m long, and enclosed an area 14m wide from north to south.

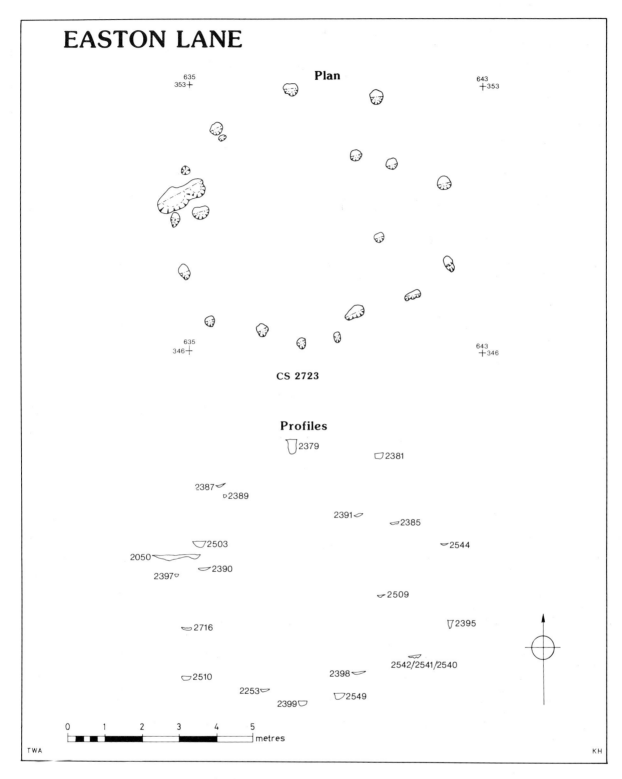

Fig 39. Easton Lane. Phase 4, Middle Bronze Age, Area B: detailed plan and profiles of CS 2723.

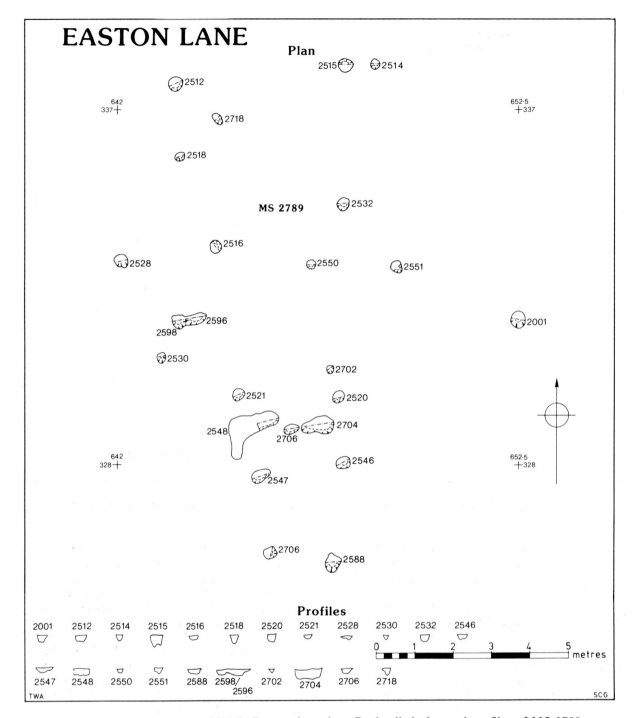

Fig 40.   Easton Lane. Phase 4, Middle Bronze Age, Area B: detailed plan and profiles of MS 2789.

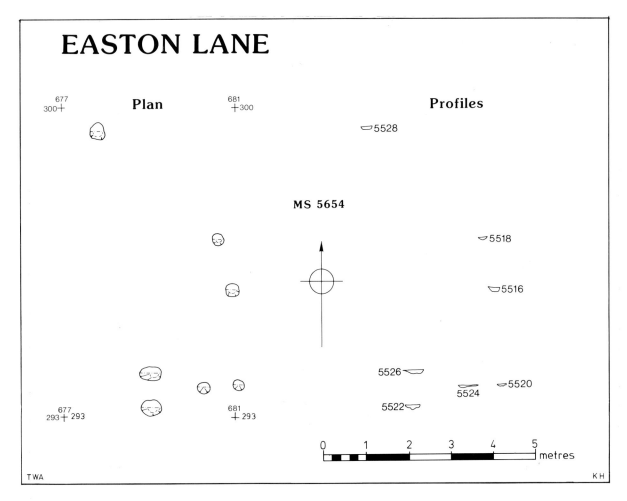

Fig 41. Easton Lane. Phase 4, Middle Bronze Age, Area B: detailed plan and profiles of MS 5654.

LS 4011 consisted of more than one line of post-holes, which may represent renewal of this line to form a southern terminal to LS 4015, 4016 and 4017 in *combination 1*.

Combination 3 incorporates elements from combinations 1 and 2 and also involves CS 4008, 4009, 5653 and MS 4010. The blank areas were considered functionally as access or courtyards. CS 4008 and 5653 were isolated to the north and east respectively, each with surrounding access or freespace of *c*3.0m-4.5m. CS 4009 and MS 4010 were separated from them by LS 4017, the southern part of LS 4015 and the western post-holes of LS 4014. Some of the post-holes not used from LS 4015, 4014 and 4016 served as additional posts and work areas for CS 4009 and MS 4010. The used parts of LS 4014 and 4015, together with LS 4011 and 4017, were linked to form an enclosure around CS 4009 and MS 4010. This enclosed a free space of *c*3.0m around CS 4009 and a yard, 6.0m east-west by 10.0m north-south, to the west of MS 4010. The eastern half of LS 4014 was re-interpreted as part of a work area within this enclosure, which consisted of a loose group of post-holes, with many possible pairs, in an otherwise open space. The cluster of post-holes to the south-west, outside the enclosure, was probably a similar work area and combinations of two- and four-post

structures can be postulated. LS 4011 could still have been a multiple fence line, or alternatively, a single fence with a small work area to the north.

It is not possible to suggest a firm chronological sequence for the various combinations except to say that CS 4009 cannot be contemporary with LS 4015 and 4016, nor the funnel on LS 4016 with MS 4010. CS 4009 appeared to have been cut by ditch 1810, although the exact sequence has been obscured by the presence of recuts in the ditch, while LS 4014, 4015, 4016 and 4017 appeared to use ditch 1810 as a boundary. The third combination with its houses and structures contradicts the implicit stratigraphic sequence.

Area E

There was one circular structure in Area E.

CS 3290 was a ring of seven post-holes about a central post-hole, with a diameter of 4.25m (Figs 54 and 55). The two largest post-holes, 3228 and 3261, may have formed an entrance 1.50m wide facing northeast. This structure was near and west of Middle Bronze Age ditch 6073/3200/7016.

Area H

This area contained three post-built structures which were attributed to Phase 4 on grounds of form,

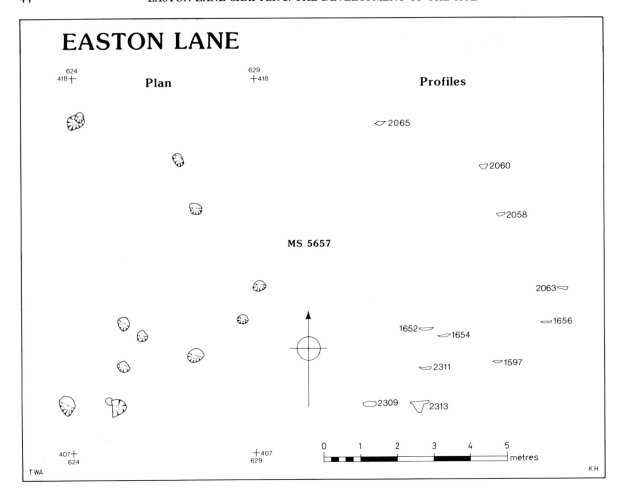

Fig 42.   Easton Lane. Phase 4, Middle Bronze Age, Area B: detailed plan and profiles of MS 5657.

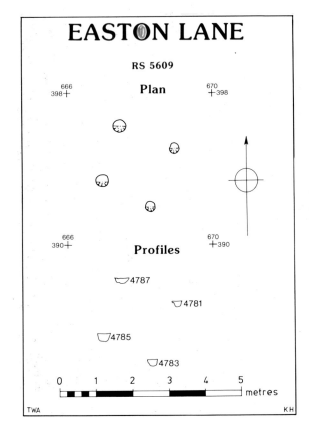

relationship to the contour and one piece of Middle Bronze Age Bucket urn (Fig 88.59) from post-hole 5345, MS 5652. They formed a compact group of one circular, one rectangular and one miscellaneous type structure (Fig 56).

CS 5636 was a circle of ten post-holes, 5.50m diameter, with two central post-holes. The largest post-holes, 5238, 5240 and 5242, formed a 1.00m wide entrance which faced south-southeast, with posts either replaced or double. Medieval pottery was found in both 5238 and 5242.

RS 5637 was a four-post structure with a length of 2.50m and a width of 1.50m. It was south of CS 5636.

MS 5652 was a group of seventeen post-holes to the northwest of CS 5636, which formed a fence ending at the west in a possible pen. The fence was 15.75m long and the possible pen 4.75m north-south and 3.00m east-west.

Area Mc

There was one post-built structure in Area Mc.

MS 5650 was a semi-circle, open to the southeast, of five equidistant post-holes which enclosed a maximum width of 4.75m (Fig 57). It was near and west of Middle Bronze Age ditch 6073/3200/7016.

Fig 43.   Easton Lane. Phase 4, Middle Bronze Age, Area B: detailed plan and profiles of RS 5609.

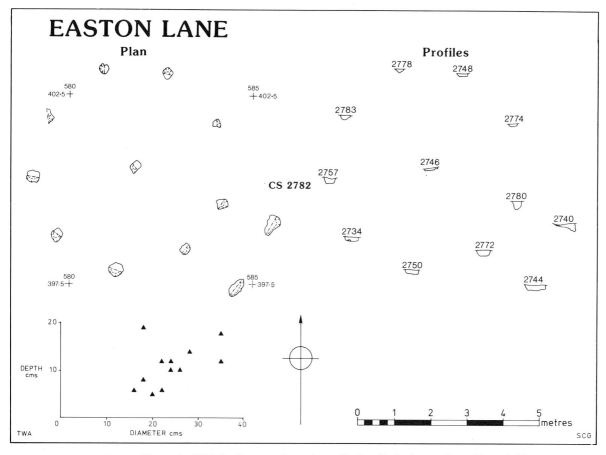

Fig 44.   Easton Lane. Phase 4, Middle Bronze Age, Area C: detailed plan and profiles of CS 2782.

Fig 45.   Easton Lane. Phase 4, Middle Bronze Age, Area C: CS 2782 from the southeast, scale 2m.

Fig 46.   Easton Lane. Area D, plan of all features.

Fig 47.   Easton Lane. Phase 4, Middle Bronze Age, Area D: general view from the southeast showing concentration of features.

Pits (Fig 58)

There were only six pits datable to the Middle Bronze Age: 166, 1498, 3691, 3749, 4691 and 4699. They were either ovoid with flat bottoms or shallow with circular or oval plans. Two further pits, 3740 and 3743, contained both Middle and Late Bronze Age pottery. The total volume of possible Phase 4 pits was 1.50m³ with a mean of 0.19m³. The only significant find was a bronze arrowhead (Fig 85.2) in pit 1498. This pit also contained rimsherds and a perforated body sherd from a Middle Bronze Age Bucket urn (Fig 88.55). Pit distribution did not relate to structure concentrations. There were two possible concentrations of pits: one group of four pits, 3691, 3740, 3743 and 3749, to the north of Area D near ditch 3692; and the other of two pits, 4691 and 4699, in Area A, which together with possible cremation 4683 and post-holes 4652 and 4726 were to the west of MS 2159. A piece of antler from pit 4699 was submitted for radiocarbon determination with a result of 3240±120bp (HAR 6116).

Two further small pits or post-holes contained Middle Bronze Age pottery. They were 6039 in Area Mc, which had a near complete Bucket urn with a row of perforations below the rim (Fig 88.53), and 6099, a possible cremation, in Area Bc, which contained 51 sherds from a single Bucket urn. Both these features were very close to, and probably associated with, the western pair of Middle Bronze Age north-south ditches (7008/6064 and 7010/7037/7049).

Four Iron Age pits in Area A contained sherds of Middle Bronze Age pottery, 409, 1391, 2154 and 4921. 2154 contained a decorated sherd of Bucket urn (Fig 88.57), and 4921 a decorated sherd of Globular urn (Fig 88.51).

Ditches (Figs 59, 60, 61 and 62)

The Middle Bronze Age ditches formed a single coherent pattern which was modified in the Later Bronze Age, Phase 5. The ditches, sometimes in parallel pairs about 6m apart, were arranged in a rectilinear pattern. They were generally of slight construction and comprised a north-south line running from Area Bc to Area Mc, a west-east line from Area Bc through Areas E, C, and B and across to A, and another north-south line running from Area A to Area D.

The north-south line from Area Bc to Area Mc was made up of three main ditches. In Area Bc there was ditch 7008 which was 0.31m-0.45m wide, mean 0.36m, 0.07m-0.25m deep, mean 0.14m, and was continued to the south in Area Mc by ditch 6064, 0.62m wide, 0.28m deep. These ran parallel to ditch 7010, width 0.30m, depth 0.12m.

The west-east line from Area Bc to Area A was made up of the following elements. In Area Bc there was ditch 7022, 0.50m wide, 0.08m deep. This line was continued east by ditch 1054, 0.40m-0.60m wide, mean 0.48m, 0.18m-0.35m deep, mean 0.26m, and ditch 972, 0.31m-0.85m wide, mean 0.64m, 0.18m-0.40m deep, 0.26m mean. These ran

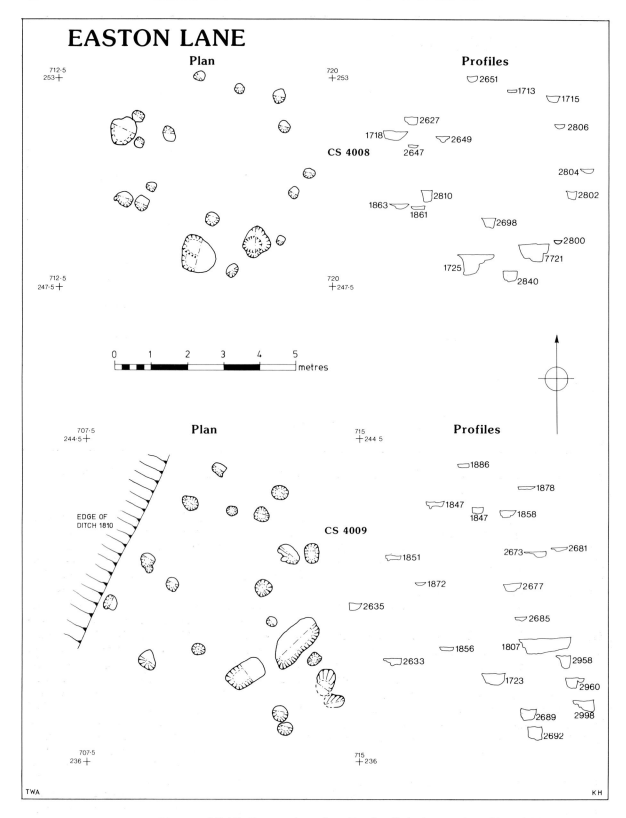

Fig 48.   Easton Lane. Phase 4, Middle Bronze Age, Area D: detailed plans and profiles of CS 4008 and CS 4009.

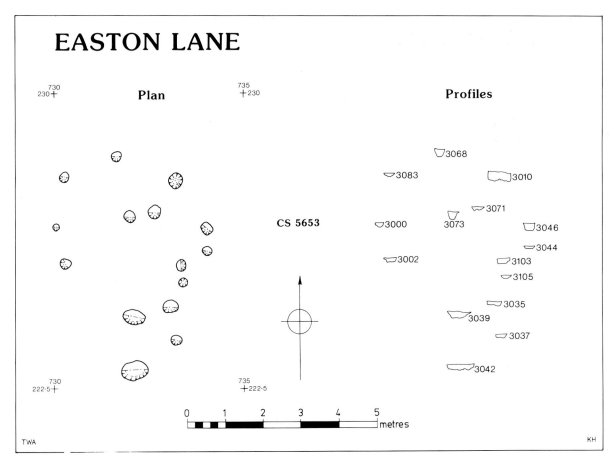

EASTON LANE

Fig 49. Easton Lane. Phase 4, Middle Bronze Age, Area D: detailed plan and profiles of CS 5653.

parallel to, and south of, ditch 7017 in Area Bc which was 0.40m wide, 0.40m deep. The line of 7017 was continued in Area B by ditch 2730, 0.42m wide, 0.12m deep, and possibly by the west end of ditch 975 in Area A.

The north-south line from Area A to Area D consisted, in Area A, of ditches 176 and 729, 0.50m-1.40m wide, mean 1.13m, 0.25m-0.74m deep, mean 0.57m, and ditch 1810, 0.80m-1.60m wide, mean 1.22m, 0.48m-0.90m deep, mean 0.69m, which ran from the southern half of Area A into Area D. The northern end of ditch 1810 appears on plan as ditch numbers 990 and 1929. In Area D parts of a parallel ditch line were recorded, ditches 2694: 0.22m-0.37m wide, mean 0.29m, 0.10m-0.22m deep, mean 0.15m and 3687; 0.14m wide, 0.05m deep. Ditches 3634 and 3673 in transect 3 probably extended the lines of 1810 and 2694 respectively.

Two further ditches in Areas A and D are considered to be part of this system. In Area A, ditch 1493, 0.68m wide, 0.30m deep, ran east at right-angles from ditch 176; and in Area D, ditch 3692, 0.68m wide, 0.23m deep, formed a right-angle against ditch 3687.

The dating of these ditches by direct reference to pottery is complicated by the sporadic and clustered nature of the evidence. Almost 40% of all Middle and Late Bronze Age pottery was recovered from two ditches, 1054 and 1810, with 154 Middle, Late

and Middle or Late Bronze Age sherds between them. From this it was assumed that ditches 1054 and 1810 were still open but probably going out of use during the Late Bronze Age. In addition, the large number of recuts which were recognised in these ditches also suggested a long period of use and management, presumably as field boundaries. The pottery from ditch 1054 included a decorated rim-sherd of Type 1A Globular urn (Fig 88.50) and a Middle to Late Bronze Age Bucket base which had been bored for use as a weight (Fig 88.58). The occurrence of Neolithic and Early Bronze Age pottery in ditch 1054, near pit 1017, reflected the proximity of the early features as a source of residual material. It is possible that ditch 1054 recut or re-used an earlier ditch line. In Area A, the dating was complicated by the concentration of later Iron Age material, but Middle Bronze Age pottery was recovered from ditch 729, which, with ditches 176, 1493 and the west end of 975, fitted well into the Middle Bronze Age Phase 4 ditch system outlined above. The only stratigraphic relationship, apart from the various recuts, was in Area Bc where a slight, east-west Middle Bronze Age Phase 4 ditch, 7017, was cut by a substantial north-south ditch, 7016.

Burials

The cemetery of two inhumations and five crema-tions in Area D, burial group 4022, has been dealt

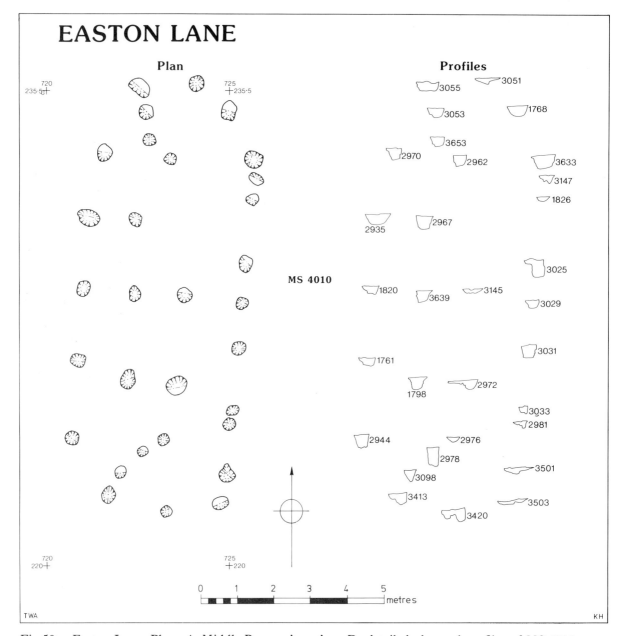

Fig 50.   Easton Lane. Phase 4, Middle Bronze Age, Area D: detailed plan and profiles of MS 4010.

with in Phase 3. A third inhumation, 3695, was 60m north of the cemetery.

Inhumation 3695 was an adult crouched burial on its right side with its head to the northwest. It was in a rectangular grave cut which also contained three sherds of Middle Bronze Age pottery (Fig 63).

In Area Bc, possible cremation 6099 contained an inverted Middle Bronze Age urn and three small fragments of cremated bone which could not be positively identified as human (Fig 63).

In Area A, west of ditch 1810, sherds of Middle Bronze Age urn (Fig 88.47) were recovered from a possible cremation, 4683, which contained two fragments of cremated bone not positively identified as human.

Phase 5. Late Bronze Age (Fig 64)

The distribution of Late Bronze Age pottery was similar to that of the more frequent Middle Bronze Age pottery. Since many features have been dated by association or by the most prevalent pottery type in the immediate area, it was especially difficult to differentiate features and structures of Phase 5 from Phase 4. However, a ditch system which replaced that of the Middle Bronze Age has been assigned to this phase, while a number of the structures described in Phase 4 may have been of Late Bronze Age date.

Fig 51.   Easton Lane. Phase 4, Middle Bronze Age, Area D: MS 4010 from the south, scale 2m.

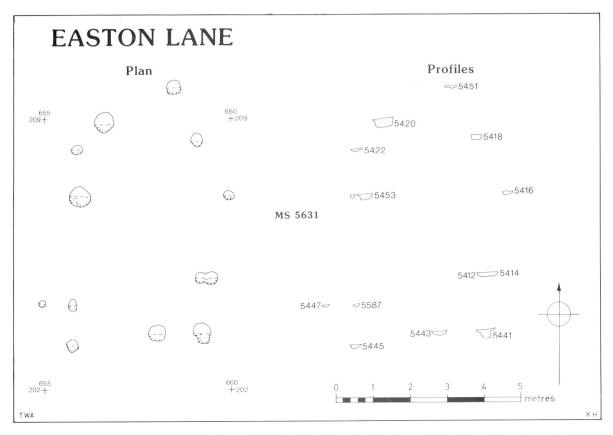

Fig 52.   Easton Lane. Phase 4, Middle Bronze Age, Area D: detailed plan and profiles of MS 5631.

Fig 53.   Easton Lane. Phase 4, Middle Bronze Age, Area D: plan of structural combinations.

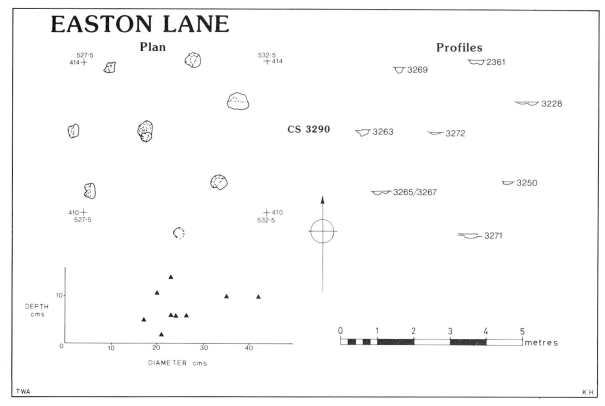

Fig 54.   Easton Lane. Phase 4, Middle Bronze Age, Area E: detailed plan and profiles of CS 3290.

Fig 55.   Easton Lane. Phase 4, Middle Bronze Age, Area E: CS 3290 with wooden pegs marking the post-holes. View from the northwest, scale 2m.

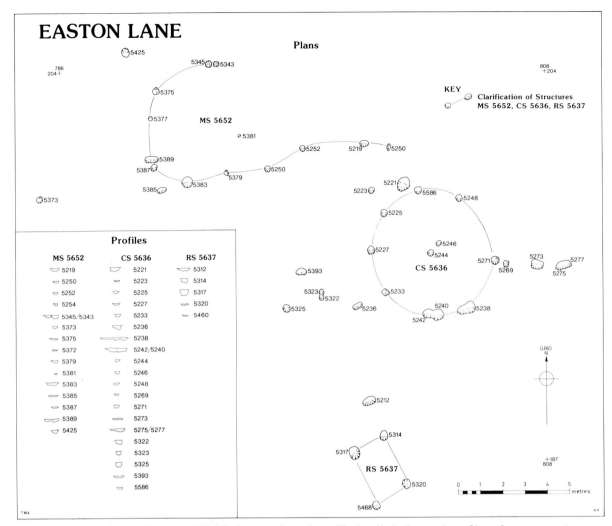

Fig 56.   Easton Lane. Phase 4, Middle Bronze Age, Area H: detailed plan and profiles of a structural group including CS 5636, MS 5652 and RS 5637.

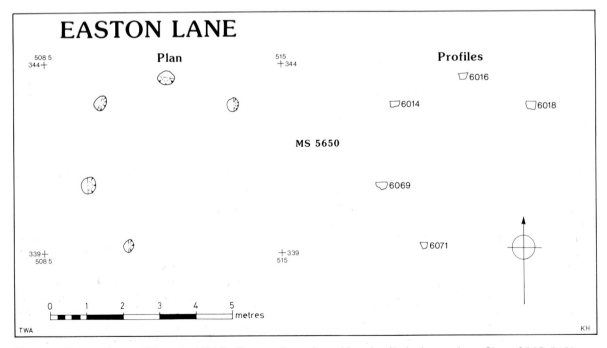

Fig 57.   Easton Lane. Phase 4, Middle Bronze Age, Area Mc: detailed plan and profiles of MS 5650.

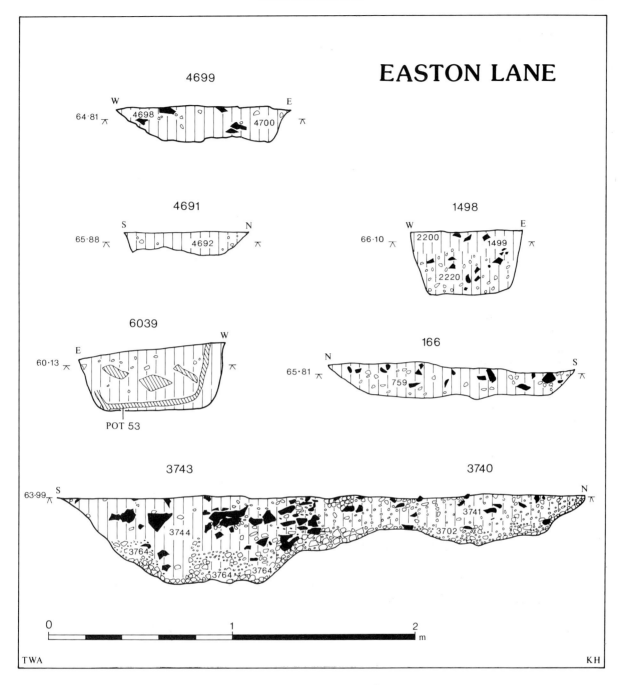

Fig 58. Easton Lane. Phase 4, Middle Bronze Age: sections of selected pits.

Structures

CS 2341 had sherds of both Middle and Late Bronze Age pottery in the post-holes, and the ovoid structure MS 2159 at a corner of the ditch system has been phased to the Middle Bronze Age because of its position even though it contained both Late Bronze Age and Early Iron Age pottery in one of its post-holes. Structures without direct dating evidence, ie CS 2723, MS 5658, MS 5654 and 5657 and RS 5609 in Area B, CS 2782 in Area C, CS 3290 in Area E and MS 5650 in Area Mc, may also have been of Late Bronze Age date. However, the overall proportion of Middle to Late Bronze Age pottery

across the site made it more likely that these were of Middle Bronze Age date.

Ditches (Fig 65)

The occurrence of Late Bronze Age pottery in ditches 176, 1810, 3274 and 6073, and the relationship between ditches 7016 and 7017, enables a sequence to be proposed for the ditch system and to separate Middle and Late Bronze Age components.

The Middle Bronze Age (Phase 4) ditch system was replaced by two larger north-south ditch lines.

The western line, running through Areas Bc and Mc, was a single ditch, variously numbered 7016 in

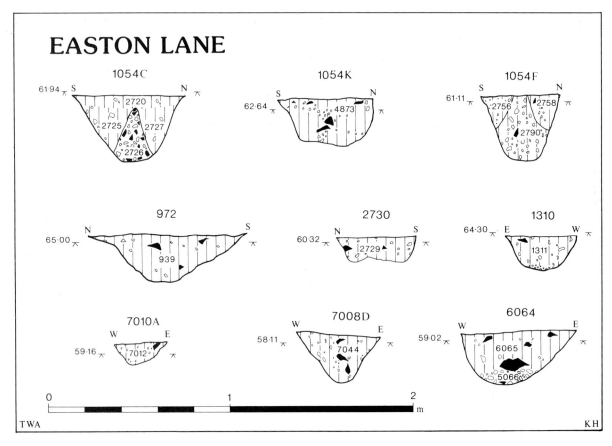

Fig 59.   Easton Lane. Phase 4, Middle Bronze Age: sections of selected ditches.

Area Bc, 3200 in Area E, and 6073 in Area Mc; and was 1.25m-1.70m wide, mean 1.51m, 0.62m-0.80m deep, mean 0.74m. 3274 probably continued this line in transect 20. Ditch 7016 cut ditch 7017 which was part of the Middle Bronze Age system.

On the east, ditch 1810 and its recuts reflect a re-use rather than a replacement of the north-south ditches in the Late Bronze Age. Both the dimensions of the ditch and the relatively high proportion of Late Bronze Age pottery support this interpretation.

Late Bronze Age pottery in ditches 1054 and 972 suggests that part of the southern line of the east-west Middle Bronze Age ditches was also re-used.

Other features and pottery finds

There were occurrences of Late Bronze Age pottery in thirty-four contexts from twenty features: eight post-holes, three pits, one gully and eight ditches. The ditches accounted for nineteen of the contexts and are mentioned above, except for ditch 511 in Area G. This short ditch occurred within pit group 653 and contained a sherd of decorated Late Bronze Age jar (Fig 88.60). Pit group 653 also contained an illustrated Late Bronze Age sherd (Fig 88.61). In addition to the ditches, only an isolated post-hole, 6000, which occurred in the north of Area Mc, has been assigned to this phase. Of the twenty features

which contained Late Bronze Age pottery, four also contained, and were dated by, Middle Bronze Age pottery and a further seven have been assigned to the Middle Bronze Age because of their associations and spatial relationships. Five later features contained residual Late Bronze Age pottery, of which one sherd of decorated Late Bronze Age jar from gully 319 in Area A, has been illustrated (Fig 88.62). In comparison, 52 features contained Middle Bronze Age pottery.

Phase 6. Early Iron Age (Fig 66)

No structures have been allocated to this phase. A limited number of Early Iron Age sherds occurred as residual material in later pits and structures, mainly in Area A. This distribution probably reflects the presence of secondary activity to the northwest of the enclosed settlement at Winnall Down.

Pits (Fig 70)

Five shallow, amorphous pits in Area A – 342, 1147, 2154, 4577 and 4917 – contained Early Iron Age pottery. The pits had a total volume of 2.24m^3 and an average of 0.45m^3. Pit 342 contained a fragment of greensand quern and was the only one not cut by later features. It seems likely that these pits were peripheral to the enclosed settlement.

Fig 60. Easton Lane. Phase 4, Middle Bronze Age, Area B: ditch 1054 showing recuts. View from the west, scale 2m.

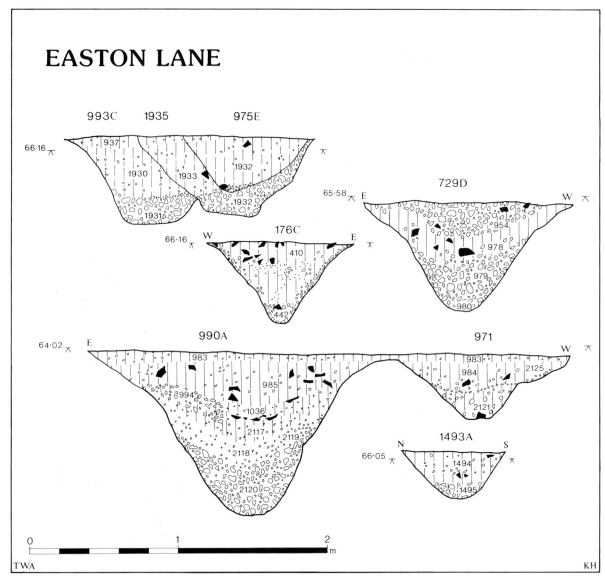

Fig 61.   Easton Lane. Phase 4, Middle Bronze Age: sections of selected ditches.

Ditches

The Late Bronze Age ditch system in Area A was still evident, if not used, throughout this phase, as the Early Middle Iron Age Phase 7 settlement related to boundaries provided by ditches 1810, 729, 176 and 1493. The system may have been modified in this phase with the construction of ditch 928.

Ditch 928/993, 0.80m-0.90m wide, mean 0.86m, 0.42m-0.73m deep, mean 0.59m, containing Early Iron Age pottery, formed a short arc, about 30m long. This arc was then recut by ditch 350/971/1011/1935, 0.70m-1.60m wide, mean 0.93m, 0.30m-0.64m deep, mean 0.39m, which extended to the south to join with and recut the northern end of Phase 4/5 ditch 1810, and again contained Early Iron Age pottery. This curving ditch system was recut again in the Middle Iron Age by ditch 975. The function of these ditches is not understood, although the arc divided the Early Middle Iron Age settlement in two.

Ditches 176 and 729 contained Early Iron Age pottery and were sufficiently extant to be used in the Early Middle Iron Age, Phase 7, as settlement boundaries. It would seem likely that ditches 176, 729, 1493 and 975 could have been re-used Phase 4 ditches in a way comparable to the re-use of Phase 4/5 ditch 1810 by ditch 350.

Phase 7. Early Middle Iron Age (Fig 67)

This phase was characterised by an unenclosed settlement containing circular gully-built structures, post-hole clusters, other auxillary structures and pits and burials. Part of the Bronze Age ditch system survived and served to delimit the settlement.

The bulk of the Iron Age pottery was found in Area A and has been divided into three phases of Early Iron Age, Early Middle Iron Age and Middle Iron Age. The Early Iron Age component has been

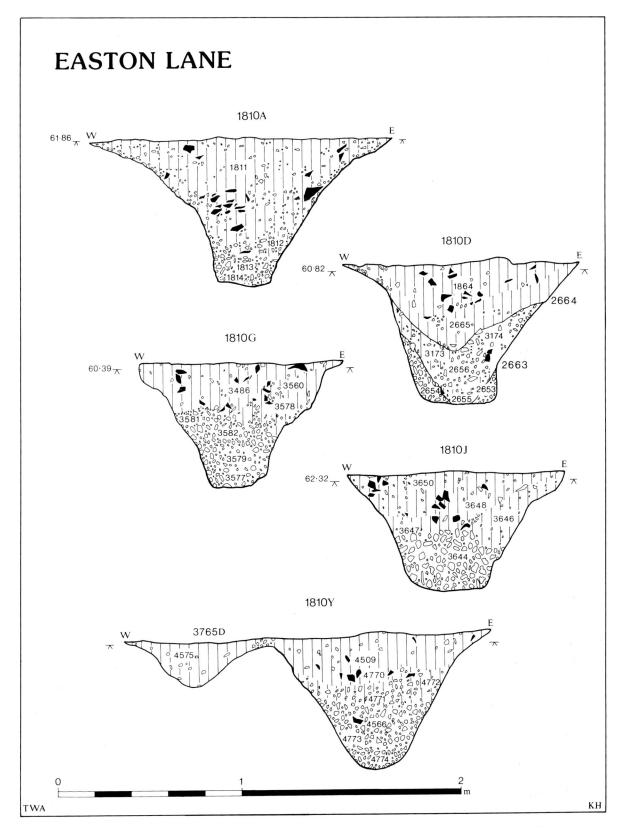

Fig 62.   Easton Lane. Phase 4, Middle Bronze Age: sections of selected ditches.

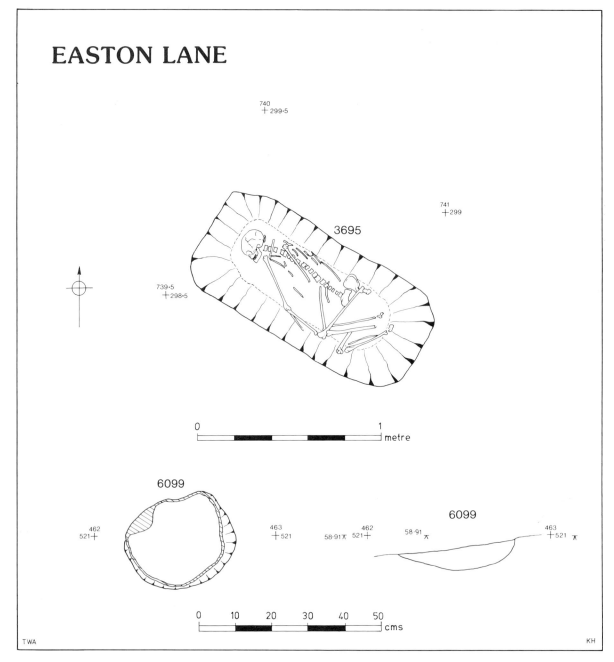

Fig 63.   Easton Lane. Phase 4, Middle Bronze Age: plan of inhumation 3695; plan and section of cremation 6099.

regarded as largely redeposited. The Early Middle Iron Age and Middle Iron Age components occurred in overlapping distributions in post-holes, gullies, pits and ditches. The structures appeared to have a higher proportion of Early Middle Iron Age pottery and, thus, are included in this phase, while the pits have been allocated between the Iron Age phases. The assignment of pits and structures to Early Middle Iron Age or Middle Iron Age was influenced by the overall view of settlement development throughout the Iron Age which was reached by combining the interpretation from this excavation with that from Winnall Down.

Structures

Fifteen gully and post-built structures, four four-post structures and numerous lengths of fence were assigned to this phase. The structures were all in Area A (Figs 68 and 69) and were divided physically into two groups by the curving ditch line formed by the Phase 6–7 ditches 928, 1935 and 975. This division may have represented a change of function or even a limited sequential development within the Early Middle Iron Age. In addition to the structures definitely assigned to this phase, the oval or sub-rectangular structure of sixteen post-holes, MS 2159,

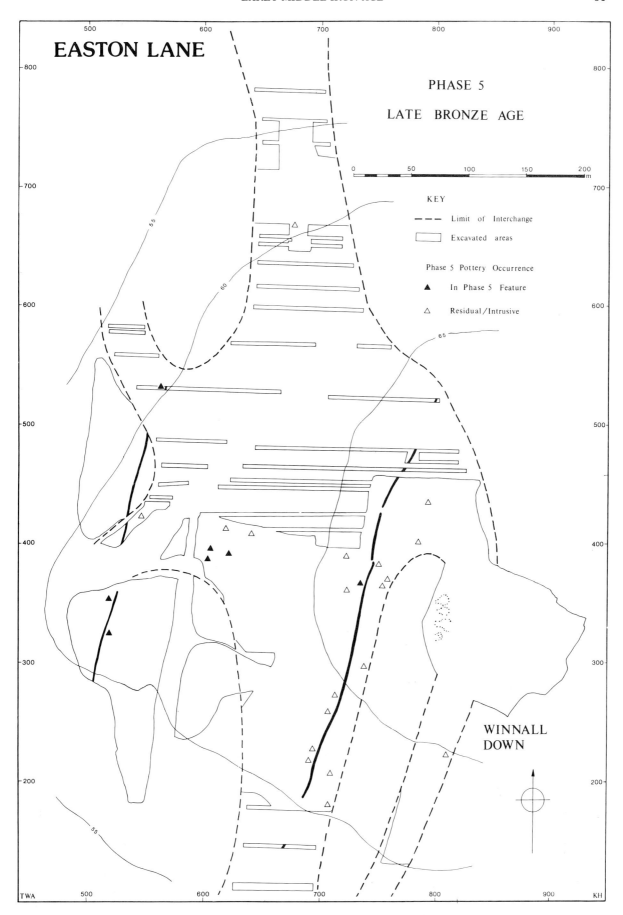

EASTON LANE

PHASE 5

LATE BRONZE AGE

KEY

– – – Limit of Interchange

☐ Excavated areas

Phase 5 Pottery Occurrence

▲ In Phase 5 Feature

△ Residual/Intrusive

WINNALL DOWN

Fig 64. Easton Lane. Distribution plan of Phase 5, Late Bronze Age, features and pottery.

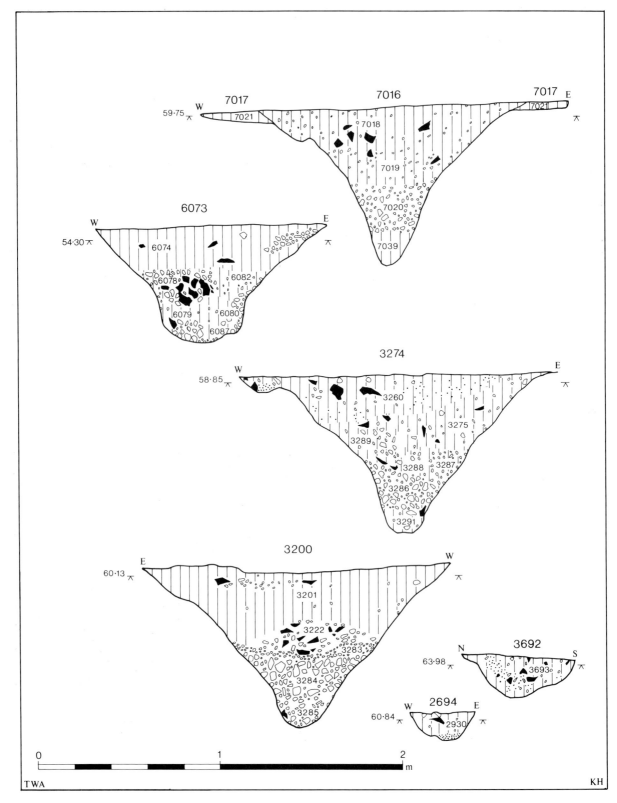

Fig 65.   Easton Lane. Phase 4, Middle Bronze Age, and Phase 5, Late Bronze Age: sections of selected ditches.

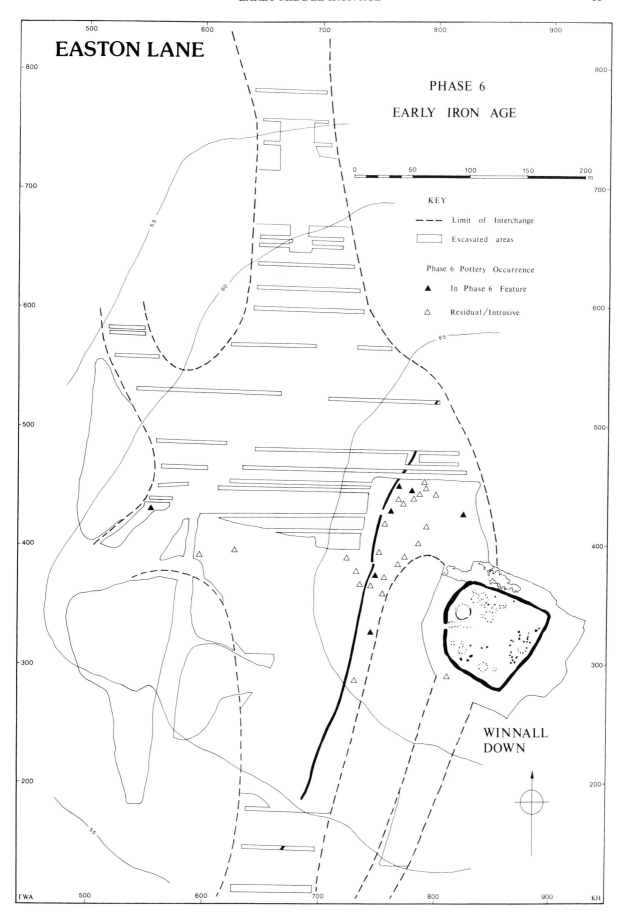

Fig 66. Easton Lane. Distribution plan of Phase 6, Early Iron Age, features and pottery.

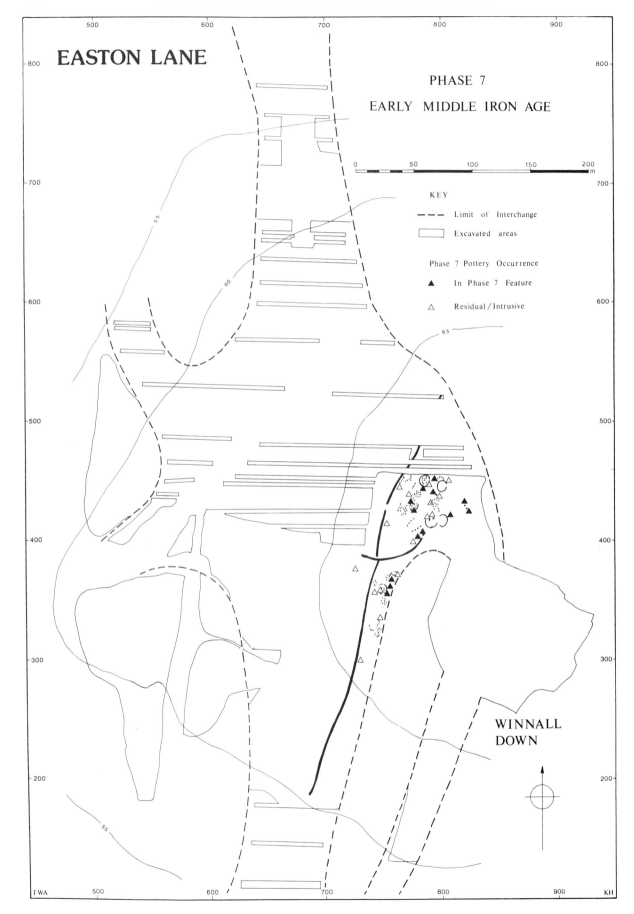

Fig 67.   Easton Lane. Distribution plan of Phase 7, Early Middle Iron Age, features and pottery.

Fig 69.   Easton Lane. Phase 7, Early Middle Iron Age, Area A: view of structures.

in the corner of the Middle Bronze Age ditch system provided a radiocarbon determination of 2220±100 BP (HAR 6118). This structure could well relate to the Iron Age, although spatially it seems best associated with the Bronze Age fields.

The northern group of structures had a clear central axis running approximately north-south which was probably a central pathway which turned southwest at its southern end to pass between LS 5645 and LS 5646. In the northern group were three circular structures, seven miscellaneous structures, two rectangular structures and a number of linear structures. They can be grouped as follows:

CS 2404 with associated structures MS 4019 and LS 5639–42;

CS 2408 with associated structures MS 2406 and RS 2407;

CS 2288 with associated structures MS 5656 and MS 4020;

MS 5622 with associated structures LS 5644 and LS 5648;

MS 2160 with associated structure RS 5647;

Discrete structures MS 5643, MS 2410, LS 5645 and LS 5646.

CS 2404, 11.25m diameter, was formed by a gully 0.16m-0.42m wide, mean 0.30m, 0.07m-0.25m deep, mean 0.16m. A 2.85m wide gap in the gully, together with two large post-holes, 908 and 907, formed a recessed entrance facing southeast. Using the relative proportions of post-ring and gully diameter from CS 2408, where the evidence for a post-ring is stronger, a post-ring of 7.2m diameter can be suggested with post-hole 112 as the central point. This ring passes through or encloses the majority of the post-holes within the structure. Two short arcs of post-holes were also

apparent. To the south the gully cut a group of earlier Iron Age pits.

MS 4019 was an oval cluster of 44 post- and stake-holes with a short section of gully extending for 9.75m east-west by 5.75m north-south. There was a hint of a five-post ring, 6.5m diameter, which enclosed the majority of the post-holes, similar to that within CS 2288, so the presence of a roofed structure cannot be entirely ruled out. Within the cluster were paired post-holes and arcs of four and five post-holes.

LS 5639, LS 5640, LS 5641 and LS 5642 were lines of four post-holes each and were 1.75m, 2.50m, 1.10m and 1.50m long respectively.

CS 2408, 15m diameter, was formed by a gully 0.53m-0.98m wide, mean 0.75m, 0.25m-0.56m deep, mean 0.37m. Longitudinal sections through the gully showed post-holes within its fill. Some reached to the base of the gully. A 5.60m wide gap in the gully with two large post-holes, 286 and 825, formed a recessed entrance facing southeast. Forty-three post- and stake-holes were found within the building. These included an irregular scoop, 287, which may have been associated with a post central to an internal ring, 9m in diameter, of five deep post-holes, 878, 889, 1172, 1174 and 1419, which was interrupted by a small undated pit, 289. There was a small oval cluster of post-holes in the southwest of the structure, 3.50m long and 2.75m wide.

MS 2406 was an oval cluster of sixteen post-holes to the north of CS 2408 which covered an area of 5.75m east-west by 4.50m north-south. It was originally thought, in the field, to have been an oval building but it could equally be interpreted as two facing arcs of four small post-holes each and a further arc of larger post-holes to the south.

RS 2407 was a small, rectangular four-post structure 1.60m by 1.00m, immediately northwest of CS 2408.

CS 2288, 10.25m diameter, was formed by a badly eroded gully which was completely absent in the northeast and southwest. Where present it measured 0.26m-0.50m wide, mean 0.30m, 0.08m-0.13m deep, mean 0.10m. There were two possible entrances. One on the east, 1.10m wide with an associated external post-hole, 52, opened onto the central path, and the other to the west, 1.20m wide with an associated internal post-hole, 74, gave access to MS 4020. Seventeen other post-holes were within the

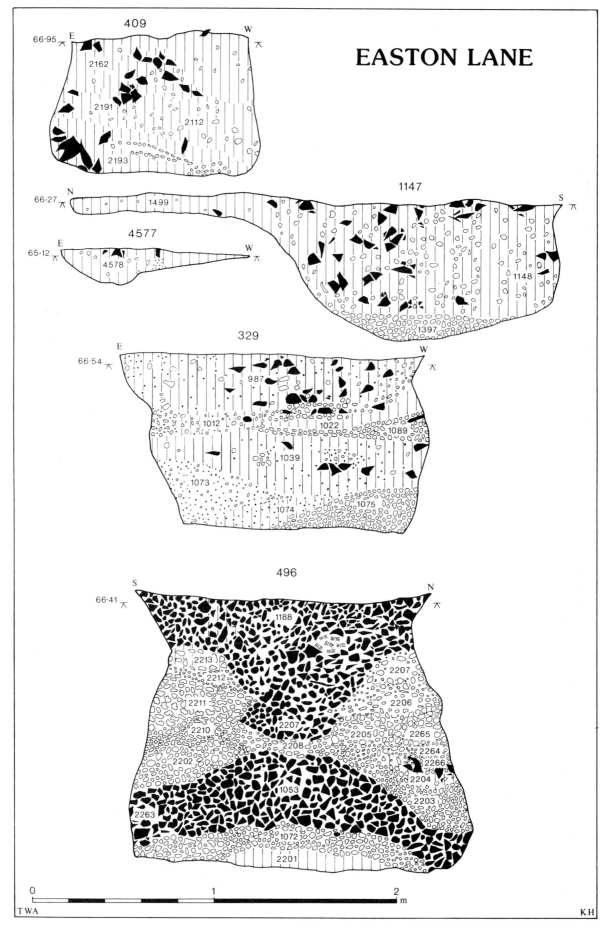

Fig 70.   Easton Lane. Phase 6, Early Iron Age, and Phase 7, Early Middle Iron Age: sections of selected pits.

building area, of which one, 1204, continued the line of the gully in the north. A ring of five post-holes, 7m in diameter, was also apparent. Within the structure were irregular feature 8 and Early Middle Iron Age pit 496.

MS 5656, an oval group of ten post-holes, 4.50m east-west by 3.30m north-south, was northwest of CS 2288; it formed a similar pairing to that of CS 2408 and MS 2406.

MS 4020 was a circular cluster, 10.50m diameter, of thirty-five post-holes and two slots. A possible outer ring of post-holes, 10m in diameter, can be identified but there are too many possible combinations for a detailed resolution of the building or sequence of buildings. Three pits and two hollows were within this area. Pit 342 was probably of Early Iron Age date.

MS 5622, gully 4901, described two-thirds of a circle with a maximum diameter 10.50m. The gully was 0.35m-0.50m wide, mean 0.40m, 0.10m-0.14m deep, mean 0.11m, and its open side faced west. Four post-holes may be related, of which one, 5577, was central. This was a complete structure with clear terminals to the gully. The open, west side was deliberate and not a consequence of subsequent erosion.

LS 5644, a line of four post-holes, 5m long, ran northeast to southwest to the north of MS 5622.

LS 5648, a line of three post-holes, 3.20m long, ran northeast to southwest to the north of MS 5622.

MS 2160, gully 319, was semi-circular in plan, open to the northeast with a maximum width of 11.60m, gully mean width 0.40m, mean depth 0.06m. The east terminal expanded to 0.65m wide while the west terminal had two small post-holes against its outer edge. Three post-holes and three pits were physically within this structure but the pits seem to post-date it.

RS 5647, a square four-poster, 1.00m across, was immediately southwest of MS 2160.

MS 5643 was an irregular series of short fence lines running east-west, to the west of and against ditch 176. These fences extended over an area 19.50m long by 5.00m wide.

MS 2410, a group of twenty-four post-holes, had been interpreted as two structures. To the north was a rough rectangle with a central division, 5.25m north-south by 4.20m east-west, and to the south an oval 5.65m north-south by 4.90m east-west.

LS 5645 and LS 5646 were fence lines of five posts each, 5.85m and 7.15m long respectively, which ran parallel from northeast to southwest. They formed the boundaries of the southern end of the central path which ran through the northern half of the settlement.

The southern group comprised two circular structures, three miscellaneous structures and two rectangular structures. They were in a loose line parallel to ditch 1810. The area to the east was outside the motorway line and thus unexcavated. They could be grouped as follows:
CS 5634 with associated structures MS 5638, RS 5659 and RS 2158;
MS 5633;
CS 5602;
MS 5632.

CS 5634, 13.50m diameter, was defined by an incomplete circular gully. It was eroded away on the west side and replaced or enlarged by gully 2105 and post-hole 4664 to the northeast. It was 0.25m-0.55m wide, mean 0.36m, and 0.06m-0.23m deep, mean 0.12m. Nineteen post-holes were within the gully, together with six pits, 4567, 4620, 4622, 4710, 4760 and 4886. Early Middle Iron Age and Middle Iron Age pottery was recovered from pits 4567, 4622 and 4886, only Middle Iron Age pottery from pit 4620, and pits 4710 and 4760 remain undated.

MS 5638 was a short arc of eroded gully, mean width 0.26m, mean depth 0.07m. Within the 8m circle so created were six post-holes, pits 407 and 409 and slot 406. Only pit 409 could be directly dated to the Early Middle Iron Age.

RS 5659, a rectangular four-post structure, length 2.20m, width 1.50m, was north of CS 5634.

RS 2158, a rectangular four-post structure, length 2.50m, width 1.45m, was immediately northwest of CS 5634.

MS 5633 was a cluster of eighteen post-holes, ten of which fell on or near to a 7m diameter ring, although the evidence is not necessarily strong enough to be considered proof of a roofed structure.

CS 5602, 12.50m diameter, was indicated by an eroded gully, with the northwest segment missing. It was 0.30m-0.50m wide, mean 0.38m, 0.09m-0.18m deep, mean 0.12m. There were six associated post-holes of which two deep ones, 4569 and 4571, formed a recessed entrance inside a 3.75m wide east-facing gap in the gully. Gully 4595 and post-hole 4737 may have formed part of a one-sided porch for this entrance. Alternatively, they may have been a small shelter for an auxillary working area, similar to auxillary structure 5632 which was associated with this structure.

MS 5632 consisted of a short arc of gully, 4516, 0.30m wide and 0.15m deep, maximum length 4.35m, and nine post-holes forming an oval cluster with maximum diameter 8.00m.

Pits (Fig 70)

Only eight pits could be attributed directly to this phase. A further nine pits contained a mixture of Early Middle Iron Age and Middle Iron Age pottery and are dealt with in Phase 8. The eight pits directly dated to this phase were: 329, 407, 409, 496, 707, 982, 1391 and 5038. Cylindrical pit 329 and irregular pit 982 occurred at the end of curving ditch 928, irregular pit 407 and cylindrical pit 409 were within structure 5658, beehive-shaped pit 496 was within structure 2288, irregular pit 707 was 7m southwest of structure 2408, irregular pit 1391 was associated with structure 2404, and irregular pit 5038 was in a group of pits 12m east of the northern half of the Early Middle Iron Age settlement. Of these, the following contained additional finds.

329 contained a chalk loomweight, a greensand weight and a fragment of greensand rotary quern.
409 contained a fragment of triangular clay loomweight, fragments of a greensand rotary quern and two saddle querns. This pit was associated with MS 5638.
496 contained fragments of a triangular clay loomweight, fragments of greensand querns and was associated with circular structure 2288.

The distribution of these pits coincided with the Phase 7 structures, except for pit 4983 which was some 20m to the east. The combined volume of these pits was 8.57m³ with an average volume of 1.07m³ (or a total of 7.44m³ and an average of 1.86m³ if pits have to be more than 0.75m deep and have a volume of 0.50m³ or more to be accepted, as only four pits meet these criteria).

Ditches

The northern and western limits of the Early Middle Iron Age Phase 7 settlement were formed by part of the Phase 4–5 ditch system. It seems that these ditches, if not actively re-used, had survived to form a recognisable physical presence around the living space. Ditches 176, 729, 928, 972 and 3765 all contained Early Middle Iron Age pottery. Some of this pottery was probably intrusive but a part probably represents the continued recutting and infilling of these ditches during this phase.

The curving ditch 928, which was recut by ditch 1935 and part of ditch 975, originated in Phase 6 and continued into this phase. This arc divided the Early Middle Iron Age settlement area and may have, in conjuction with LS 5645 and LS 5646, formed part of a rather grand entrance which led into the northern half of the settlement area.

Burials

Three burials and four occurrences of human bone were discovered in Area A.

Disturbed burial 1035 was that of an infant 1–3 years old which was cut into Phase 4 ditch 990 (Fig 71).

Burial 4978 was that of a contracted skeleton of an adult male aged 35–45 years with the head to the north (Fig 71). The skeleton was arranged with the legs drawn up beneath the torso, which was prone. The grave was an irregular oval 0.50m deep, 1.30m long and 0.50m wide which cut Phase 4–5 ditch 1810.

Layer 354 in ditch 176 contained the disturbed burial of a female adult of which about half the skeleton survived. Layer 354 also contained fragments of bone from the skeleton of a male adult.

None of these were directly datable but their stratigraphic relationships and proximity to the Phase 7 settlement suggests that they were all of Early Middle Iron Age date.

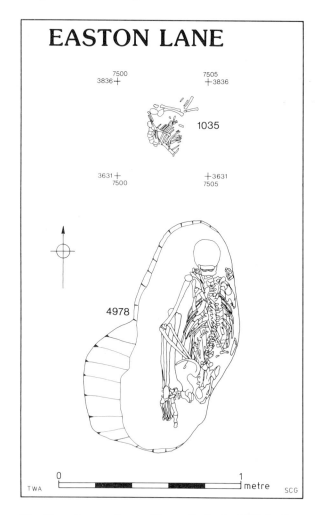

EASTON LANE

1035

4978

0   1
TWA   metre   SCG

Fig 71.   Easton Lane. Phase 7, Early Middle Iron Age: burials 1035 and 4978.

A few fragments of adult human bone were recovered from post-hole 907 and pit 409.

Some fragments of cremated human bone were found in post-hole 169.

Phase 8. Middle Iron Age (Fig 72)

The majority of Middle Iron Age, Phase 8, material came from Area A and consisted of a few features that were stratigraphically later than Phase 7 or could be distinguished on ceramic grounds. While it is possible that the Early Middle Iron Age settlement contained elements that continued through into the Middle Iron Age it seems most likely that such Phase 8 features as have been identified represented activity peripheral to the focus of the Middle Iron Age settlement which had returned to the area of the earlier enclosed settlement at Winnall Down.

Pits (Figs 73 and 74)

Eight pits were directly attributed to this phase. They were 8, 17, 1100, 4620, 4921, 4928, 4951 and 4983. A further eight contained both Middle Iron Age pottery and earlier, presumably residual, material. These were pits 238, 316, 317, 4560, 4567, 4622, 4886 and 4933. 17, 4622, 4921, 4951 and 4983 were beehive-shaped, 316, 317, 4620 and 4928 were cylindrical and the rest were of irregular shape. 4921, 4928, 4951, 4933 and 4983 occurred in a linear north-south group 30m long and 10m-20m east of the northern half of the Early Middle Iron Age settlement; 8 occurred within the arc of structure 2288; 17 and 238 were close to structure 2410; 316, 317 and 1100 were within the area of structure 2160; 4567, 4620, 4622 and 4886 were within the area of structure 5634; and 4560 cut the gully of structure 5602. Of these, the following contained additional finds.

Irregular-shaped pit 238 contained a fragment of greensand rotary quern.

Cylindrical pit 316 contained a bone spindle whorl, fragments of two greensand rotary querns and was associated with MS 2160.

Cylindrical pit 317 contained a triangular clay loomweight, fragments of two greensand rotary querns and was associated with MS 2160.

Irregular-shaped pit 1100 contained a fragment of greensand quern, a flint scraper and was associated with MS 2160.

Irregular-shaped pit 4560 contained a bone implement, a cylindrical clay spindlewhorl, six chalk loomweights and was associated with CS 5602.

Irregular-shaped pit 4567 contained fragments of clay loomweight, a sarsen weight, a chalk loomweight, a damaged greensand saddle quern and was associated with CS 5634.

Beehive-shaped pit 4622 contained a fragment of triangular clay loomweight and was associated with CS 5634.

Beehive-shaped pit 4921 contained a fragment of greensand quern.

Cylindrical pit 4928 contained a fragment of greensand quern.

Beehive-shaped pit 4983 contained a flint scraper and a few fragments of human bone.

The combined volume of all these pits was 50.68m³ with an average of 3.17m³ (or total of 48.02m³ and an average of 4.00m³ if pits are defined as being more than 0.75m deep and have a volume of 0.5m³ or more; only eleven pits meet these criteria).

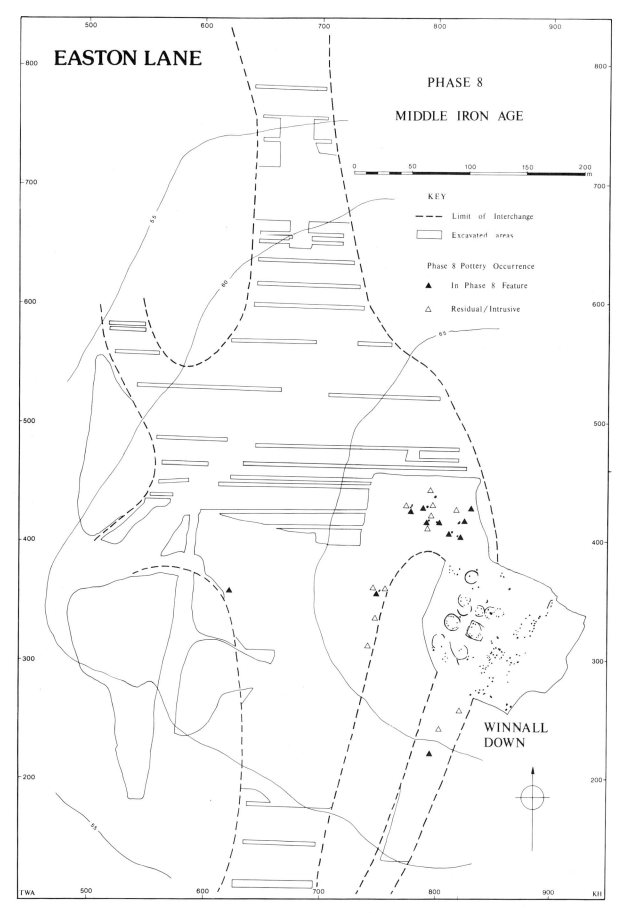

Fig 72.   Easton Lane. Distribution plan of Phase 8, Middle Iron Age, features and pottery.

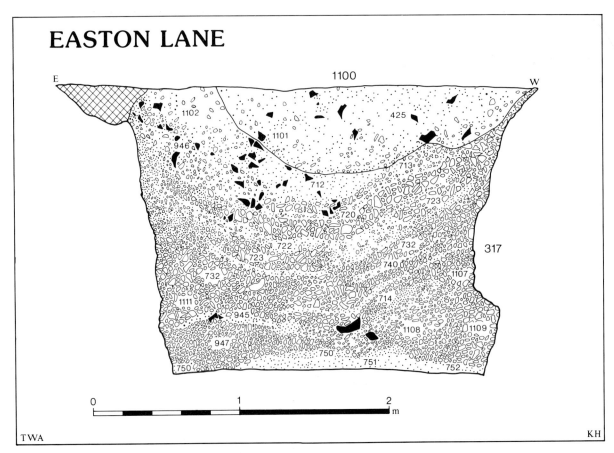

Fig 73.   Easton Lane. Phase 8, Middle Iron Age: section of pits 1100 and 317.

Ditches and other features

Ditch 975 was stratigraphically later than ditches 928 and 1935 but could not be dated on ceramic grounds. It could therefore be included in this phase. However the function of the curved ditch, although not obvious, would seem to be connected with the Early Middle Iron Age settlement and most likely predates Phase 8.

Middle Iron Age pottery was discovered in the following additional features.

Area A: post-hole 34 in MS 2410, post-hole 230 in MS 4019, post-hole 4602 in MS 5633, and post-hole 4906.
Area B: slot 1619 in CS 2373.
Area H: post-hole 5019, pit 5347 and ditch 5302.

None of these could be considered significant, and are believed to represent intrusive material.

Phase 9. Late Iron Age/ Early Roman (Fig 75)

Only a limited amount of pottery attributable to this phase was recovered. However, most of it occurred within a small area, Area H (Fig 76), where it served to date securely a sequence of small enclosures which were first encountered during the Winnall Down excavation. Conquest period pottery was also recov-ered from post-hole 1992 and pit 1100 in Area A, and natural feature 2537 in Area B.

Enclosure ditches and structure

The ditches (Fig 77) formed the southern extent of the enclosure system excavated at Winnall Down (Phase 6 periods ii and iii). Two of the Winnall Down ditches, 6732 and 6740, were partly re-excavated and numbered respectively as Easton Lane Interchange 5293 and 5007. The ditches were in two main sequences (Fig 78). The earliest was 5007, a shallow, 0.50m wide ditch with gently sloping sides and 0.10m deep, which formed the western limit of the enclosure system. At its southern end it formed a right-angle and was traced to the west for 5m. The second part of the sequence was formed by the larger ditches, 5039, 5042, 5293, 5295 and 5302, which defined a series of three enclosures. These enclosures are lettered D, E and F to maintain the sequence from Winnall Down. The ditches around enclosure D, 5042 and the northern part of 5293, were 1.50m wide and 0.60m deep and 1.48m wide and 0.67m deep respectively. Around enclosure E were ditches 5042, 5302 and the southern part of 5293. 5302 was 1.40m wide and 0.58m deep. The west and south sides of F were formed by ditches 5295 and 5039 whose respective dimensions were 2.20m wide by 0.85m deep and 1.80m wide by 0.60m deep. From the plan it looks as

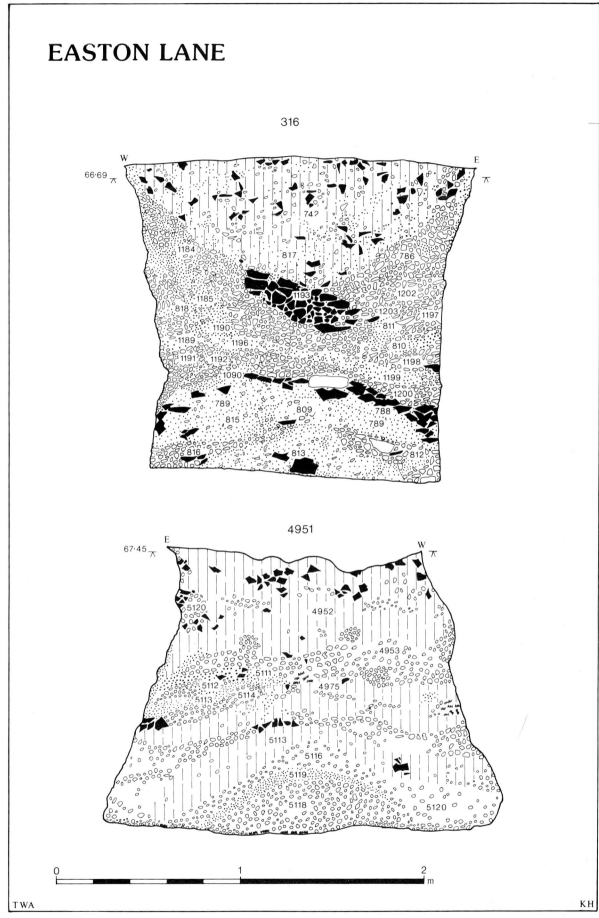

Fig 74. Easton Lane. Phase 8, Middle Iron Age: sections of pits 316 and 4951.

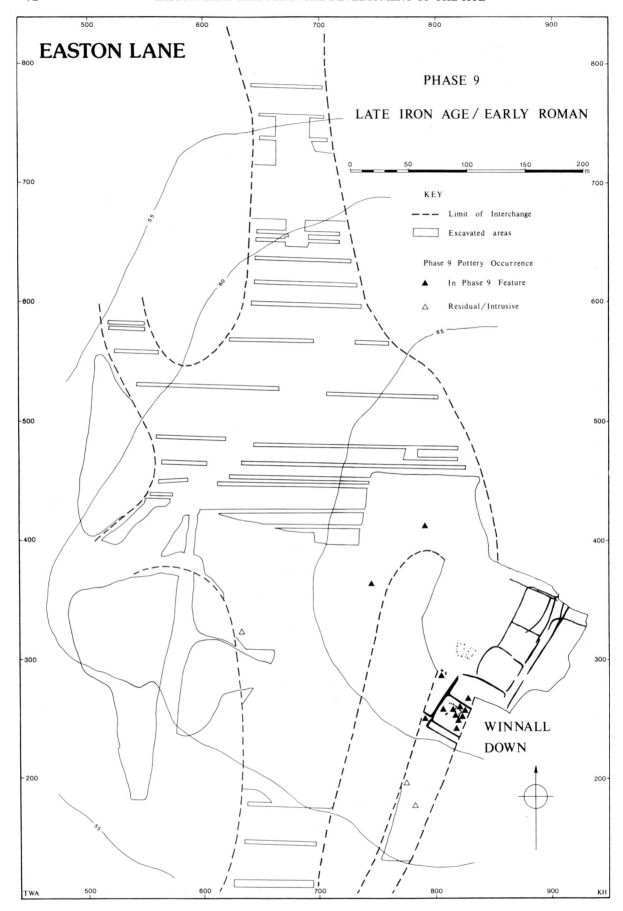

Fig 75.   Easton Lane. Distribution plan of Phase 9, Late Iron Age/Early Roman, features and pottery.

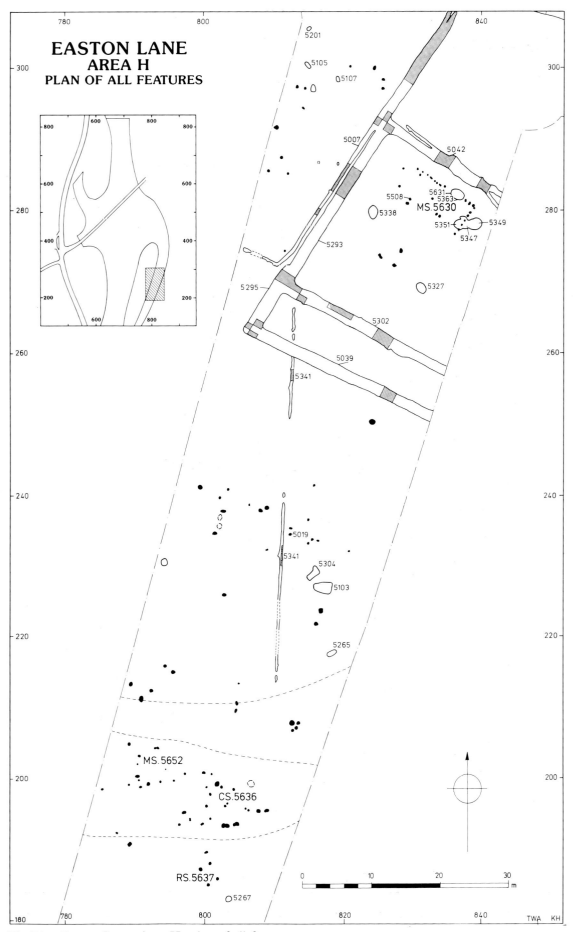

Fig 76.   Easton Lane. Area H, plan of all features.

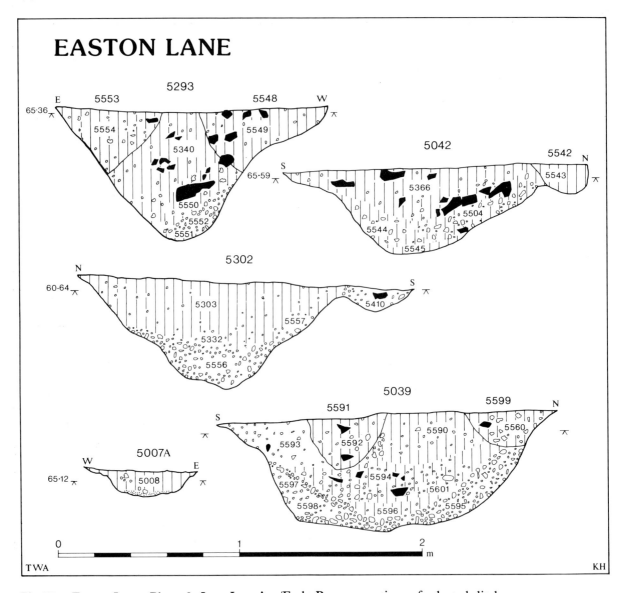

Fig 77.   Easton Lane. Phase 9, Late Iron Age/Early Roman: sections of selected ditches.

if enclosure F was an addition to the sequence, but the archaeological evidence does not demonstrate this. The enclosures covered an area of about 150m north-south by 50m east-west.

Within enclosure E and aligned on it was a post-built structure, MS 5630. This consisted of twenty-two post-holes which formed a right-angle with sides of 9.75m and 4.75m length. The longer side was interrupted by pits 5361 and 5363. Eight other post-holes occurred within the immediate area of this structure.

Pits

Five pits were assigned to this phase: 5347, 5349, 5351, 5361 and 5363. The largest, although shallow, was 5351 with a volume of 2.18m³. The rest were small steep-sided pits. No special finds were recovered from these features. Their total volume was 4.84m³, mean 0.97m³. All five pits occurred within the ditched enclosures and one, 5351, predated post-hole structure 5630, since two post-holes cut it.

Burials (Fig 79)

Five human skeletons were found in Area H. Only one was directly dated, but all were assigned to this phase because of their proximity to the ditched enclosure and the lack of features from other phases in their immediate vicinity.

Most of the skeleton of a foetal/neonate was recovered from layer 5337 in ditch 5624, a recut of enclosure ditch 5295.

5263 was the skeleton of an old male in a disturbed, contracted position with his head to the north. The burial had been tightly packed into a sub-rectangular pit, 5107, 0.39m deep, 0.75m long by 0.46m wide.

5264 was the skeleton of a woman aged 35–45 years in a crouched position with her head to the northwest. The burial had been tightly packed into a rectangular pit, 5105, 0.22m deep, 1.00m long by 0.55m wide.

5338, a large oval grave-cut 0.28m deep, 1.64m long by 1.32m wide, contained at least two individuals. These were a woman aged 17–25 years, 5424, and most of the skeleton of a foetal/neonate which was not recognised during excavation. The adult was in a crouched position with her head to the southeast.

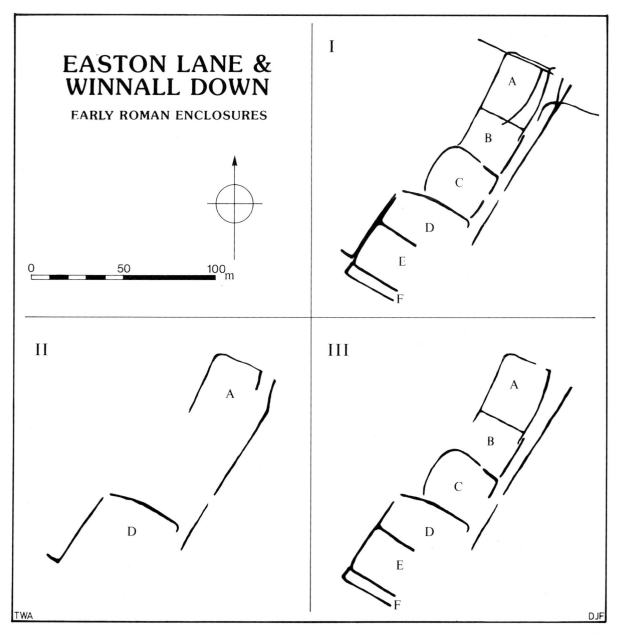

Fig 78. Easton Lane. Phase 9, Early Roman, Area H: plan of enclosures, incorporating information from Winnall Down.

Phase 10. Late Saxon and Medieval (Fig 80)

Medieval pottery occurred throughout the site but much of it was intrusive, especially in Areas B and D. The overall lack of protective stratification, and the position of some sherds in natural features and the upper fills of earlier features, suggests a widespread pattern of disturbance. Many of the features provisionally dated to Phase 10 were post-holes or shallow pits. The phase has been subdivided into Late Saxon and Medieval.

Late Saxon Enclosure MS 5635 (Fig 81)

In Area F, a Late Saxon, rectangular ditched enclosure was discovered. It had a maximum external length of 40m and a width of 16.50m. The ditches, 634 and 5459 (Figs 82 and 83), were 0.40m–1.00m wide, mean 0.70m, and 0.20m-0.35m deep, mean 0.29m, and had irregular 'U' shaped profiles. The long axis ran west-northwest to east-southeast and there was a 1.35m wide gap in the centre of the short eastern side. The ditches contained the bow of a fibula, an iron strip, a fragment of iron horseshoe, three fragments of Mayen lava, a small fragment of fired clay possibly from a loomweight, and a perforated oyster shell. The only feature to be found within the enclosure was pit 654 which contained a rectangular iron ring and a bone plaque, and whose section suggests a possible post-pipe and packing. The enclosure cut pit 5456 and was cut by pit 5461, which contained an iron punch and a fragment of

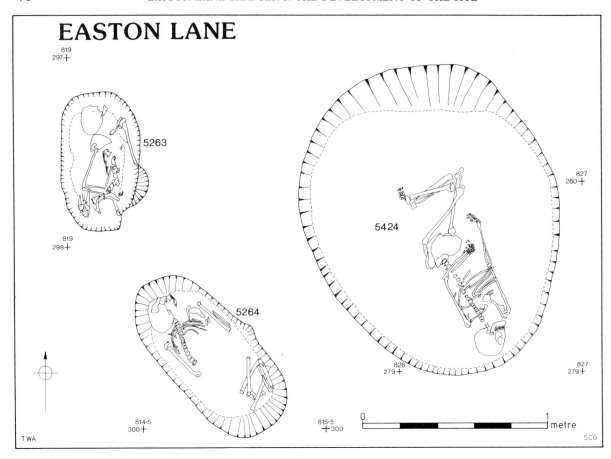

Fig 79.   Easton Lane. Phase 9, Early Roman, Area H: detailed plans of burials.

worked antler. The overall dimensions and lack of associated structural evidence strongly suggests that this was not a roofed structure. However, the amount of pottery and other finds recovered from the enclosure could not have been derived from purely agricultural activities.

Late Saxon pits (Fig 82)

Area F contained seven pits: 600, 610, 612, 621, 631, 654 and 5461. Of these, only 612, 621 and 631 were less than 0.60m deep; however, only 654, which occurred within the rectangular enclosure, contained an appreciable amount of pottery. Pit 600 contained articulated vertebrae and ribs from a horse (Fig 84) which displayed pathology consistent with having been ridden. It seems likely that this pit group may have been associated with the rectangular enclosure.

Medieval pits

Most of the pits assigned to this phase were shallow and/or amorphous. These included 3585 in Area A; 89, 870, 1308 and 1627 in Area B; 2812 in Area D; 5265, 5267 and 5304 in Area H; and 7052 in Area Mc. However, pit 7059 in Area Mc was of reasonable size and shape, as was pit 5103 in Area H, which contained a sheep skeleton (Fig 82).

Medieval pottery was found throughout pit group 653 in Area G, although the amount of intercutting between pits made it impossible to assign specific pits to this phase. The pottery date has been applied to the general disturbance.

Medieval ditches

A number of short sections of ditch were discovered. They formed parts of one or more systems of rectilinear field boundaries which included those found at Winnall Down.

In Area A there was a short east-west ditch, 4596, 0.35m wide and 0.10m deep; in Area D a north-south ditch, 3569, 0.50m wide and 8.20m long; in Area H a discontinuous north-south ditch, 5341, 0.65m wide, 0.12m deep and with a total length of 52.40m (probably continuous with ditch 1100 from Winnall Down); in Area Mc a discontinuous east-west ditch, 6067/6097, c1.00m wide and 0.32m deep; and in transect 3 there was a short section of north-south ditch, 3660, 0.40m wide and 0.16m deep.

Feature 509, transect 24, was a sand-filled natural fault which contained a reasonable amount of Medieval pottery. It was oval in plan, 12.00m by 6.50m, and at least 1.00m deep. It may have been used as a quarry.

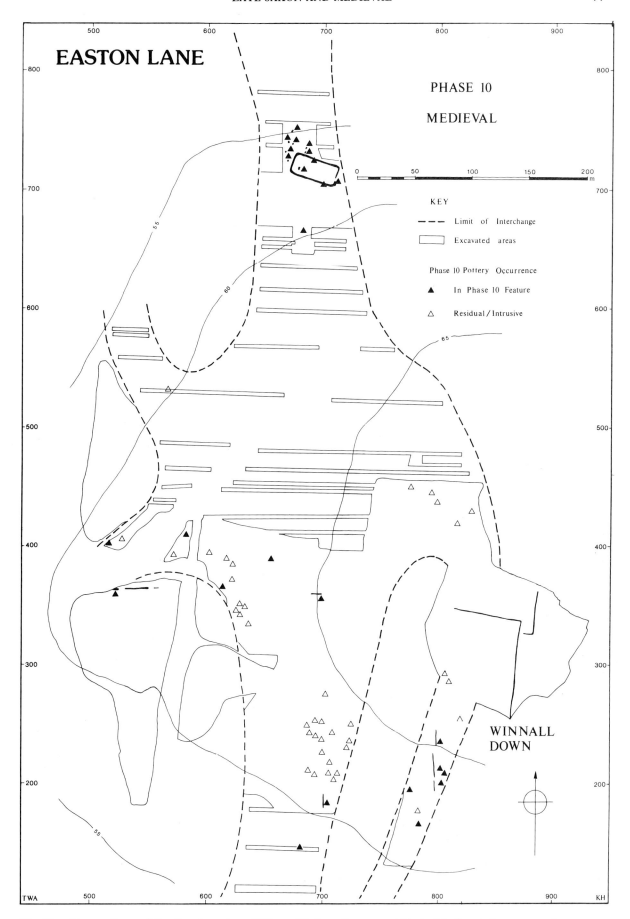

Fig 80. Easton Lane. Distribution plan of Phase 10, Late Saxon and Early Medieval, features and pottery.

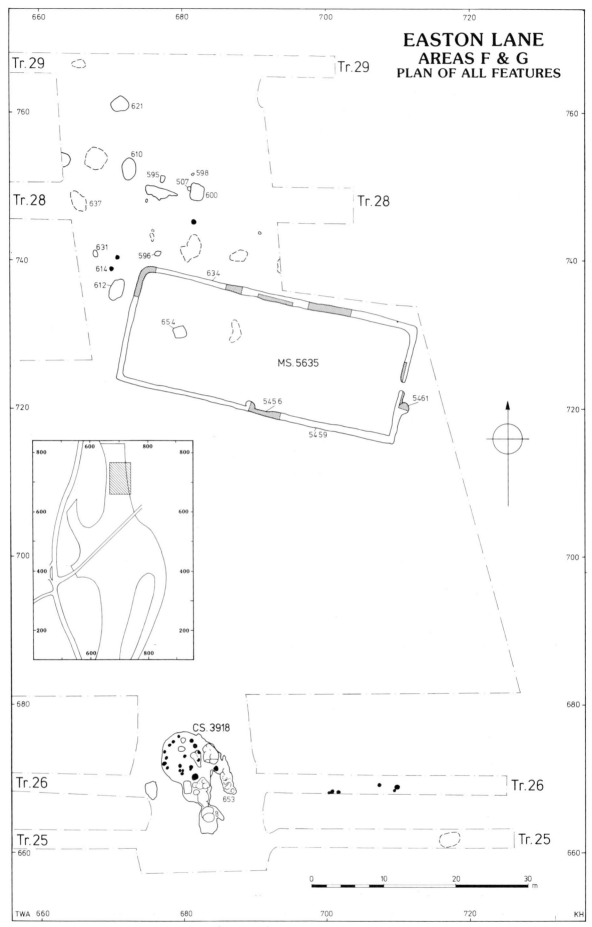

Fig 81.　Easton Lane. Areas F and G, plan of all features.

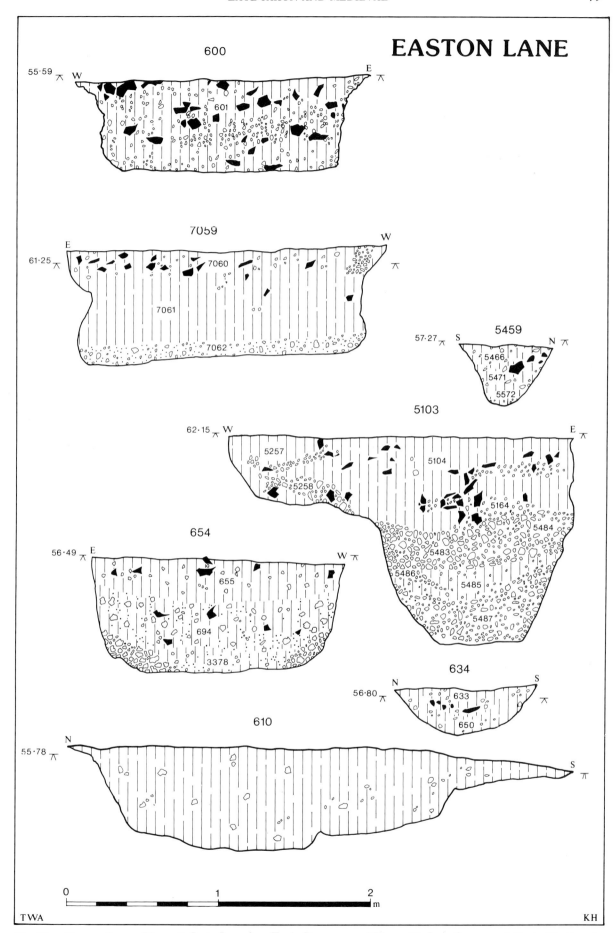

Fig 82. Easton Lane. Phase 9, Late Iron Age/Early Roman, and Phase 10, Late Saxon and Early Medieval: sections of selected pits and ditches.

Fig 83.   Easton Lane. Phase 10, Late Saxon and Early Medieval, Area F: MS 5635 ditch 634 from the west, partially excavated. 2m scale in the foreground; 0.5m horizontal and 0.20m vertical scales against the section.

Fig 84.   Easton Lane. Phase 10, Late Saxon and Early Medieval, Area F: pit 600 from the south; 0.5m and 0.20m scales.

Chapter 3

The Finds

Finds of metal, by D E Farwell with a contribution by C J Gingell

Table 7 summarises the distribution of metal objects by phase.

Table 7. The distribution of metal objects by phase. NP=Not Phased.
Nails and other small iron objects frequently appear as intrusive material.

| Object | Phase | | | | | | |
	2/3	4/5	6–8	9	10	NP	Total
Bronze							
Arrowhead	–	1	–	–	–	–	1
Awl	1	–	–	–	–	–	1
Buckle	–	–	–	–	1	1	2
Fibula	–	–	–	–	1	–	1
Pin	–	1	–	–	–	–	1
Rings	–	–	–	–	–	2	2
Nails and Miscellaneous	1	2	2	1	2	6	14
Iron							
Buckle Plate	–	–	–	–	1	–	1
Padlocks	–	–	–	–	2	–	2
Punch	–	–	–	–	1	–	1
Nails and Miscellaneous	4	14	3	1	13	13	48
	6	18	5	2	21	22	74

Copper alloy (Fig 85)

1. Awl, round section, one end drawn out into a point, the other flattened to a chisel end. Length 29mm. SF 3 in Phase 3, Early Bronze Age, cremation 507, Area F.

Arrowhead, by G J Gingell
2. Tanged arrowhead. SF 224 in Phase 4, Middle Bronze Age, pit 1498, Area A.

    This object consists of a slender triangular blade terminating in an oval tang flanked by short barbs. Length 36.8mm; width 20.1mm; weight 1.7g. Throughout, it consists of thin sheet metal; maximum thickness 0.96mm at centre of blade. The edges are eroded; the point, small areas of the blade and the tips of the both the tang and the barbs are missing. Otherwise, the surface condition is good, the metal overlain by patches of thin black patina with pitting containing a little powdery oxide.

    The shape does not appear to result from casting, but to have been from a small bar or rod. On one surface a very slight, flat midrib is flanked by broad bevels, the other surface being almost flat. A few hammer marks are discer-

nable on the bevel of the blade, but the etched surface does not show honing marks under magnification. The barbs appear to have been cut away from the tang with a cold chisel, leaving a weak constriction at the top of the tang. The resulting groove has been ground or 'filed' with a very narrow edged tool (<0.4mm wide).

Alternative interpretations of this object are i) a razor, ii) a tanged arrowhead. Both razors and arrowheads are usually castings. Although the short flat tang does bear a faint resemblance to the tangs of bifid razors, the combination of a triangualar blade and barbs is not found on any British razor.

Until recently the only certain finds of bronze arrowheads from Britain were the tanged arrowhead from the Penard Hoard, Gower; and a larger example, a chance find from Water Dean Bottom, Enford, Wilts. The writer has now identified a spurred arrowhead from a later Bronze Age settlement at Rowden, Winterbourne Steepleton, Dorset (Woodward forthcoming).

Tanged arrowheads are found in European grave groups and occasionally in hoards, almost entirely distributed to the west of the Rhine. Mercer's survey (1970) shows that the form occurs in France, Spain and the Oberpfalz of Germany during the Tumulus and Urnfield periods (Bronze B onwards) and can be expected to have lasted until Halstatt B. The Penard find of Bronze D/Halstatt A date may suggest that the type belongs to the beginning of the Late Bronze Age in Britain. The example from Easton Lane would appear to be a crude copy of the continental form; only the Penard find, with its Breton links, and that from Water Dean Bottom can be closely paralleled with examples from Europe.

3. Pin, bent, head formed from strip wound round shaft, traces of solder or plating. Probably intrusive. Length (bent) 30.5mm. SF 264 in Phase 4, Middle Bronze Age, post-hole 1591, part of structure 2375, Area B.

4. Strip, 8mm wide, folded over to form square 8mm by 7mm with a triangular shaft. Possible clasp. SF 1 in post-hole 20 associated with Phase 7, Early Middle Iron Age, structure 2410, Area A.

5. Wire or bent shank, the tip missing. Diameter of wire tapers from 1.7mm to 1.0mm. Formed into loop. Diameter 15mm. SF 362 in Phase 9, Early Roman, ditch 5295, Area H.

6. Bow of fibula with part of the hinge intact, traces of white metal coating on hinge and at hinge end of bow. Longitudinal and transverse decoration, five transverse rods within the metal of the bow. Length 44mm. SF 620 in Phase 10, Late Saxon, ditch 5459, Area F.

7. Buckle, bar with lobed ends and broken side pieces, damaged but probably of single-sided D-shaped form, section half-octagonal and half-worn smooth with facets surviving on the outer surfaces only. Length 27mm. SF 5 in Phase 10, Medieval, quarry 509, transect 24.

8. Strip, bent tapering fragment with punched decoration,

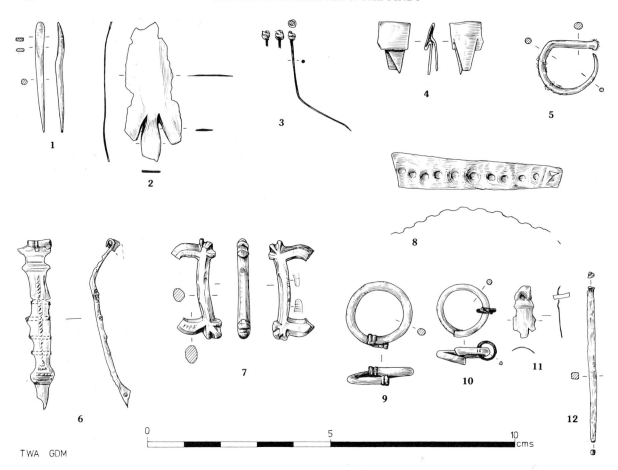

Fig 85.   Easton Lane. Objects of copper alloy and iron.

punch face uneven. Length 45.5mm; width varies from 5mm to 9mm; 0.4mm thick. SF 237 in Phase 10, Medieval, ditch 3569, Area D.

9. Circular ring, 17.3mm diameter, overlapped terminals, plain shank formed of round-sectioned wire, ends in two grooves and two expansions. Diameter of wire 2.5mm. SF 298 in unphased pit 5201, Area H.

10. Circular ring, 14mm diameter, overlapped terminals, no decoration other than a small interlocked glass ring. Metal ring shank, 1.7mm diameter, glass ring diameter 5.3mm, 1mm wide. SF 299 in unphased pit 5201, Area H.

11. Fragment of thin sheet terminal, one end pierced by rivet, still attached, the other end tri-lobate. Length 14mm, length of rivet 4mm. SF 274 in unphased post-hole 2852, Area D.

Not illustrated are a very small irregular fragment from Phase 2, Late Neolithic, pit 1017, Area B; two very small fragments from Phase 4, Middle Bronze Age, post-hole 1858, Area D; a small fragment from Phase 4, Middle Bronze Age, post-hole 5238, Area H; a small fragment of thin sheet, 4mm square, from post-hole 418 which was associated with Phase 7, Early Middle Iron Age, structure 2406, Area A; and a nail, circular to sub-rectangular shaft tapering slightly to a blunt point, slightly domed circular head, length 39mm, diameter of head 10mm, from unphased post-hole 614, Area F.

Also not illustrated are five objects recovered from the topsoil: a thimble, flattened rectangular fragment, decorated on outer face with two pairs of inscribed lines above and below twenty-two columns of small circular punch marks, length 23mm, width 14mm; a strapend buckle, single sided with prong still attached, strap formed from single folded strip with one rivet, buckle formed from worked bar with folded strip over end rib, overall length 36mm; a ferrule, damaged elongated cone formed from

folded sheet, one rivet hole punched through one layer of metal at join, white metal (or solder) present along seam and around outside of metal at narrow end, length 42mm, head 10mm by 7mm, point 5mm by 2mm; a damaged rectangular sheet with seven rivet holes surviving from a pattern of two rows of four, surface scored, length (straightened) 63mm, width (straightened) 28mm; and a folded sheet with parallel inscribed lines, length 25mm, width 20mm.

Lead

Not illustrated. Two pellets or shot were recovered. One from Phase 4, Middle Bronze Age, pit 3058, Area D, and the other from Phase 4, Middle Bronze Age, post-hole 3131, Area D. Both were probably intrusive.

Iron (Fig 85)

The occurrence of small iron objects, mainly nail fragments, as intrusive material in Late Neolithic and Bronze Age contexts reflects the pattern of Medieval disturbance in the upper fills of earlier features.

Nails and possible nail fragments were recovered from the following Phase 2, Late Neolithic, features: pits 1017 and 80 in Area B; pit 6091 in Area Mc; and from post-hole 3829 in Area G. None are illustrated.

Nails, possible nail fragments and irregular fragments were recovered from the following Phase 4 and 5, Middle and Late Bronze Age, features: post-holes 966 in Area A, 1650 in Area B, 1794, 2637 and 3721 in Area D and 5240 in Area H; in ditches 1929 and 1810 in Area A, 1054 in Area B and 3765 in Area D; and in pit 3058 in Area D. None are illustrated.

Two finds of iron were made from Phase 7, Early Middle Iron Age, features, neither of which were illustrated. In Area A there was a small fragment of iron strip from post-hole 1115 which was associated with structure 2408, and in Area D there was a nail

TWA GDM

head from post-hole 4648 which was associated with structure 5633.

A nail was recovered from Phase 9, Late Iron Age/ Early Roman, post-hole 5508 in Area H.

12. Punch, square section, 3mm thick, tapering slightly by 0.5mm to each end, one end burred and slightly deformed, the other flat. Possibly a nail or rivet punch. Length 82mm. SF 304, in Phase 10, Medieval, pit 5461, Area F. Possibly derived from structure 5635.

Six other objects were recovered from Phase 10, Late Saxon and Medieval, features; none are illustrated. They were a fragment of cylindrical brazed casing from a barrel padlock, length 73mm, maximum diameter 47mm, from quarry 509, transect 24; a small fragment of cylindrical brazed casing with a ribbed outer surface from a barrel padlock, length 42mm, width 33mm, from pit 610, Area F; an irregular, damaged fragment with four rivet holes and traces of white metal plating from a buckle plate, length 25mm, width 22mm, 1mm thick, from quarry 509, transect 24; an irregular rectangular strip, broken end cut and partly rolled, possibly part of a buckle plate, length 30mm, width 18mm, 2mm thick, from ditch 634, Area F; a crudely folded rectangular ring, length 33mm, width 22mm, from pit 654, Area F; and a fragment of horseshoe with one attached nail, nail 29mm long, fragment length 45mm, nail hole diameter 5mm, from ditch 5459, Area F.

Nails and nail fragments were recovered from the following additional Phase 10 contexts: pits 600 and 621 in Area F, 1308 in Area B, 3585 in Area D and 7052 and 7059 in Area Mc; ditches 634 in Area F, 3569 in Area D and 3660 in transect 3; and quarry 509 in transect 24. None are illustrated.

Nails and nail fragments were recovered from the following unphased contexts: pits 389 and 1055 in Area B, 3689 in Area D, 3802 in Area G and 6083 in Area Mc; post-holes 2852 and 2866 in Area D; ditch 522 in transect 21; and natural features 78 in transect 19, 637 in Area F, 3095 and 3514 in Area D and 4949 in Area A. None are illustrated.

The Neolithic and Bronze Age Pottery, by Ann B Ellison

The Neolithic and Bronze Age assemblage from Easton Lane comprises 841 sherds and seven near complete vessels. Much of the material (54%) was of Middle or Late Bronze Age date, but all earlier phases were well represented (Table 10). Of the sherd material, 108 items possessed diagnostic form or decoration and a selection of these feature sherds, together with the seven more complete vessels are illustrated below (Figs 86 to 88). In view of the great variety of styles represented, decorative techniques employed, and the wide distribution of the material across the site, descriptions of these key terms are also provided.

In order to provide the maximum amount of chronological information it was decided to characterise as much of the material as possible and this was achieved by designing a detailed fabric classification. A series of 16 fabric types was identified macroscopically. Detailed descriptions may be found in the site archive, but the main characteristics are summarised in Table 8. By careful analysis of the featured sherds it proved possible to assess the date ranges of each fabric and these are also shown in Table 8. It should be noted that whilst some fabric types are specific to particular forms of a single period (eg D2 – Grooved ware; A5 – Middle Bronze Age fine ware), many of them occur in a variety of

types through time. Thus, fabric D1 was used for Grooved ware, Beakers and Early Bronze Age urns, fabric A7 may belong to Grooved ware or Late Bronze Age vessels, and fabric C5 might denote pottery of Late Neolithic, Beaker, Early Bronze Age, Middle Bronze Age, or Late Bronze Age date. Sometimes it was possible to determine a closer date for single sherds on the grounds of further characteristics such as texture, surface treatment and sherd thickness. Using this data it was then possible to ascribe period designations to almost all the sherd material and thus to provide a substantial contribution to the dating evidence for the site as a whole. The occurrence of pottery by context and details of the feature sherds (numbers 1000–1115) are recorded in the archive, while a summary of the incidence of Neolithic and Bronze Age pottery across the site is given in Tables 8–10 and Figs 86 to 88.

Phase 1A. Early Neolithic

Thirty-six sherds of Early Neolithic fabric were identified. Feature sherds include fragments from plain round-based bowls, of average diameter 14cm, and a single sherd bearing an oval lug and incised decoration, possibly belonging to the Ebbsfleet style.

Illustrated items (Fig 86)

1. Rim of bowl. Fabric D4. Context 82, pit 1017, Area B.

2. Rim of bowl. Fabric C4. Context 3217, MBA ditch 1054, Area B.

3. Applied oval lug with vertical perforations; incised inclined lines above and below lug. Fabric D3. Context 3357, pit group 653, Area G.

Phase 2A. Late Neolithic

One hundred and sixty-five sherds of Late Neolithic type were identified. Some fragments of Peterborough ware were recovered, but most of the items were from a series of distinct Grooved ware vessels found mainly in pit 1017, which contained the Late Neolithic burial. The minimum number of vessels represented is six, four in fabric D1, one in fabric D2 and one in fabric D3.

Illustrated items (Fig 86)

Peterborough ware

4. Plain rim with internal moulding. Fabric D4. Context 82, pit 1017, Area B.

5. Shoulder fragment decorated with inclined rows of twisted cord-impressions above and below the carination. Mortlake style. Fabric D4. Context 24, amorphous feature 23 in Iron Age occupation area A.

6. Two joining shoulder fragments, decorated with paired rows of oval impressions. Mortlake style. Fabric D4. Context 3769, pit 3768, Area D.

7. Sherd from lower body, decorated with uneven rows of fingernail impressions. Fengate style. Fabric D3. Context 1019, pit 1017, Area B.

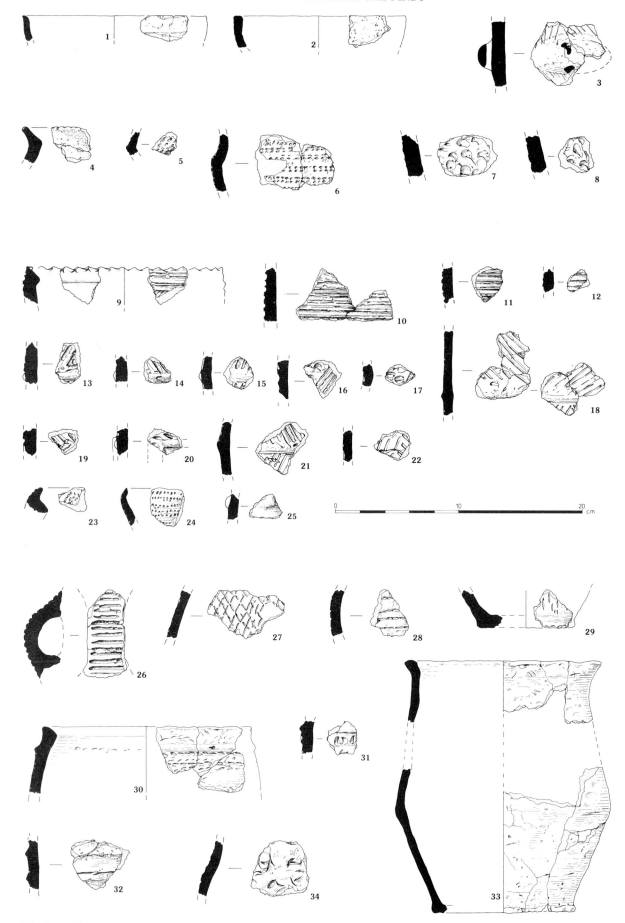

Fig 86.   Easton Lane. Early Neolithic, Late Neolithic and Beaker wares.

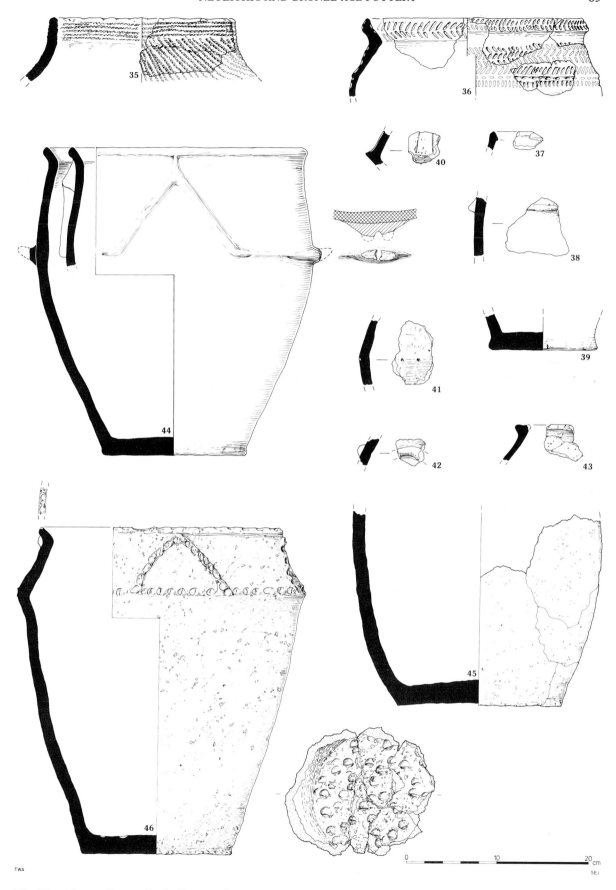

Fig 87.   Easton Lane. Early Bronze Age urns.

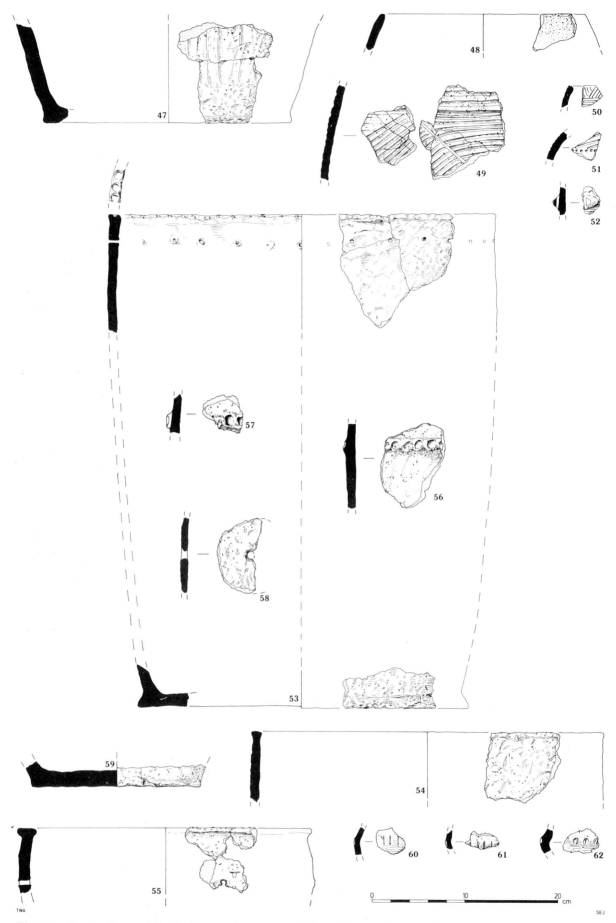

Fig 88.   Easton Lane. Middle Bronze Age urns and Late Bronze Age vessels.

Table 8. Neolithic and Bronze Age Pottery: the occurrence of fabrics by period.
/ = occurrence – = non-occurrence

Fabric Code	Early Neo	Late Neo Peter-boro	Late Neo Grooved Ware	Beaker	EBA Urn	Biconical Urn	MBA Fine	MBA Coarse	LBA	Abbreviated Fabric Description
										Flint inclusions (F)
A5	–	–	–	–	–	–	/	–	–	sparse small and medium F
A6	–	–	–	–	–	–	/	–	–	dense small and medium F
A7	/	–	/	–	–	–	–	–	/	moderate medium and large F
A8	–	–	–	–	–	/	–	/	–	dense medium and large F
A9	–	–	–	–	–	–	–	/	/	moderate medium and large F
										Grog mixtures (G)
D1	–	–	/	/	/	–	–	–	–	grog
D2	–	–	/	–	–	–	–	–	–	G with sparse shell
D3	–	/	/	–	–	–	–	–	–	G with sparse flint
D4	–	/	–	–	–	–	–	–	–	G with sparse medium and large F
D5	–	–	–	/	/	–	–	–	–	G with sparse large F
										Sand inclusions (S)
C4	/	/	–	–	–	–	–	–	–	S with sparse medium F
C5	–	/	–	/	/	–	–	/	/	S with sparse small and medium F
C6	–	–	–	/	–	–	–	–	–	S with sparse small F and G
										Shell Inclusions (Sh)
E1	/	–	/	–	–	–	–	–	–	moderate medium and large Sh
E2	/	–	/	–	/	–	–	/	–	moderate small Sh
										Chalk inclusions
F1	–	–	–	–	–	–	–	/	–	chalk

8. Sherd from lower body, decorated with irregular fingernail impressions of varying depth. Fengate style. Fabric D3. Context 1018, pit 1017, Area B.

Grooved ware

9. Rim sherd with internal bevel, decorated with parallel grooves on the body and overlapping finger-tip impressions on the top of the rim. Fabric D1. Context 1044, pit 1017, Area B.
   Two further similar rim sherds (not illustrated) from contexts 1018, pit 1017 Area B and 1056, MBA ditch 1054, Area B.

10. Two joining sherds with grooved decoration. Fabric D2. Contexts 1040 and 1049, pit 1017, Area B.

11 and 12. Two body sherds with grooved decoration, from the same vessel. Fabric D2. Context 1018, pit 1017, Area B.

13 and 14. Two grooved body sherds from a single vessel with a plain applied cordon. Fabric D1. Fig 86.14 shows a grain impression on the cordon. Context 1019, pit 1017, Area D.

15. Body sherd with grooved decoration above and below an applied cordon. Fabric D1. Context 1018, pit 1017, Area B.

16 and 17. Two sherds from a single vessel decorated with grooves and fingernail rustication. Fabric D1. Contexts 1018 and 1019, pit 1017, Area B.

18. Six body sherds with grooved decoration above and below a raised cordon; also a simple base angle (not illustrated). Fabric D2. Context 3257, pit 3256, transect 18.

19. Body sherd with grooved chevron decoration. Fabric D2. Context 1018, pit 1017, Area B.

20. Body sherd with plain horizontal applied cordon, the finger-tip impressed terminal of a vertical applied cordon, grooves above the cordon and a fingernail impression below. Fabric D2. Context 1018, pit 1017, Area B.

21. Body sherd with grooved decoration above and below a narrow raised cordon. Fabric D3. Context 1018, pit 1017, Area B.

22. Body sherd with grooves. Fabric D3. Context 1018, pit 1017, Area B.

23. Rim sherd with internal moulding and, on the exterior, faint traces of twisted cord decoration. Fabric E1. Post-hole 1703, Area D.

Table 9. Neolithic and Bronze Age Pottery: the occurrence of pottery (number of sherds, near complete vessels are counted as 1) by fabric and feature area.

Period	Neo		Late Neo			Neo/BA			Neo/EBA		EBA		E/MBA	MBA		M/LBA
Fabric code	C4	E1	D2	D3	D4	A7	C5	F1	D1	E2	D5	C6	A8	A5	A6	A9
Neolithic features																
Area B	10	–	33	11	25	17	4	–	38	–	30	–	–	1	–	4
Area G	4	5	1	10	–	20	24	–	1	3	2	2	3	1	1	6
EBA cemeteries																
Area F	–	–	–	–	–	–	–	–	9	–	–	–	–	–	–	–
Area D	–	–	–	–	–	–	–	–	–	–	–	–	3	–	–	–
EBA features																
Area Mc	1	–	–	–	–	4	–	–	2	–	6	8	–	–	–	–
MBA occupation areas																
Area Mc	1	–	–	–	–	21	1	–	–	–	–	–	1	1	–	–
Areas B,C,E	5	1	–	–	–	10	4	–	1	–	–	–	–	1	23	27
Area W	–	–	–	–	–	3	–	–	–	–	–	–	12	–	–	5
Areas D,H	–	–	1	–	–	3	1	–	–	–	–	–	8	–	2	6
MBA ditches																
7008, 7010	–	–	–	–	–	2	3	–	–	–	1	–	–	–	–	58
3200, 6073	–	–	–	–	–	–	3	–	–	–	–	–	–	–	1	–
1054, 972	4	–	–	1	1	15	27	–	3	–	6	–	–	6	5	105
1810	–	–	–	–	–	1	20	–	–	–	1	–	4	–	2	17
3692	–	–	–	–	–	–	8	–	–	–	1	–	–	–	3	3
Residual: in Iron Age ditches																
Area A	–	–	–	1	–	1	1	–	1	–	1	–	–	–	–	2
in Iron Age occupation area																
Area A	–	1	–	1	–	3	16	13	1	–	1	1	1	2	14	24
in Saxon enclosure																
Area F	–	–	–	–	–	–	18	–	–	–	–	–	–	–	–	–
Other	4	–	–	–	–	–	4	–	1	2	–	1	2	–	2	2
TOTALS	28	7	35	24	26	100	134	13	57	5	49	12	34	12	53	259

GRAND TOTAL: 848

24. Hooked rim sherd from a bowl, decorated by horizontal rows of small impressions executed by the points of a round-toothed comb. Fabric D1. Context 1018, pit 1017, Area B.

25. Sherd with part of a plain applied knob. Fabric D2; probably Grooved ware. Context 1019, pit 1017, Area B.

Phase 3. Beaker Wares

26. Strap handle decorated with horizontal grooves. Fabric D4. Probably Southern Handled. Pit 852, cut into pit 80, Area B.

27. Body sherd from upper body of Beaker, decorated with very irregular incised lattice design. Late Style: S4. Fabric D4. Pit 6085, Area Mc.

28. Body sherd from rounded shoulder of Beaker, decorated with worn lines in twisted cord. Probably Late Style. Fabric C6. Pit 6091, Area Mc.

29. Base angle decorated with fingernail impressions. Fabric D5. Pit 6091, Area Mc.

30. and 31. Rim and body sherds, domestic vessel with internal rim bevel, horizontal ridges and rows of fingernail impressions. Fabric C6. Pit 6091, Area Mc.

32. Body sherd from a ridged domestic vessel. Fabric A7. Pit 6091, Area Mc.

33. Plain beaker with everted rim and low sharp carination. Form could be Early or Middle Style. Fabric D1. Pit 6053, Area Mc.

Table 10. Neolithic and Bronze Age Pottery: the occurrence of pottery (number of sherds) by period and feature area.

Phase: Period:	1 Earlier Neolithic	2 Late Neolithic	3 Beaker	3 EBA	4 MBA	4/5 M/LBA	5 LBA dated	Not	TOTAL
Neolithic features									
Area B	10	101	3	34	1	4	–	20	173
Area G	10	23	4	6	6	3	21	10	83
EBA cemeteries									
Area F	–	–	–	9	–	–	–	–	9
Area D	–	–	–	3	–	–	–	–	3
EBA features									
Area Mc	1	–	–	–	2	–	1	21	25
Areas B,C,E	5	1	–	–	26	25	11	4	72
Area W	–	–	–	–	2	5	2	11	20
Areas D,H	1	1	–	–	11	4	–	4	21
MBA ditches									
7008, 7010	2	–	–	1	51	7	–	3	64
3200, 6073	–	–	2	–	1	–	1	–	4
1054, 972	3	5	–	11	80	46	13	15	173
1810	–	–	4	2	13	10	16	–	45
3692	–	–	–	1	3	10	1	–	15
Residual: in Iron Age ditches									
Area A	1	1	1	1	2	–	–	1	7
in Iron Age occupation									
Area A	1	4	4	4	34	24	4	3	78
in Saxon enclosure									
Area F	–	14	3	–	–	–	1	–	18
Other	–	–	6	–	6	–	1	5	18
TOTALS	36	165	30	72	238	148	72	87	

GRAND TOTAL : 848

34. Shoulder sherd from a domestic vessel with random, paired fingernail impressions. Fabric A7. Pit 6053, Area Mc.

Phase 2B. Early Bronze Age Urns (Fig 87)

35. Large portion of simple rim and collar from a Collared urn, decorated with cord-impressed lines inside the upper rim and on the collar. Form indeterminate. Fabric D1. Cremation 507, Area F.

36. Rim and shoulder of vessel with internal moulding. Incised herringbone decoration on the rim chamfer, the internal moulding and above the shoulder; a row of oval impressions on a slight raised cordon at the shoulder and a row of vertical incisions immediately below. Fabric D4. Enlarged Food Vessel urn.
Context 82 in pit 80, Area B.

37 –39. Rim, body and base sherds of a Collared urn. Internal rim bevel and plain lower collar fragment; no decoration surviving. Fabric D5. Context 82 in pit 80, Area B. Context 2790, MBA ditch 1054, Area B.

40. Collar fragment from a Collared urn, decorated with widely-spaced vertical incised lines. Fabric C5. Context 2790, MBA ditch 1054, Area B.

41. Shoulder fragment, decorated with a row of oval impressions. Collared urn. Fabric D1. Pit 600, Area F.

42. Sherd from upper body of a Biconical urn, bearing part of an applied plain cordon, probably a horseshoe-shaped handle. Fabric A8. Context 712, pit 317, residual in Iron Age occupation area A.

43. Flat-topped rim of a bipartite urn. Fabric A6. Context 772, natural feature 364 within CS 2375, Area B.

44. Bipartite urn with internal rim bevel, raised shoulder cordon, complex applied cordons forming two inverted-V 'handles' and two applied lugs, damaged, but possibly of the mammilated type. Biconical urn; Inception Series. Fabric A8. Cremation 1705, Area D.

45. Lower body of bipartite or bucket-shaped urn; no decoration surviving. Fabric A8. Cremation 1700, Area D.

46. Bipartite urn with rows of finger-tip impressions on the top of the rim and at the shoulder; four applied cordon horseshoe handles decorated with finger-tip impressions; the interior of the base impressed with random finger-tip indentations. Biconical urn; Supplementary Series. Fabric A8. Cremation 1705, Area D.

Phase 3A. Middle Bronze Age Urns (Fig 88)

47. Base angle of urn with vertical finger-smearing on exterior. Fabric A8. Context 4684, cremation 4683, Area A.

48. Simple plain rim. Type I Globular urn. Fabric A5. Context 772, natural feature 364 with CS 2375, Area B.

49. Upper body sherds, decorated with shallow-tooled lines. Type I Globular urn, possibly the same vessel as Fig 88.48 above. Fabric A6. Context 2362, natural feature 364 with CS 2375, Area B.

50. Rim sherd, decorated with shallow-tooled lines. Type I Globular urn. Fabric A5. Context 2738, MBA ditch 1054, Area B.

51. Upper body sherd decorated with shallow-tooled lines and a row of circular impressions. Type I Globular urn. Fabric A6. Context 4925, pit 4921, residual in Iron Age occupation, Area A.

52. Half a vertically perforated, plain horizontal lug. Fabric A7. Context 3424, post-hole 3423, Area D.

53. Rim and base angle from Bucket urn; decorated with a row of finger-tip impressions on the top of the rim and a row of perforations, bored from outside before firing, below the rim. Fabric A8. Context 6040, pit 6039, Area Mc.

54. Plain rim, slightly expanded. Bucket urn. Fabric A8. Context 3757, post-hole 3756, MS 5658, Area D.

55. Expanded T-shaped plain rim of urn with a slightly bipartite profile; one perforation surviving possibly from a row below the rim. Fabric A7. Context 1499, pit 1498 in Iron Age occupation area, transect 18.

56. Body sherd with raised cordon decorated with finger-tip impressions. Bucket urn. Fabric A8. Context 1749, post-hole 1748, Area D.

57. Body sherd with applied cordon decorated with finger-tip impressions. Bucket urn. Fabric A9. Context 2112, pit 2154, Area A.

58. Base of urn, bored as a weight. Fabric C5. Context 2738, MBA ditch 1054, Area B.

59. Base of a Bucket urn. Fabric A9. Context 5346, post-hole 5345, MS 5652, Area H.

Phase 3B. Late Bronze Age Vessels

60. Shoulder sherd decorated with vertical slashes, possibly executed by a flint tool. Fabric C5. Context 512, pit group 653, Area G.

61. Shoulder sherd decorated with a row of vertical fingernail impressions. Fabric C5. Context 678, pit group 653, Area G.

62. Shoulder sherd decorated with a row of fingertip impressions. Fabric C5. Context 4908, gully 319, Iron Age structure 2160, Area A.

Discussion

The Easton Lane assemblage includes a remarkable variety of ceramic styles dating from all periods of the Neolithic and Bronze Age and provides a very significant contribution to our knowledge of ceramic development both in the county of Hampshire and in the Wessex region. The Grooved ware sherds and the Biconical urns are of particular significance but the most important aspect is regarded to be the recovery of so much diagnostic material from such a wide range of domestic and funerary contexts within a very limited block of prehistoric landscape.

Excavated sites of Neolithic date are rare in Hampshire and the occurrence of Early Neolithic plain wares, Peterborough ware and Grooved ware at Easton Lane is notable. Both major styles of Peterborough ware are represented, and two of the Fengate sherds were associated with Grooved ware in the Neolithic burial pit 1017. Such associations are rare and, although early Beaker material is present on the site, neither the Peterborough or Grooved wares are associated with Beaker material. Thus the site does not appear to comply with the patterns of secular and ritual division outlined by Thorpe and Richards (1984); however, Neolithic burials are rare indeed and different sets of ceramic regulation may apply in specific funerary contexts. The Grooved ware vessels belong to the Durrington Walls style. The rim, Fig 86.23, matches Durrington Walls form 136 (Wainwright and Longworth 1971, 57, Fig 20) and many of the decorative motifs can be paralleled at the type site (eg Fig 86.14 and 16; Wainwright and Longworth 1971, Figs 26a top, and Fig 27 centre). Previously the only Grooved ware known from Hampshire comprised scatters of small sherds within the mound material of three Bronze Age round barrows in various areas of the county and a pit beneath a fourth at Latch Farm, Christchurch (Wainwright and Longworth 1971, 276–7).

The Beaker material at Easton Lane includes an interesting group of rusticated 'domestic ware', a Late Style sherd and an Early or Middle Style plain Beaker from a series of features in the southwest sector of the site (Fig 86.27–34) and the remarkable ridged handle (Fig 86.26) which probably belonged to a Southern Handled Beaker. This was associated with the Enlarged Food Vessel described below and can be paralleled on a Handled Food Vessel from Balmuick, Perth, and a Handled Bowl from Whitwell, Dorset (Clarke 1970, 417.1081 and 409.1035).

Three styles of Early Bronze Age urn are represented. A minimum of five Collared urns include plain vessels, one with a row of stabs on the shoulder (Fig 87.41) and the upper portion of an urn with simple rim and concave collar and carrying cord-impressed decoration on the collar and inside the rim (Fig 87.35). This vessel probably belongs to Longworth's Secondary Series and bears some similarities to the urn from Stockbridge, Hants (Longworth 1984, Plate 209 b). The Enlarged Food Vessel urn (Fig 87.36) does not belong to the series of Ridged Food Vessel urns usually found in southern England. In contrast to these sparsely-decorated urns, known from Dorset (Forde-Johnston 1965) and from Amesbury 71 and Shrewton 23 in Wiltshire (Christie 1967, 350; Green and Rollo-Smith 1984, 299), the Easton Lane vessel bears complex herringbone decoration which is more characteristic of Yorkshire Vase Food Vessels, but can be matched in the south on the Food Vessel from the Bishop's Waltham barrow (Ashbee 1957, Fig 9).

In his recent analysis of Biconical urns, Tomalin has defined an Inception Series of urns, characterised by one or more of nine formal characteristics and a silicous fabric type, all of which may be matched on the Continent during the Early Bronze Age (Tomalin 1983). A Supplementary Series includes further Biconicals which have silicous temper, usually flint, but lack the definitive formal traits of the Inception Series. The Biconical urns from Easton Lane are some of the best provenanced vessels belonging to these groups. The urn with complex plastic decoration, possibly mammilated lugs and flint temper (Fig 87.44) is a fine addition to the Inception Series. The decoration can be matched on the vessels from Amesbury 68, Wilts (unpublished, Salisbury Museum), and Bere Regis 46b, Dorset (Calkin 1964, Fig 14, 8), while the profile is similar to the plain lugged urn from Roke Down, Bere Regis (Warne 1866, Pl IV, 4). The second Biconical urn (Fig 87.46), decorated with rows of finger-tip impressions and four finger-tip impressed horseshoes, and also tempered with flint, belongs to Tomalin's Supplementary Series. Other urns closest to this example in form, albeit with only two horseshoes, are those from Bulford 71a, Wilts (Abercromby 1912, no 373), and Hythe, Hants (Godden 1966). An urn from Odiham, Hants, possesses four horseshoe handles, but does not have a flint-tempered fabric (Willis 1954).

It is of particular interest that these two Biconical urns at Easton Lane were associated in the same feature; indeed, they were placed one inside the other. The Inception Series urn had been deposited upright in the pit and around it had been placed large portions or slabs of the Supplementary Series urn, which seemed to have been carefully dismembered for the purpose. A few fragments had been deposited within, or had fallen into, the interior of the complete urn, just above the level of the cremated bones (Figs 25, 27 and 28). The rite of 'slab' burial recalls the phase C Barrel urn interments at Kimpton, Hants (Dacre and Ellison 1981, 159–165), but cannot be paralleled further afield. The rite may have been more widespread in the Early Bronze Age but the fact that urns of this date, most of which were excavated in the nineteenth century, survive intact in museum collections, militates against this. On the other hand, fragments of urns, and even those of large size, may not have been retained from antiquarian excavations. The proximity and probable association of a second burial contained in a Biconical or Bucket urn (Fig 87.45) and the inhumation burials, one of which included the amber and shale or lignite necklace, is of particular interest and chronological significance.

The Middle Bronze Age assemblage conforms to the Central Wessex group defined elsewhere (Dacre and Ellison 1981, 173–183). There is a minimum of five Type I Globular urns represented, similar to those excavated on the Winnall Down Trading Estate immediately west of the Easton Lane site. In particular, the filled triangle motif and row of circular impressions (Fig 88.49–51) can be matched in Winnall Pits A and B (Hawkes 1969, Fig 2.1–3). Some of the Bucket urns have finger-tip impressed cordons on top of the rim, and rows of perforations below the rim (Fig 88.53 and 55) are more commonly found in eastern England, especially East Anglia (Longworth and Ellison forthcoming).

Although the later Bronze Age Post Deverel-Rimbury plain ware tradition does not appear to be represented in the present assemblage, a group of plain, hooked-rim and finger-smeared jars was associated with the Late Bronze Age structures immediately west of the main Winnall Down enclosure (Fasham 1985, 61, Fig 51). However, the Bronze Age sequence is now completed by the occurrence of a substantial quantity of sherds characterised by a hard, Late Bronze Age fabric, some of which definitely derived from shouldered jars with impressed decoration on the line of the shoulder (Fig 88.60–62). These belong to the Late Bronze Age decorated tradition of the eighth to seventh centuries BC and are well-matched in the assemblage from the ring-ditch on Easton Down (Fasham 1982, 36, Fig 16, P40 and P41).

Later Prehistoric Pottery, by J W Hawkes

Introduction

A consideration of the later prehistoric pottery from Easton Lane obviously involves reference to the Winnall Down sequence, although the complementary nature of the two groups with little overlap in fabrics has not necessitated a completely integrated approach.

The computer-based recording used for Winnall Down enabled a large number of investigations and analyses to be undertaken which could not be replicated by the manual methods available for the processing of bulk records from Easton Lane. The Trust for Wessex Archaeology (manual) pottery recording system incorporates much of the philosophy and design of the MARC3 system, and at the archival level, the range of recorded attributes for the Winnall Down and Easton Lane assemblages is virtually identical. The disparity between manual and computerised recording is more pronounced at levels of advanced or complex analyses where considerations of time and finance preclude the full exploitation of the collected data (Fasham and Hawkes 1980).

Such limitations are, in this particular case, not overly restrictive. The spatial analyses carried out for Winnall Down are less appropriate for Easton Lane where a comparatively small quantity of later prehistoric and Roman pottery was dispersed over a wide area. At Easton Lane, there were 2,728 sherds from 1 hectare of Iron Age settlement (and that from within a total excavated area of 5 hectares). By comparison there were 8,645 sherds of Iron Age pottery from an area of 1.26 hectares at Winnall Down, at a density 2.5 times greater than Easton

Lane. Over 56% of the contexts from which the Easton Lane pottery derived were secondary or tertiary contexts in ditches or pits, and many of the remainder were post-holes, slots, gullies, cleaning layers and non-archaeological features containing only very small quantities; 77.5% of contexts with pottery contained less than ten sherds, and 39.3% contained only one sherd (in terms of weight, 80.5% of contexts with pottery contained less than 100g, and 41.2% contained less than 10g).

Method

The pottery was sorted into fabric groups on the basis of visible inclusions, counted and weighed. Featured sherds (rims, bases, decorated and perforated sherds) were individually classified by type and by vessel form where possible. This information on featured sherds, together with diameters, percentage present and surface treatment where appropriate, has been subject to limited analysis by computer, all other aspects being recorded as a paper archive.

Chronology and Phasing

There is little in the way of internal evidence to assist the construction of a chronology for the Easton Lane pottery. There was no useful intercutting stratigraphy, and cursory examination of pottery from the very few sequences of pit deposits available does not suggest that any of these groups need be considered to represent an extended time span. No radiocarbon samples relevant to the Iron Age were available.

It has therefore proved necesary to rely on external models to impose a chronological scheme. The divisions proposed for Danebury (Cunliffe 1984) are based on varieties of vessel form and decoration which are relevant to other parts of Hampshire, and which can be used as a reference against which

incomplete or interrupted sequences can be measured (Fig 89). Such an exercise suggests that Easton Lane and Winnall Down should be regarded as essentially complementary assemblages, areas of overlap between the two groups being confined to parts of the Early Iron Age and latest Iron Age/Roman period represented by very small collections of pottery from both sites, and for the Middle Iron Age, where material comparable to Danebury cp7 forms the bulk of the Winnall Down assemblage, but is present only in negligible quantities at Easton Lane. Arguments in favour of a continuity between Winnall Down Phases 3, Early Iron Age, and 4, Middle Iron Age (Hawkes in Fasham 1985, Fig 49 and supporting text), must now be acknowledged to be overstated, although conservative elements particularly within the flint tempering tradition do undoubtedly exist.

There has been no formal quantification of residuality or intrusion; the occurrence of obviously intrusive Medieval pottery in earlier contexts suggests the problem may be common. In areas of the site lacking quantities of readily identifiable anachronistic material, redeposition may be widespread but undetectable; wherever distinctive forms, fabrics or decorative types have occurred in apparently undisturbed contexts, this information has been used to provide phasing. The scope for intra-site analysis is thus severely limited by the reliance on external chronologies and the subsequent incorporation of the pottery information into the site phasing.

Fabrics

Twenty-one fabrics are associated with the Iron Age and Roman periods, plus Samian and amphorae. These fabrics are arranged in groups according to

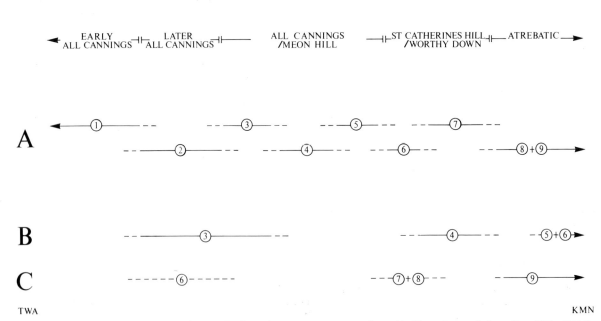

Fig 89.   Easton Lane. Comparison of phased pottery groups for: A) Danebury (after Cunliffe 1984); B) Winnall Down (after Fasham 1985); C) Easton Lane.

their principal inclusions (Table 11) and are described in summary form only. Full fabric descriptions are held in archive.

The criteria for the fabric divisions are based on the physical constituents of the pottery body without any expectation that they should necessarily represent distinct chronological periods, sources or manufacturing techniques. An informal assessment of the vessel forms represented (Table 12) does allow some suggestions of chronological separation to be made, however (Fig 90).

Fabrics B2/B4/C3 are rare, distinctive and readily identifiable with Early Iron Age vessel forms; fabrics B1/B3/C4 are equally distinctive and are associated only with undecorated saucepan pots and related vessels. Fabric A1 is the same as Winnall Down fabric 3. At Easton Lane it is associated with undecorated saucepans, and the three examples of decorated saucepan and also (rarely) with post-saucepan forms; at Winnall Down it also comprised the bulk of the developed, decorated saucepan tradition missing from Easton Lane. Fabric A2 is a flint-tempered fabric less well-sorted, more variable and coarser than A1, broadly comparable to Winnall Down fabric 2. Found in the same vessel forms, it is associated with post-saucepan forms significantly more frequently than A1. Inevitably broadly defined, A2 may also incorporate elements of the pre-saucepan flint-tempered tradition which, together with fabrics A3 and A4, form a very small proportion of the assemblage. Heavily sand-tempered fabrics (C1, C2, C5, C10, D1 with grog, A5 with sparse flint) dominate the later Iron Age period, fabrics C1 and C5 at least incorporating

Table 11. Quantities of later prehistoric and Roman pottery by fabric.

Later Prehistoric – Roman Pottery		No	Wt in g
A1	Well-sorted flints up to 2mm = Winnall 3	499	9,243
A2	Ill-assorted flints up to 3mm	803	12,686
A3	As A2 with added sand and rare black igneous temper	20	179
A4	Very dense fine flints less than 1mm	7	62
A5	Sparse flint, abundant micaceous sand (LIA/RB)	5	98
	Total Group A	1,334	22,268
B1	No visible temper, little or no added sand = Winnall 27	963	7,791
B2	Micaceous haematite-coated bowl fabric	9	54
B3	As B1 with added vegetable temper	94	1,632
B4	As B2 with very sparse fine flint	2	4
	Total Group B	1,068	9,481
C1	LIA/RB Micaceous sandy ware	160	1338
C2	Black-burnished type ware	1	4
C3	As C1 with larger quartz inclusions	3	46
C4	As C1 with occassional chalk	11	249
C5	Wheel-turned greywares	50	460
C6	Corfe Mullen type ware	3	10
C7	Mica-dusted red sandy RB fine ware	21	84
C8	Slightly micaceous red sandy ware	2	51
C9	Very sparse grog in sandy matrix	41	218
C10	Miscellaneous oxidised RB sandy wares	5	89
	Total Group C	297	2,549
D1	Sparse grog and chalk in sandy matrix	5	54
E1	Sparse shell in sandy matrix	3	6
Samian		10	137
Amphorae		11	224
	Total Miscellaneous	29	421
	Overall Total	2,728	34,719

Table 12. Later prehistoric and Roman vessel forms by fabric.

	Saucepans			Jars/Bowls					Other Forms				
	S1	S2	S3	J1	J2	J3	J4	J5	D/L	X1	X2	X3	X4
A1	10	12	3	7	4	5	–	–	–	–	–	–	–
A2	2	3	–	–	9	4	1	–	–	–	–	–	–
A3	1	–	–	1	–	1	1	–	–	–	–	–	–
A4	–	1	–	–	–	–	–	–	–	–	–	–	–
A5	–	–	–	–	–	2	–	–	–	–	–	–	–
B1	10	5	7	7	1	–	–	–	–	–	–	–	–
B2	–	–	–	–	–	–	–	–	–	3	–	–	–
B3	2	3	1	2	–	–	–	1	–	–	–	–	–
C1	–	1	–	–	3	2	1	3	2	–	1	1	–
C3	–	1	–	–	–	–	–	–	–	–	–	–	–
C4	1	–	–	–	–	1	–	–	–	–	–	–	–
C5	–	–	–	–	–	–	–	5	–	–	–	2	1
C9	–	–	–	–	1	–	–	1	–	–	–	–	–
Total	26	26	11	17	18	15	3	10	2	3	1	3	1

Key to Vessel Forms

Saucepan Pots	S1 Straight–sided	Jars/Bowls	J1 Slack–shouldered	Other Forms	D/L Dish or lid
	S2 Incurving sides		J2 Shouldered		X2 RB beaker
	S3 Outflaring sides		J3 Bead rim		X1 Furrowed bowl
			J4 Necked and everted		X3 Cordoned jars
			J5 Everted		X4 Flanged bowls

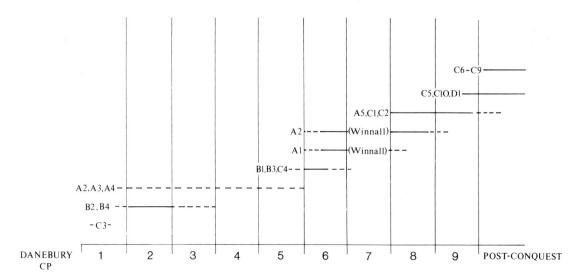

Fig 90.   Easton Lane. Easton Lane pottery fabrics related to the Danebury ceramic phases.

wheel-thrown vessels. Fabrics C6-C9 are a range of distinctive post-conquest wares.

No petrological examination has been carried out on the fabrics. Examination by thin section of pottery from Winnall Down (Fasham 1985, 60–61) revealed no evidence for any distinctive or necessarily non-local groups.

Early Iron Age (Phase 6)

Evidence for the Early Iron Age is extremely limited; only fabrics B2, B4 and C3 are necessarily of this period, forms identified being haematite-coated furrowed bowls (Fig 91.1–2) and round-bodied bowls (Fig 91.3–4), possibly also originally haematite-coated but with badly abraded surfaces. Scratch-cordoned bowls, which formed the majority of the identifiable haematite-coated vessels from a small assemblage at Winnall Down, are absent.

The single sherd of the micaceous sandy fabric C3 is of a thin-walled vessel with a design of recessed dots infilled with white paste set in a triangular or lozenge-shaped border (Fig 91.5). Stylistically an Early All Cannings type of decoration, the sherd is comparable in fabric to contemporary examples from central Wiltshire (C Gingell pers com) and is unlikely to be local to Easton Lane.

Typologically, the slack-shouldered jar (Fig 91.6) is also best considered an Early Iron Age vessel. In a densely flint-gritted fabric, it is finer and thinner-walled than the majority of examples from Winnall Down. It is possible that other sherds of this period are unrecognised amongst the flint-tempered group.

None of this material was recovered from contexts themselves identifiable as Early Iron Age, and presumably derived from a settlement focus within the Phase 3 enclosure at Winnall Down.

Middle Iron Age (Phases 7 and 8)

The Middle Iron Age component of the Easton Lane

assemblage can be compared to cp 6 at Danebury (Cunliffe 1984), comprising undecorated saucepan pots to the virtual exclusion of all other vessel forms. The saucepan pots are consistent in fabric and largely repetitive in shape; although essentially straight-sided vessels (eg Fig 91.10 and 14), variations exist with rounded profiles resulting in incurving upper sections (eg Fig 91.7–8) or flaring profiles (eg Fig 91.15).

Fabrics divide into two groups: fine sandy wares (B1 and, with added organic material, B3) and flint (A1 and A2). At Winnall Down the flint fabrics, in particular A1, continued into a later phase where they occurred as decorated saucepans often with expanded rims (Danebury cp 7), represented at Easton Lane only by the illustrated examples (Fig 91.18–20). At Winnall Down, undecorated flint-tempered saucepans were only very rarely associated with sandy examples, and it seems likely that there was a transition from sand to flint fabrics within the plain saucepan phase, here used to differentiate Phases 7 and 8.

Surface treatment in the form of external burnishing is common on the flint-tempered fabrics, but is also present on sandy fabrics where its true incidence is likely to be substantially underestimated because of easily abraded, flaking surfaces.

Analysis of vessel diameter (the only extant measurement of size) reinforces the impression gained from the Winnall material of a tightly defined range consistent on both sites (Fig 92). Comparisons between flint-tempered and sand-tempered examples (archive) reveals no significant differences in the range or absolute values of vessel diameter.

Late Iron Age/Roman (Phase 9)

Finds of pottery datable to the post-saucepan, Late Iron Age through to the Early Roman period, were almost entirely confined to Area H in the southern

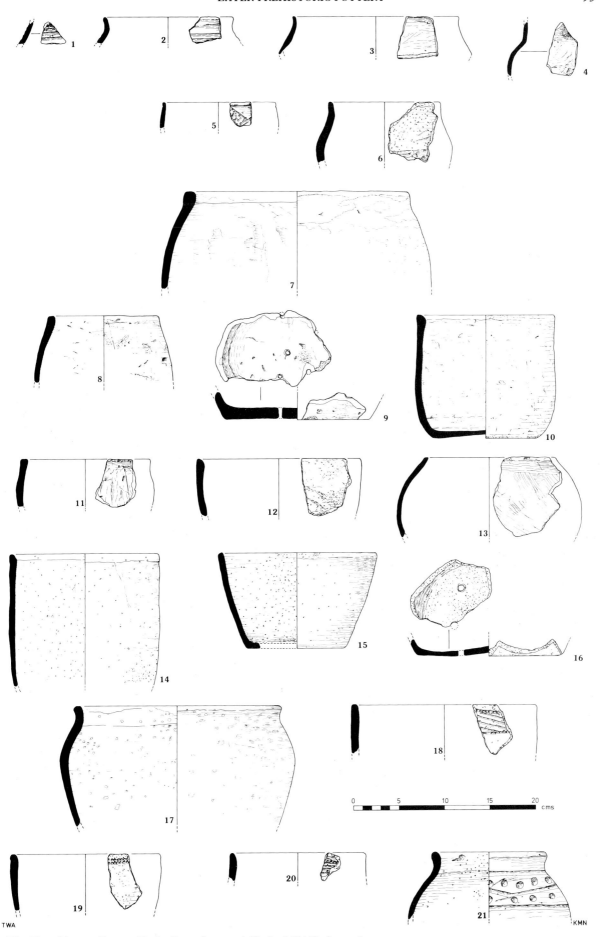

Fig 91.   Easton Lane. Early Iron Age and Early Middle Iron Age pottery.

Wide variety of graphics e tabulated material

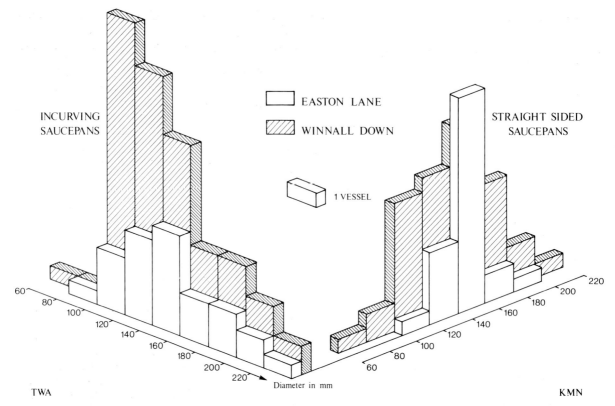

Fig 92.   Easton Lane. Comparative vessel sizes for selected categories of saucepans from Easton Lane and Winnall Down.

extension of the Roman enclosure system at Winnall Down, deriving from ditch fills or pits within or immediately adjacent to the enclosures. The small quantity recovered (essentially the Group C fabrics, plus samian and amphorae) is reflected by the restricted range of forms; the date range proposed for the longer, more varied, Winnall Down assemblage (end of first century BC through to mid-second century AD) would adequately encompass all the pottery from this phase. Correlation of fabrics with those from Winnall Down, associations of forms to fabric, and details of distribution are held in archive.

Illustrated Items (Fig 91)

1. Rilled body sherd from Furrowed Bowl (vessel type X1). Fabric B2. Featured Sherd (FS) 156, context 4504 ditch 4731, Area D.

2. Furrowed Bowl (X1). Fabric B2. FS 223, context 4833 pit 4622, Area D.

3. 'Haematite-coated' bowl. Fabric B2. FS 239, context 4714 ditch 3765, Area A.

4. 'Haematite-coated' body sherd. Fabric B2. FS 62, context 985 ditch 990, Area A.

5. Decorated body sherd, All Cannings Cross type. Fabric C3. FS 88, context 2192 pit 409, Area A.

6. ? Tripartite jar (J2). Fabric A1. FS 5, context 37 post-hole 36, Area A.

7. Incurving saucepan (S2). Fabric B1. Co-joining sherds FS

63, context 1075 pit 329 Area A, and FS 71, context 1074 pit 329, Area A.

8. Incurving saucepan (S2). Fabric B1. Co-joining sherds FS 70, context 1022 pit 329 Area A, and FS 77, context 1075 pit 329, Area A.

9. Perforated base. Fabric B1. FS 68, context 1074 pit 329, Area A.

10. Straight-sided saucepan (S1). Fabric B3. Co-joining sherds FS 100, 101, 102, 105 all from context 2193 pit 409, Area A.

11. Saucepan or jar (J1). Fabric B3. FS 87, context 1333 post-hole 908, Area A.

12. Straight-sided saucepan (S1). Fabric A2. FS 91, context 2191 pit 409, Area A.

13. Bowl (J2). Fabric B1. FS 40, context 723 pit 317, Area A.

14. Straight-sided saucepan (S1). Fabric A1. FS 3, context 65 pit 17, Area A.

15. Outflaring saucepan (S3). Fabric A1. FS 125, context 4716 pit 4560, Area D.

16. Perforated base. Fabric A1. FS 173, context 4753 pit 4933, Area A.

17. Jar (J2). Fabric A2. FS 134, context 934 ditch 928, Area A.

18. Decorated straight-sided saucepan (S1). Fabric A1. FS 53, layer 1023, Area A.

19. Decorated straight-sided saucepan (S1). Fabric A1. FS 22, context 468 pit 238, Area A.

20. Decorated saucepan or jar. Fabric A1. FS 167, context 4993 pit 4928, Area A.

21. Decorated jar (J2). Fabric A1. FS 57, context 1063 ditch 975, Area A.

Fig 93

22. Jar (J2). Fabric A2. FS 14, context 351 pit 238, Area A.

23. Decorated sherd. Fabric A2. FS 38, context 711 pit 707, Area A.

24. Bead-rim jar (J3). Fabric A2. FS 15, context 351 pit 238, Area A.

25. Bead-rim jar (J3). Fabric A2. FS 148, context 5340 ditch 5293, Area H.

26. Bead-rim jar (J3). Fabric A1. FS 17, context 351 pit 238, Area A.

27. Bead-rim jar (J3). Fabric A2. FS 139, context 5348 pit 5347, Area H.

28. Wheel-turned base. Fabric C4. FS 153, context 5366 ditch 5042, Area H.

29. Bead-rim jar (J3). Fabric C4. FS 152, context 5366 ditch 5042, Area H.

30. Bead-rim jar (J3). Fabric C1. FS 195, context 5294 ditch 5293, Area H.

31. Beaker (X2). Fabric C1. FS 142, context 5348 pit 5347, Area H.

32. Everted jar (J5). Fabric C1. FS 244, context 5296 ditch 5295, Area H.

33. Perforated base. Fabric C1. FS 144, context 5367 pit 5349, Area H.

35. Cordoned jar (X3). Fabric C5. FS 140, context 5348 pit 5347, Area H.

36. Everted jar (J5). Fabric C5. FS 202, context 5294 ditch 5293, Area H.

37. Lid (D/L). Fabric C1. FS 194, context 5294 ditch 5293, Area H.

38. Lid (D/L). Fabric C1. FS 213, context 5043 ditch 5042, Area H.

The Samian, by S M Davies

Drag 37 base; probably Central Gaulish; ? early second century AD. Context 98, clearance layer.

Abraded body sherd; possibly South Gaulish; ? late first century AD. Context 1860, clearance layer.

Abraded rim sherd, glossy slip. Drag 37; Central Gaulish; late first century (to early second century) AD. Phase 9 Early Roman, context 5294, ditch 5293, Area H.

Two rims, two bases and two decorated body sherds, probably all from the same vessel. Drag 37; Central Gaulish; Trajanic. One of the body sherds is decorated with double-bordered ovolo, with the tongue ending in a rosette, probably in the style of Frontinus (cf La Graufensque). Only a small frag-

ment of the decoration below survives, probably a foliate design. The moulded decoration on the other body sherd is poorly finished and not at all clear. One base carries part of the lowest border of decoration, with S-shaped gadroons, each with three (+) small grooves across the central area, bordered by a continuous running scroll. Phase 9, Early Roman, context 5296 ditch 5295.

Plain body fragment, possibly from small cup (Drag 27?). South Gaulish, late first century AD. Phase 9, Early Roman, context 5348 pit 5347, Area H.

The Amphorae, by S M Davies and R Seager-Smith

Body sherd of a Dressel 20 amphora. This type originated in southern Spain and carried olive oil. Imports arrived in Britain in the Late Iron Age and the form remained in use until the late third century AD (Peacock and Williams 1986). Natural feature 2537, Area B.

Ten sherds from a Pelichet 47 amphora. This type originated in southern France, and is commonly found in Britain. Its date range is from mid-first century AD to the third century AD. It does not seem to appear before AD 60 in British contexts (Peacock and Williams 1986, 142–3). Phase 9, Early Roman, context 5296 ditch 5295, Area H.

Late Saxon and Medieval Pottery, by J W Hawkes

Introduction

A total of 216 sherds of Late Saxon pottery weighing 1,080g and 218 sherds of later Medieval pottery weighing 1,052g were recovered from the excavations.

Late Saxon

The Late Saxon material was found almost exclusively in Area F contexts within the gullies of struc-634/5459 or from features nearby. The pottery has been sorted by fabric and form, and all featured sherds are illustrated. Four fabrics are identified.

EM 1: abundant fine flint, added sand and sparse chalk, also represented as voids usually on the inside of the vessel.

EM 2: added sand, fabric usually reduced. The fabric is not diagnostic but occurs in association with EM 1 and is not consistent with the range of sand-tempered fabrics from the later Medieval period.

EM 3: as EM 1 but without chalk inclusions or voids.

EM 4: as EM 1 but with distinctive red oxidised surfaces.

Quantities of each fabric are given in Table 13.

The stamped Chichester-type pitcher (Fig 94.5) is regarded as pre-Conquest in Winchester and

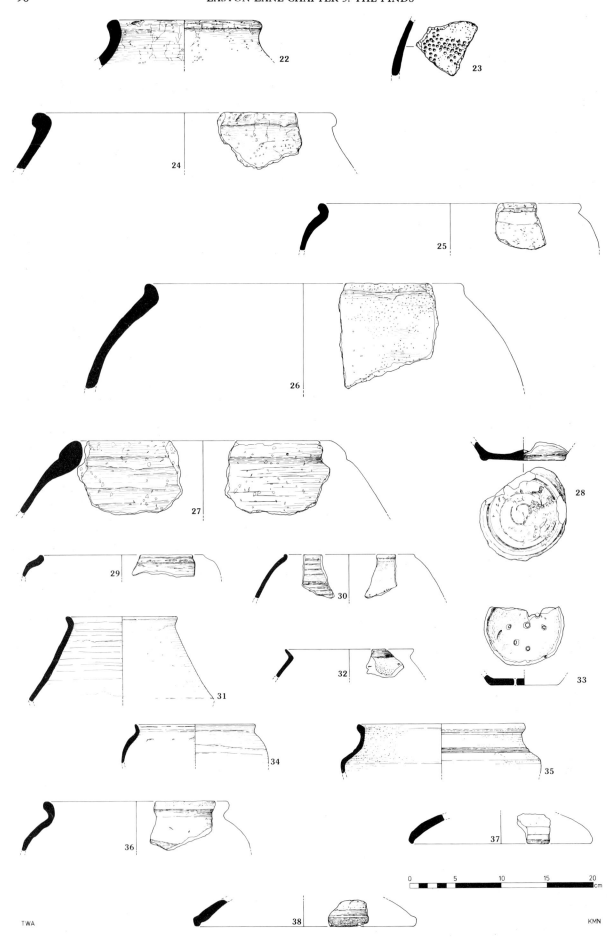

Fig 93.   Easton Lane. Late Iron Age/Roman pottery.

Table 13. Late Saxon pottery by fabric.

Fabric	Number	Wt in g
EM 1	192	978
EM 2	18	64
EM 3	3	19
EM 4	3	19
Total	216	1,080

Southampton, and although other forms represented are less diagnostic, the technique of turntable-added rims to coil-built bodies (*eg* Fig 94.1) also indicates a Late Saxon date. Identifications and observations have been provided by Duncan Brown.

Illustrated Items (Fig 94)

1. Jar, Fabric EM1. Featured Sherd (FS) 510, context 650 ditch 634, Area F.
2. Jar, Fabric EM1. FS 502, context 633 ditch 634, Area F.
3. Jar, Fabric EM1. FS 504, context 5460 ditch 5459, Area G.
4. Jar, Fabric EM3. FS 501, context 633 ditch 634, Area F.
5. Stamped pitcher, Fabric EM1. FS 503, context 633 ditch 634, Area F.
6. Shoulder from jar, Fabric EM4. FS 505, context 647 ditch 634, Area F.
7. Base, Fabric EM1. FS 509, context 655 pit 654, Area F.

Medieval

The later Medieval pottery was more widely dispersed, occurring in 137 different contexts of which less than 50 can be suggested as being of Medieval date, and only ten of which contained more than 25g of pottery. The majority of the identifiable material can be suggested as being of fourteenth century date; there are no obviously non-local wares represented. The pottery has been recorded in summary form only, descriptions of fabrics for individual sherds, tabulations of featured sherd types and contextual information can be found in archive. No discussion is presented here.

Flint and the Burial Group in 1017, by P A Harding with a Note on the Antler Spatulae by S Olson

The excavation of the Easton Lane Interchange produced only 43 cores, 917 flakes and 573 broken flakes from all contexts. The contents of four small assemblages are shown in Table 14, and summarised below.

Pit 1017, Area B. This Late Neolithic phase feature contained flint from three context groups:

i) grave goods associated with inhumation 2752 included six barbed and tanged arrowheads and a cache of retouched and unretouched flakes, of which two refit;

ii) flakes in mint condition from the grave backfill in immediate association with the burial. They included core preparation, trimming and rejuvenation flakes, many of which refit. The fill also included one flint hammerstone and one flake scraper;

iii) derived material from the upper fills of the feature including an end/side scraper and a reworked ground flint axe fragment.

All three are technologically similar and analysis has been based on an amalgamated sample. There is no evidence of core tool production.

Pit 5456, Area F. This Late Neolithic, Phase 2, feature contained flint knapping waste from a flake industry using both prepared and unprepared cores. Core tools were also manufactured.

Pits 6053, 6083, 6085 and 6091 were four small Late Neolithic, Phase 2, features in Area Mc. The samples, from a flake industry, included 15 end scrapers, which suggests that the material may have had a domestic rather than an industrial origin. As the pits were excavated in the watching brief, only 6053 was fully excavated, and the other three were half-sectioned; total contents are therefore incomplete.

Pit group 653, Area G. This feature produced the

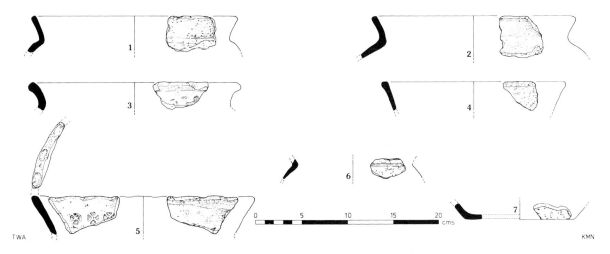

Fig 94. Easton Lane. Late Saxon pottery.

Table 14. Distribution of flint from four assemblages by type.

Feature	Context	Cores	Core Frags	Flakes	Broken Flakes	Burnt Material	Retouched
5456	5457/5458	9	–	142	157	–	9
1017	1049	–	–	5	1	–	8
(2752)	Grave Goods						
	1049 Grave Fill	2	–	20	27	–	1
	1018/1019 Tertiary Fill	3	–	46	22	1	3
6053	6054/6061	–	–	28	11	–	6
6083	6084	–	–	7	5	1	4
6085	6086	–	–	2	1	–	1
6091	6092	2	1	37	9	–	4
653		3	1	188	74	–	12

largest proportion of complete flakes (20%) and retouched material from the excavation. Results of the analysis of this assemblage are shown in Fig 99, for comparative purposes, but have not been described in detail. The horizontal distribution of material, Fig 10, indicates a concentration of flint flakes within the area of the post-holes, CS 3918.

This report aims to describe and compare the technology and products of the first three groups.

Raw material

Flint occurs in the Upper Chalk, both as nodules and thin bands of poor quality tabular flint. The nodules, which are irregular and lobed in shape, measure up to 100mm maximum dimensions and weigh 500–600g. They have a hard chalky cortex up to 10mm thick and thermal flaws. Flint of sufficient quality was available however and a wide range of tools was manufactured. The flint is grey-brown when fresh with light grey inclusions.

Two flakes of Bullhead flint were found in 5456. This distinctive flint, which has an orange band below green cortex, occurs locally in the Reading Beds near East Stratton or in clay-with-flints as derived nodules.

Pit 1017

Material associated with burial 2752

Six barbed and tanged arrowheads in mint condition and of Green's (1980, Fig 46) Green Low type were found in a disturbed group near the presumed pelvic region of skeleton 2752. They measure from 28mm to 32mm long, from 22mm to 25mm wide, which is within the mean for Green Low arrowheads (Green 1980, Table VIII.2), and are 3–4mm thick. All have slightly convex edges which taper to delicate points. The absence of impact fractures suggests that these arrowheads were never used. They have wide concave bases with square-ended tangs and broad slop-

ing barbs. This design maximizes the length of the barbs but reduces the need for deep notches, the formation of which can often cause the barbs and/or tang to break during manufacture (Fig 95.2). Two arrowheads retain areas of the ventral surface of the flake from which they were made but precise details of the blanks are obscured by the bifacial covering retouch. There is no reason to believe that blanks were removed from specially prepared cores.

These arrowheads form an unusually large group. Green (1980, Table VIII.I) records only three instances of six barbed and tanged arrowheads in a single grave, where one or two are normal. Unfortunately, few instances occur which demonstrate how the arrowheads/arrows were included in the grave; four barbed and tanged arrowheads were located by the feet of an inhumation at Dairsie, Fife (Anon 1886–7) with points to the north, as if hafted; at Mucking (Jones 1975) eleven barbed and tanged arrowheads lay in a group with the long axis parallel to the spine; and in grave 203, Barrow Mills, Radley, Oxon, five barbed and tanged Green Low arrowheads, which were undoubtedly hafted, were found against the right side of the body near the feet (Halpin in prep). The Easton Lane skeleton was disturbed and, although the arrowheads were located together, it is uncertain whether they were *in situ*. Firm conclusions about their orientation or hafting cannot be made, although the general location compares well with these published examples.

Green Low arrowheads occur throughout England but are more common in a zone which extends east from Bournemouth towards Sussex and the Lower Thames, but which avoids Wessex (Green 1980, Fig 51). Easton Lane is situated on the margin of this zone. Arrowheads of this type are often found with inhumations of Late Beaker date (Steps 4–7 Green 1980, 130). Clarke (1970, 203) associates them with Southern Beakers (S1-S4), as in grave 203, Barrow Hills (Halpin in prep), where the Beaker was of

Clarke's S4 type (Lanting and van der Waals Step 7 1972) but at Winterbourne Monkton barrow 9 they were found with an N2 Beaker. Three occurred at Wimbourne St Giles (Annable and Simpson 1964, 39) with an inhumation, a fabricator, bronze dagger, copper awl, Beaker (not preserved) and a V-perforated button. Aceramic inhumations have also included Green Low arrowheads without Beakers. Six were found in a matched set at Sixpenny Hill, Sharrow, Yorkshire (Green 1980, 304), and one occurred at Aldwinkle 1, Northamptonshire (Green 1980, 373), associated with two bone spatulae.

The combination of Green Low arrowheads with antler spatulae is not unique; at Wetton Mill, Staffs (Green 1976), they occurred in a rock shelter and a spatulae was included in Grave 203, Barrow Hills, Radley (Halpin in prep). Green Low arrowheads do not occur with Food Vessels or with Urns.

Radio-carbon dates of 1850±150 bc were obtained for two sites from Fifty Farm, Suffolk (BM-133), where Green Low arrowheads were associated with Southern Beakers, and from Chippenham barrow 5, Cambridgeshire (BM-152), where Beaker sherds were also present. Additional dates of 1550±150 bc (BM-75) from Windmill Hill (Smith 1965, 11) and 1324±51 bc (BM-669) for Mount Pleasant (Burleigh et al 1972, 397) suggest slightly later dates, although this final date was obtained from the tertiary silt of the ditch.

Retouched and unretouched flakes
Four flakes and blades, Fig 95.9,10 and 12, of which two pieces refit, were located in a small cache near one of the hands in the southwest corner of the grave. An additional piece, Fig 95.11, lay approximately 0.30m to the northeast. They were all in mint condition and appear to have been selected for their cutting edges. The four unbroken pieces average 82mm in length and although one blade, Fig 95.9, has direct low angle scaled retouch along both edges the remainder have either total or partial natural backing. Plain butts predominate and the negative flake scars suggest that the core had no more than one striking platform.

A collection of flint flakes produced deliberately for a burial were also found at Chilbolton, Hampshire (Russel forthcoming). Two flakes refitted and others had been retouched or utilized before deposition.

Two more cortical flakes (Fig 95.7 and 8) and one naturally backed flake with stepped and scaled edge retouch (Fig 95.13) were found in the pelvic region. Their original association with the burial is not certain.

Grave fill
The material from the grave fill found in direct association with the inhumation comprises 47 pieces of waste flint and two cores in mint condition. Most of the material was found in small isolated groups which may represent individual tips which were backfilled from the surface. Twenty-eight flakes (59%) have been refitted to at least one other piece but none refit to the grave goods. Relevant results of

metrical analysis of a combined sample from the grave fill and tertiary fill are shown in Fig 99. Basic data is retained in archive. The results for breadth:length ratios indicate similarities in shape to those from pit 5456 (see below, 105). However, the technology is considerably different. Most flakes are large with thick, unweathered chalky cortex. They illustrate identifiable stages of platform/core preparation including alternate flaking, trimming and core correction/rejuvenation. The two cores did not produce usable flakes and were abandoned because of unsuccessful preparation. The semi-spherical nature of the nodules, which were probably removed from the pit during its original excavation, made it difficult to prepare a successful flaking angle from the striking platform. A group of refitted flakes show that some cores were rejuvenated by rotating the core rather than by modifying the existing striking platform.

An end scraper with regular abrupt retouch around the distal end of a broad non-cortical flake and a flint hammerstone were also found with this material. The hammerstone weighs 426g and is made from a spherical nodule with weathered cortex. It has a pitted surface flattened by hammering at one end. It is not possible to ascertain whether the flint waste, and these two artefacts in particular, formed part of the original grave goods, although flint scrapers are known from graves of this type (Bateman 1848, 59–60; Halpin in prep). An antler found in the grave is described with the faunal remains (see below).

Upper fills
Three cores and 46 unbroken flakes were found in the upper fills, 1018 and 1019. Examination has shown that although some weathered pieces were present others were similar in both condition and technolgy to the material from the grave fill. There were no refits. This material therefore probably represents core preparation and trimming waste derived from working flint encountered during the construction of the shaft. The three cores all produced unprepared flakes by alternate percussion. They are heavier than the cores from pit 5456, where platform modification prolonged potential core productivity.

The upper fills included an end/side scraper made on a large flake and a reworked ground flint axe fragment (Fig 95.15). The scraper has a convex edge modified by direct, regular, abrupt/semi-abrupt retouch. The flint axe fragment consisted of the blade of a well-ground implement which had probably snapped in the haft. The snap had been thinned subsequently by bifacial flaking into a semi-discoidal knife. These pieces, together with a fabricator (Fig 95.14) from context 1042, may be contemporary with the Later Neolithic pottery from the feature.

Antler spatulae and bone awl, Figs 96 and 97
Four spatulae of red deer antler and a bone awl were found near the barbed and tanged arrowheads. The spatulae were in a good state of preservation but were broken in situ and disturbed.

V. detailed!

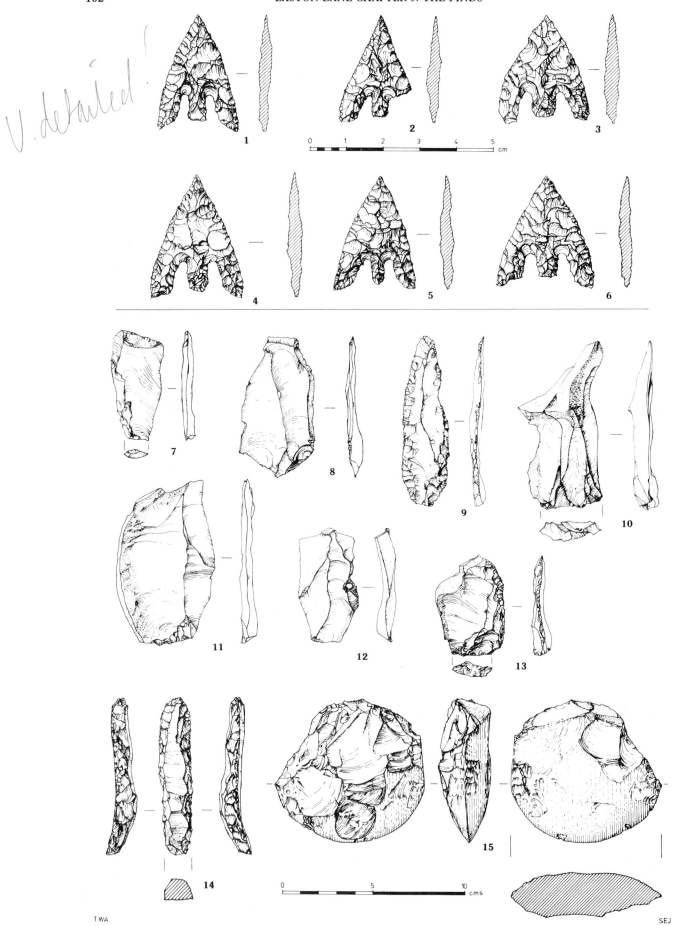

SEJ

Fig 95.   Easton Lane. Flint objects from burial 2752.

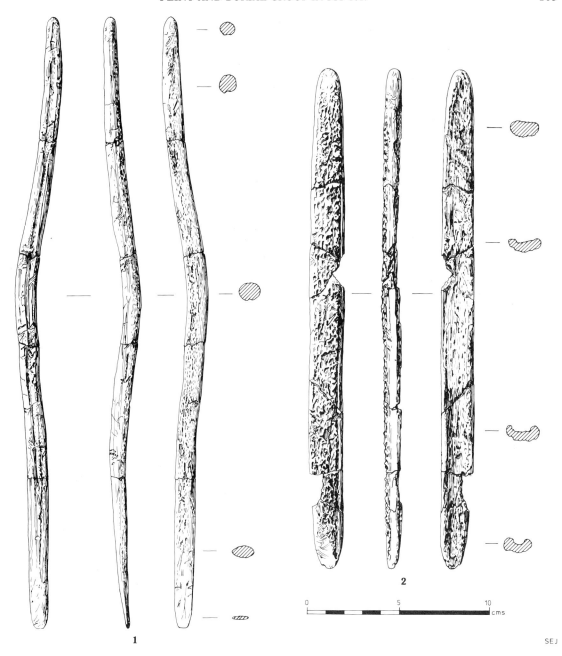

Fig 96.   Easton Lane. Antler spatulae from burial 2752.

1.   Spatula. Straight in plan and profile. Exterior surface unmodified; marrow probably present but largely decomposed resulting in crescentic cross section. Edges smoothed with some parts rounded and others slightly faceted. Ends generally rounded with additional striae. 270mm long by 20mm wide. SF 204/167.

2.   Spatula. Straight in plan and slightly curved in profile. Exterior surface unmodified; marrow present. Oval cross section. Edges smoothed and rounded with longitudinal striae. Tips: one rounded, one flattened with fine striae. 220mm long by 14mm wide. SF 165.

3.   Spatula. Twisted in plan and profile (possibly post-depositional). Exterior surface smoothed, marrow rounded. Oval cross section. Edges lightly faceted by smoothing. Tips: one rounded, one flattened, both have fine striae. Approximately 328mm long by 13mm wide. SF 205.

4.   Spatula. Twisted in plan and profile (possibly post-depositional). Exterior surface lightly smoothed; marrow flat.

Plano-convex cross section. Edges rounded with longitudinal striae extending onto exterior surface. Tips: one rounded, one flattened with faint striae. Approximately 340mm long by 15mm wide. SF 166.

5.   Awl, made from a deer or sheep metatarsus, broken into two pieces. Length 119mm. SF 155.

Manufacture and use

Large splinters of antler were probably removed by the groove and splinter technique, using flint flakes which are as efficient as burins for this task. The edges are striated and faint 'chattermarks' are also visible on some pieces, features which are typical of antler tools made with stone implements (Newcomer 1974, 148). The four spatulae were submitted to Dr Sandi Olsen (Institute of Archaeology) for

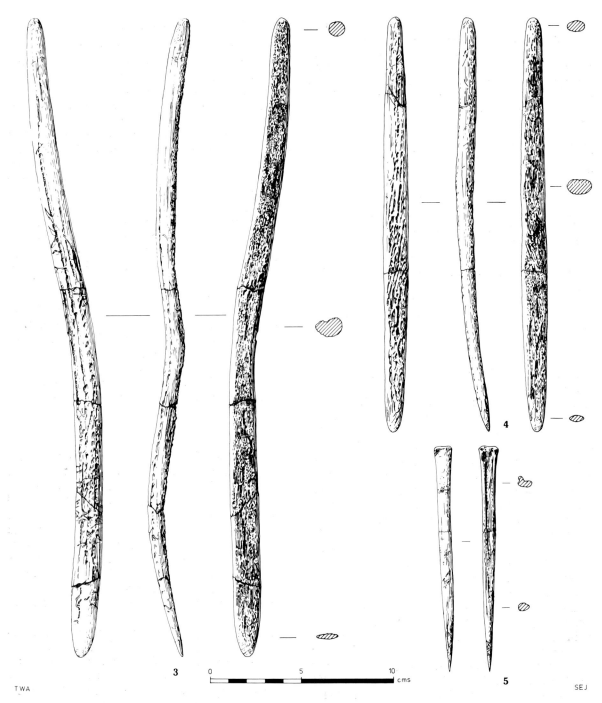

Fig 97.   Easton Lane. Antler spatulae and bone awl from burial 2752.

examination of manufacture and use wear traces. She reported:

No actual trace of the manufacturing technique remains. The blank was smoothed, especially along the edges, by longitudinal scraping with a stone tool.

The use wear at the ends with a round cross-section resembles that found on experimental (pressure) flakers, that is, parallel transverse striations on the end, sometimes forming a facet, and pitting of the tip. Longitudinal striae caused from slippage are also sometimes present running from the tip up the shaft a short distance.

The spatulate end bears some fine transverse striae running across the surface above the tip which may either be from abrading with granular stone during manufacture or from use on an abrasive material. This end may have been used as a (pressure)

flaker for notching (barbed and tanged) arrowheads. The indentation which should form along the end would have been obliterated by re-sharpening. This would fit very nicely with the function of the other end.

Although a very small amount of polish may be seen at the spatulate tip on at least one specimen, it is not developed sufficiently enough to indicate use on leather or plants. It is more likely that this is localised handling polish.

The function of spatulae of both antler and bone has never been answered satisfactorily. Smith and Simpson (1966), drawing on the work of Semenov (1964, 175), interpreted them as leather-working tools, possibly burnishers, despite noting that few of the associations were with other leather working tools. The connection of spatulae with archery equipment was first made by Clarke (1970, 203) when he remarked on the frequency with which they occurred with male burials (100%) accompanied by archery equipment (72%). This association was particularly strong at Aldwinkle 1, with its Green Low arrowheads, and at Green Low (Bateman 1848, 59–60) itself where three barbed and tanged arrowheads were found near the pelvis of a male inhumation with three spatulae and a bone awl. The burial was also accompanied by a Beaker, an iron ore nodule, a scraper and a dagger, grave goods which are remarkably similar to those from Easton Lane. Clarke's interpretation was not disputed by Ashbee (1978), although Green (1976) describing the spatulae from Wetton Mill retained Smith and Simpson's interpretation, as did Fleming (1971, 161) when discussing leatherworking in Bronze Age Wessex.

The possibility that the Easton Lane spatulae are pressure flakers, based on the evidence of wear traces, provides a credible alternative interpretation of their function.

It provides a plausible tool ('fabricator') for both barbed and tanged arrowhead manufacture and for the formation of the barbs in particular. The flattened ends of the two largest spatulae can be inserted into the notches of all six arrowheads from Easton Lane. It does not explain, however, why spatulae usually occur only in graves.

Ceramic associations with spatulae are more diverse than with Green Low arrowheads. They include spatulae with Clarke's Primary and Developed Southern Beakers as at Mouse Low, Deepdale, Staffs (Clarke 1970), Amesbury G.51, Wilts (Ashbee 1978), and grave 203 Barrow Hills, Oxon (Halpin in prep), and Ravenstone, Bucks (Allen 1981), where an unaccompanied cenotaph was excavated. A beaker of Clarke's European type (Lanting and van der Waals Step 2 1972) was found in grave 4660, Barrow Hills (Halpin in prep), and at Chilbolton, Hampshire (Russel forthcoming), while at Mere a Wessex Middle Rhine Beaker, a spatula and bracer had been deposited. Wessex Graves at Amesbury G.85, Roundway G.6 (ApSimon 1954) and West Overton G.6b (Smith and Simpson 1966) have also included spatulae. A recently excavated barrow at Irthlingborough, Northants, included a middle to late Beaker with three spatulae, up to 400mm long, which were made from animal ribs (Halpin pers com).

Spatulae from aceramic burials are known (Green 1980, 138) but are rare and, in addition to typical examples from Aldwinkle, include perforated examples which may have served separate functions. Cremations, both with and without urns, have also been found with spatulae. Burials of this type have been discussed by Smith and Simpson (1966); some include archery equipment, arrowshaft smoothers at Amesbury G.85 and at Roundway G.5 (Annable and Simpson 1964, 51) which also included a barbed and tanged arrowhead.

Pit 5456 – fills 5457 and 5458

This pit contained dumped waste, including chips, from an adjacent knapping floor. Refitting flakes were present in the lower fill (5457), where most of the flint was concentrated.

Nine cores were found, of which at least four produced no usable flakes. There were four single platform cores and two more with a second striking platform. These six cores produced elongated and squat flakes from both prepared and unprepared striking platforms. Abrasion of the striking platform, which removes overhang and strengthens the core edge, and faceting, which modifies the flaking angle, were present. Two faceting chips were refitted to one of the cores. Core rejection resulted from a failure to maintain the angle of percussion, although refitting core rejuvenation tablets indicates that systematic rejuvenation was sometimes used to maintain production.

There are also two exhausted, semi-discoidal cores which have slightly domed flaking surfaces with converging flake scar patterns. The backs of the cores are steeply prepared and partially cortical. Control of the flaking angle ensured flake production beyond that of the single and double platform cores so that these two cores were the smallest from the pit.

Flakes

The unbroken flakes were analysed and relevant results are shown in Fig 99. Diagnostic flakes were apparent, eg blades and thinning flakes, but the sample size prevented separate analysis of individual types. Most flakes are preparation and trimming flakes which were removed to construct or maintain the shape of the core, particularly the discoidal cores where preshaping was more important. There were insufficient blades (13% 2:5 breadth:length ratio) for these to be regarded as intentional products and two from platform preparation were refitted to a semi-discoidal core (Fig 98.16).

The assemblage also includes approximately 25 flakes classified as 'thinning/finishing flakes' from core tool manufacture. They are thin, broad flakes with narrow butts, which are often faceted, and have feathered edges and plunging profiles (Newcomer 1971). Their function as core tool thinning flakes is, however, less certain, despite the evidence for core tool production on the site. The cross section of the core tool is thick and the flake scars suggest that the flakes should be shorter with a less plunging profile. It seems more likely that these 'thinning' flakes were derived from trimming discoidal or Levallois cores. A flake from the upper fills has been classified as an atypical Levallois flake (Bordes 1961, 31). It has centripetal preparation, regular edges, a faceted butt and was probably removed by hard hammer percussion. There is, however, a patch of cortex on the dorsal surface and the axis of percussion does not correspond to the axis of morphology. This implies that the shape of the flake was not prepared precisely before its removal from the core. Small 'thinning/

finishing' flakes recorded amongst the chips, including two which refit, may have resulted from faceting.

The use of discoidal and semi-discoidal cores has resulted in more variation of recorded scar patterns on the dorsal surfaces of flakes from these cores than on flakes from single platform cores.

Chips

One hundred and eight chips were recovered from a sieved sample. They suggest that, although retouched implements are present, retouch phases cannot be identified. Most chips result from blank production. Platform abrasion and faceting chips (Newcomer and Karlin 1987) were recorded, of which two faceting chips were refitted to the core. The remaining chips are undiagnostic and result from the impact of the hammer on the striking platform. Chips of this type are produced during all phases of flint knapping.

Pits 6053, 6083, 6085 and 6091

The high ratio of scrapers to flakes from these features suggests that the contents may represent domestic refuse, including unretouched flint tools, rather than industrial waste. The material from 6091, however, does appear to contain some debris from small-scale knapping. It includes two cores, one of which is failed, and simple refits. The cortex suggests that the raw material might be derived from no more than two nodules, with the majority from one. The cortex is present on the core and an end scraper (Fig 98.9) which has been refitted to a flake. The core has two striking platforms, the first prepared by simple flaking and the second, at 90 to the first, formed by a thermal fracture. Elongated ridged flakes with broad butts were removed from this striking platform before production was terminated by a thermal fracture near the base of the core. The scraper is made on a preparation flake with a dipping distal end.

Sixty-nine flakes from 6053, 6083 and 6091 were amalgamated for analysis to maximise the sample available. Relevant results from this sample are shown in Fig 99. The values for breadth:length ratios indicate large numbers of elongated flakes with lengths which exceed 30mm. The analysis also shows that the flakes were produced from cores which were predominantly flaked from a single direction. Negative flake scars rarely deviate through more than 90° and butts are both broad and unprepared. The flakes and the core are therefore comparable in all respects.

Results from other Late Neolithic/ Early Bronze Age industries (Pitts 1978a, 1978b) show, in contrast, that squat flakes normally predominate in these periods. Flakes which are less than 30mm in length are also common amongst waste flakes regardless of raw material size: see pit 5456 from Grimes Graves where 67% were less than 30mm (Saville 1981, 27); and retouched pieces consistently exceed 30mm in length. The results also show that 26% of the flakes from the pits are 'distal trimming flakes' (Harding 1986b) – flakes with a cortical distal end. These flakes were considered to be amongst the most suitable blanks for conversion into retouched tools at Rowden, Dorset (Harding 1986b), despite forming only a minority of retouched flakes at that site. The flakes from Easton Lane therefore may be tools rather than mere large waste flakes.

Fifteen flake scrapers were found in the excavated areas of the pits. They have been made on ridged flakes which were struck from single platform cores and generally exceed 30mm in both length and breadth. The scaping edges, which are convex in plan, range from 104mm to 14mm (mean 42.3mm) in length. They have been manufactured by regular, direct retouch at the distal end, although there are two side scapers and one double end scraper.

The large number of scrapers and the presence of a scraper with a refitting flake demonstrates that these tools were disposable. They could be made quickly when they were required. The scraper with its associated waste flake (Fig 98.9) was probably made for immediate use near its place of manufacture rather than reunited with its flake in a centralised refuse pit. The relationship of domestic activity with flint knapping has also been demonstrated elsewhere. A Beaker pit at Dean Bottom on the Marlborough Downs (Harding 1986a) contained retouched material which could be refitted to flakes, although larger quantities of knapping debris, including debitage and retouch chips were also present.

Discussion

The assemblages from Easton Lane are broadly contemporary, but still provide interesting comparisons of production, technology and function. Extensive industrial activity is absent but small-scale core preparation and non-specialised flake production was found near burial 2752. This contrasts with evidence of specialised flake production identified by the distinctive by-products and core tool manufacture found in pit 5456. This specialised flake technology was probably a small component of the industry and existed alongside non-specialised production, which is represented in the pit by single and double platform cores. Core tool production was clearly not a monopoly of industrial centres.

Evidence also exists for the function of finished tools, both in a ceremonial context, as grave goods in burial 2752, and as domestic artefacts in pits 6053, 6083, 6085 and 6091. These groups also demonstrate possible differences in the expendability of individual objects. The barbed and tanged arrowheads are unlikely to have been made immediately before their inclusion in the grave, but the refitting flakes of the cache suggests some deliberate production and selection for the ceremony; unfortunately the grave goods cannot be associated with the flint waste in the feature. The refits from pit 6091 demonstrate that scrapers were also expendable. These non-specialised tools can be made easily and production was undoubtedly high. The presence of large flakes in this retouched, tool-dominated assemblage has been used to suggest that unretouched flake tools, which are impossible to recognise with certainty, are present. Tools of this type undoubtedly dominate flint assemblages but go largely unrecognised.

The following flints are illustrated (Figs 95 and 98):

Fig 95.
1. Barbed and tanged arrowhead. SF24 in inhumation 2752 in pit 1017, Area B.
2. Barbed and tanged arrowhead with broken barb. SF25 in inhumation 2752 in pit 1017, Area B.
3. Barbed and tanged arrowhead. SF26 in inhumation 2752 in pit 1017, Area B.
4. Barbed and tanged arrowhead. SF27 in inhumation 2752 in pit 1017, Area B.
5. Barbed and tanged arrowhead. SF28 in inhumation 2752 in pit 1017, Area B.
6. Barbed and tanged arrowhead. SF154 in inhumation 2752 in pit 1017, Area B.
7. Cortical flake. SF156 in inhumation 2752 in pit 1017, Area B.
8. Cortical flake. SF157 in inhumation 2752 in pit 1017, Area B.
9. Retouched flake. SF159 in inhumation 2752 in pit 1017, Area B.
10. Two refitting flakes. SF160/161 in inhumation 2752 in pit 1017, Area B.
11. Blade. SF158 in inhumation 2752 in pit 1017, Area B.
12. Blade. SF162 in inhumation 2752 in pit 1017, Area B.
13. Naturally broken flake with stepped and scaled retouch. SF168 in inhumation 2752 in pit 1017, Area B.
14. Fabricator. SF130 in pit 1017, Area B.
15. Ground axe fragment formed into semi-discoidal knife. SF29 in pit 1017, Area B.

Fig 98.
1. End scraper on a flake. SF803 in pit 6083, Area Mc.
2. End scraper on a flake with faceted butt. SF804 in pit 6083, Area Mc.
3. Side scraper on a flake. SF806 in pit 6083, Area Mc.
4. Side/end scraper on a flake. SF805 in pit 6083, Area Mc.
5. End scraper on a flake. SF807 in pit 6085, Area Mc.
6. End scraper on a flake. SF809 in pit 6091, Area Mc.
7. End scraper on a flake. SF810 in pit 6091, Area Mc.
8. End scraper on a flake. SF808 in pit 6091, Area Mc.
9. End scraper on preparation flake, refitted to a flake. SF811 in pit 6091, Area Mc.
10. End scraper on a flake. SF308 in pit 6053, Area Mc.
11. End scraper on a flake. SF796 in pit 6053, Area Mc.
12. Side scraper on a flake. SF797 in pit 6053, Area Mc.
13. Side scraper on a flake. SF800 in pit 6053, Area Mc.
14. Double end scraper on a flake. SF798 in pit 6053, Area Mc.
15. End scraper on a flake. SF799 in pit 6053, Area Mc.
16. Two blades refitted to a semi-discoidal core. Pit 5456, Area F.

Stone Objects

Table 15 summarises the distribution of stone artefacts by phase.

Querns

Saddle querns (Fig 100)

1. Damaged saddle quern, worn. Greensand. 150mm square, 55mm thick. SF 134 in Phase 7, Early Middle Iron Age, pit 409, Area A.
2. Almost complete saddle quern, subrectangular, worn. Greensand. Length 323mm, width 194mm, 80mm thick. SF 147 in Phase 7, Early Middle Iron Age, pit 409, Area A.
3. Almost complete saddle quern, subrectangular, worn. Greensand. Length 295mm, width 165mm, 65mm thick. SF 328 in Phase 8, Middle Iron Age, pit 4567, Area A.
   Not illustrated. Irregular chipped fragment of sarsen boulder,

Table 15. The distribution of stone artefacts by phase.

| Object | Phase | | | | | | | |
	4	6	6/7	7	7/8	9	NP	Total
Greensand								
Weight	–	–	–	1	–	–	–	1
Saddle Quern	–	–	2	–	1	–	–	3
Rotary Quern	–	–	–	–	3	–	1	4
Fragments	7	1	2	1	7	1	2	22
Sarsen								
Weight	–	–	–	–	1	–	–	1
Saddle Quern	–	–	–	1	–	–	–	1
Fragments	–	–	2	–	–	–	1	3
Carrstone								
Fragments	1	1	–	–	–	–	1	3
Chalk								
Weight	–	–	–	–	7	–	–	7
	8	2	6	3	19	1	5	45

signs of wear. Length 180mm, width 125mm, 215mm thick. SF 89 in Phase 7, Early Middle Iron Age, post-hole 358 associated with structure 2288, Area A.

Also not illustrated were a small fragment of greensand saddle quern from Phase 6, Early Iron Age, pit 342, Area A; a small fragment of greensand saddle quern from Phase 7, Early Middle Iron Age, post-hole 222, Area A; and a small damaged saddle quern of very coarse red sandstone from Phase 4, Middle Bronze Age, post-hole 1538 associated with structure 2375, Area B.

Rotary querns (Fig 101)

4. Six fragments of lower stone. Greensand. Projected radius 185mm, depth of central hole 35mm. SF 13/19 in Phase 8, Middle Iron Age, pit 316, Area A.
5. Two fragments of upper stone of 'beehive' type. Greensand. Width 700mm. SF 60 in Phase 8, Middle Iron Age, pit 317, Area A.
6. Five fragments of an upper stone. Greensand. SF 776 in Phase 8, Middle Iron Age, pit 317, Area A.

Not illustrated were a small fragment of a sarsen rotary quern from Phase 7, Early Middle Iron Age, post-hole 117 associated with structure 2404, Area A; three small fragments of greensand rotary querns from Phase 7, Early Middle Iron Age, pit 409, Area A, Phase 7, Early Middle Iron Age, pit 496 and Phase 8, Middle Iron Age, pit 238; and a small fragment of a dark, ferruginous sandstone rotary quern from unphased pit 3063, Area D.

In addition there were some stone fragments which could not be readily assigned to type.

7. A sandstone quern, heathstone, oval, damaged edges and flat worn surface. Maximum diameter 180mm, 80mm thick. SF 183 in unphased pit 3063, Area D.

Not illustrated are very small fragments of greensand from the following contexts: Phase 2, Late Neolithic, pit 80 Area B, and mixed phase pit group 653, Area G; Phase 4, Middle Bronze Age, post-holes 387, 1591, 1593 and 2367 Area B, 1731 Area D, and ditches 990 Area A and 1054 Area B; Phase 7, Early Middle Iron Age, pits 329 and 496 and post-hole 83 associated with structure 4020 and Phase 8, Middle Iron Age, pits 317, 1100, 4921 and 4928, all from Area A; and Phase 9, Early Roman, ditch 5042, Area H.

Small sarsen fragments were recovered from Phase 7, Early Middle Iron Age, pit 409 Area A and from unphased pit 3745, Area A.

A very small fragment of 'carrstone' was recovered from Phase 6, Early Iron Age, ditch 350, Area A.

Mayen Lava
Not illustrated. Three small rounded fragments. SF 85 in Phase 10, Late Saxon, ditch 634, Area F.

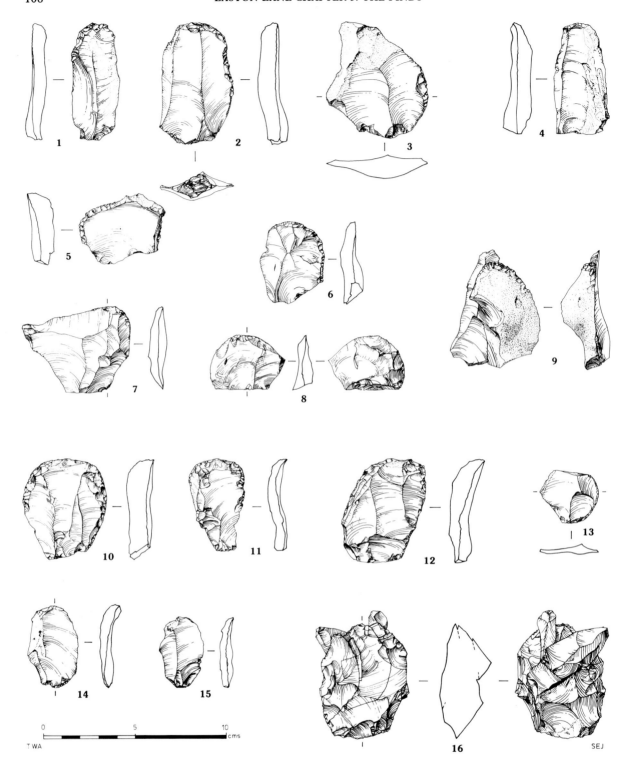

Fig 98.   Easton Lane. Flint objects.

Weights (Figs 101 and 102)

8.   Fragment of stone weight, with the remains of an iron
        attachment in a central hole, possibly from a pear-shaped
        weight. Danebury type W1. Greensand. Projected maxi-
        mum diameter 103mm, projected maximum weight
        1320g. SF 54 in Phase 7, Early Middle Iron Age, pit 329,
        Area A.

9.   Weight, almost complete, smoothly pecked surface,
        symmetrical form, slightly convex base, with fragment of

an iron attachment at top. The attachment seems to be
too slight for the weight of the object. Sarsen. Height
140mm, maximum width 150mm, projected maximum
weight 4500g. SF 290/296 in Phase 8, Middle Iron Age,
pit 4567, Area A

10.   Cylindrical chalk weight with a rounded triangular sec-
        tion and a single perforation at the top. Weight 1150g.
        SF 283 in Phase 8, Middle Iron Age, pit 4560.

11.   Irregular chalk weight with a single perforation. Weight
        930g. SF 284 in Phase 8, Middle Iron Age, pit 4560.

5456 SAMPLE 142

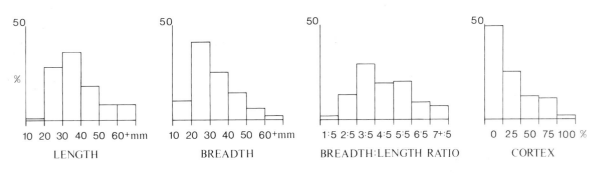

2752 SAMPLE 66

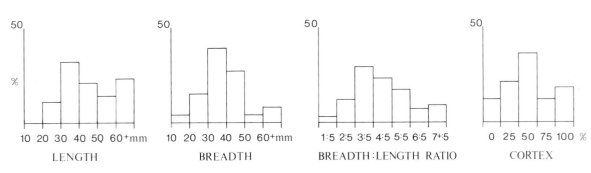

6092,6084,6061 SAMPLE 69

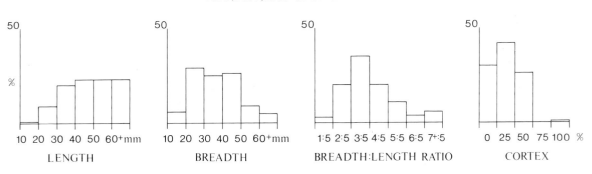

653 SAMPLE 119

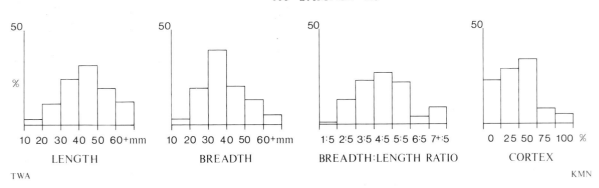

TWA   KMN

Fig 99.   Easton Lane. Flint bar charts.

12. Cylindrical chalk weight with an oval section and a single perforation at the top. Weight 940g. SF 287 in Phase 8, Middle Iron Age, pit 4560.

13. Cylindrical chalk weight with an oval section and a single perforation at the top. Weight 1080g. SF 288 in Phase 8, Middle Iron Age, pit 4560.

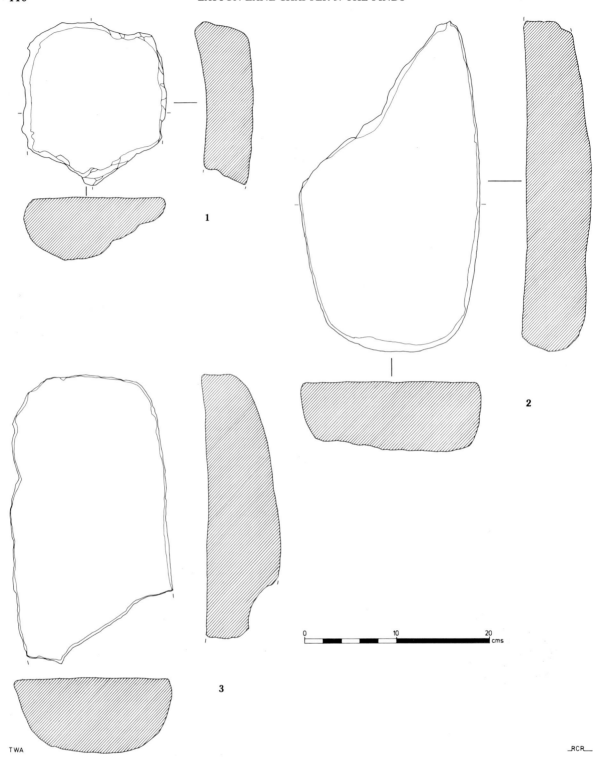

TWA

RCR

Fig 100.   Easton Lane. Saddle querns.

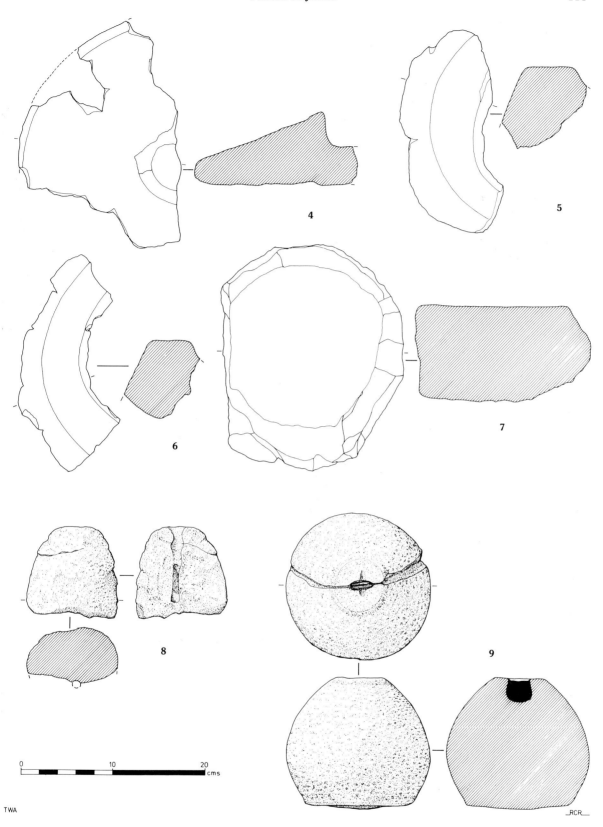

Fig 101. Easton Lane. Rotary querns and stone weights.

14.   Irregular chalk weight with a single perforation. Weight 1180g. SF 294 in Phase 8, Middle Iron Age, pit 4560.

15.   Damaged chalk weight, roughly oval form with a single perforation. SF 295 in Phase 8, Middle Iron Age, pit 4560.

16.   Irregular chalk weight with a trapezoidal section and a single perforation. Incomplete, possibly hung horizontally from two perforations. Weight 1020g. SF 292 in Phase 8, Middle Iron Age, pit 4567.

Not illustrated. Fragments of a possible oval chalk weight with a single incomplete hole. SF 43 in Phase 7, Early Middle Iron Age, pit 329.

Clay Objects (Fig 102)

Loomweights
Cylindrical and triangular forms were present.

17.   A damaged cylindrical loomweight with a central perforation 25mm diameter. SF 62 in unphased layer 165, Area B.

Not illustrated are fragments from two loomweights from Phase 2, Late Neolithic, pit 4775 in Area B; and fragments from a possible loomweight in Phase 4, Middle Bronze Age, post-hole 1718 in Area D.

18.   A damaged triangular loomweight with three perforations, estimated total weight 1880g. SF 9 in Phase 8, Middle Iron Age, pit 317, Area A.

Not illustrated from Area A are a small fragment of loomweight from Phase 7, Early Middle Iron Age, pit 409; four small fragments, possibly from a loomweight, from Phase 7, Early Middle Iron Age, pit 496; and a fragment of loomweight from Phase 8, Middle Iron Age, pit 4622.

Some small fragments of possible loomweights were recovered from the following features: Phase 2, Late Neolithic, pit 4775, Area B; Phase 5, Late Bronze Age, ditch 3765, Area A; Phase 8, Middle Iron Age, pit 4567, Area A; Phase 10, Late Saxon, ditch 634, Area F; unphased pit 4697, Area A; and unphased pit 7014, Area Bc.

Spindlewhorl
19.   Complete cylindrical form, roughly made, with a central perforation 5mm diameter. Height 46mm, diameter 30mm, weight 60g. SF 282 in Phase 8, Middle Iron Age, pit 4560, Area A.

Amber beads, by S J Shennan (Fig 103)

The amber beads from grave 3058 at Easton Lane place the burial clearly in the tradition of 'Wessex' Early Bronze Age graves from which by far the great majority of British prehistoric amber finds are known. Their co-occurrence with shale beads (Fig 103.28–30), as here, is also common. The following report will comment on the beads from two points of view: their quantity and their typology.

Quantity

Approximately 27 beads were found in grave 3058, which places it amongst the richest amber finds from prehistoric Britain, in number of beads if not in weight of amber. Only ten other finds are known to have had this many or more beads and nine of these are 'Wessex' burials: Kingston Deverill G5 (Grinsell 1957, 218); Little Cressingham (Clarke et al 1985, 275–6); Mold (Clarke et al 1985, 277–8); Norton Bavant G1 (Grinsell 1957, 185); Shrewton G5J (Green and Rollo-Smith 1984, 273–5, 309–10); Upton Lovell G2e (Clarke et al 1985, 279–80);

Wilsford cum Lake G47, 49 and 50 (Grinsell 1957, 198); Wimbourne St Giles G8 (Annable and Simpson 1964, 58, Grinsell 1959, 170); Winterslow JFSS 3 (Grinsell 1957, 213); and South Chard, Tatworth, Somerset (Gray 1966, 284). Four of these finds include spacer-beads, pointing to their relatively frequent but clearly not universal connection with large numbers of beads.

Within this group of burials, all within the same tradition, the contexts and associations are variable. Five are inhumations and six cremations. Two have shale beads associated with the amber, as at Easton Lane. Other associations include bronze daggers or knife-daggers (Little Cressingham, Norton Bavant, Upton Lovell and Wimbourne St Giles), faience beads (Kingston Deverill, Norton Bavant?, Tatworth and Wilsford cum Lake?), and gold items (Little Cressingham Mold, Upton Lovell and Wilsford cum Lake).

Typology

The beads from Easton Lane grave 3058 fall into two clearly defined types: small disk beads, which make up the majority, and small long 'oblate' beads.

The second of these is very restricted in numbers, occurring at only eight sites altogether in Britain. Six, including the Easton Lane examples, are 'Wessex' burials: Felmersham, Bedfordshire (Hall and Woodward 1977); Southwick (Corney et al 1969); Wilsford cum Lake G16 (Grinsell 1957, 214); Wimbourne St Giles (Grinsell 1959, 170); and Winterslow (Grinsell 1957, 203). Of these all except Easton Lane are cremations.

There is a strong pattern of association of this type with shale beads, which occur at Easton Lane, Felmersham, Southwick, Wilsford and Winterslow. Other associations include Collared urns (Felmersham and Winterslow), but nothing else occurs more than once.

Small disk beads, the more common type at Easton Lane, are also the most common type generally in Britain and occur in finds of all periods from the Neolithic to the Late Iron Age; however, inasmuch as amber occurs predominantly in the Early and Middle Bronze Age, the majority of finds of disk beads belong to this period.

The date of the burial

The radiocarbon date for this burial seems far too late in the context of the amber. As already indicated, amber in this quantity in burials appears to be a distinctive Early to Middle Bronze Age phenomenon on the basis of other finds. The disk beads could be this late but the long beads appear to be distinctive of the Early Bronze Age. Apart from the 'Wessex' burials listed above, the other two finds are a very uncertain association from Mid-Nithsdale in Scotland (unpublished) and a bead from a Bronze Age layer in a cave in Derbyshire, possibly associated with Bell Beaker sherds (Wilson nd).

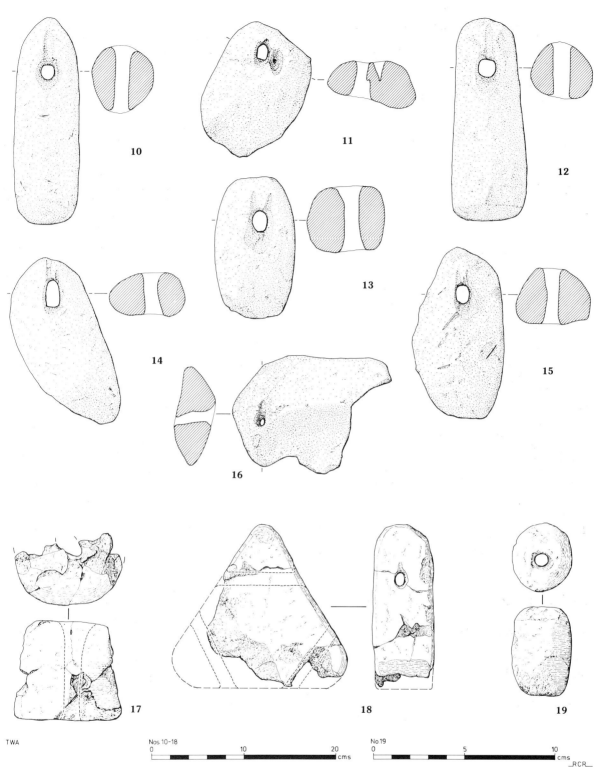

Fig 102. Easton Lane. Chalk weights and clay loomweights.

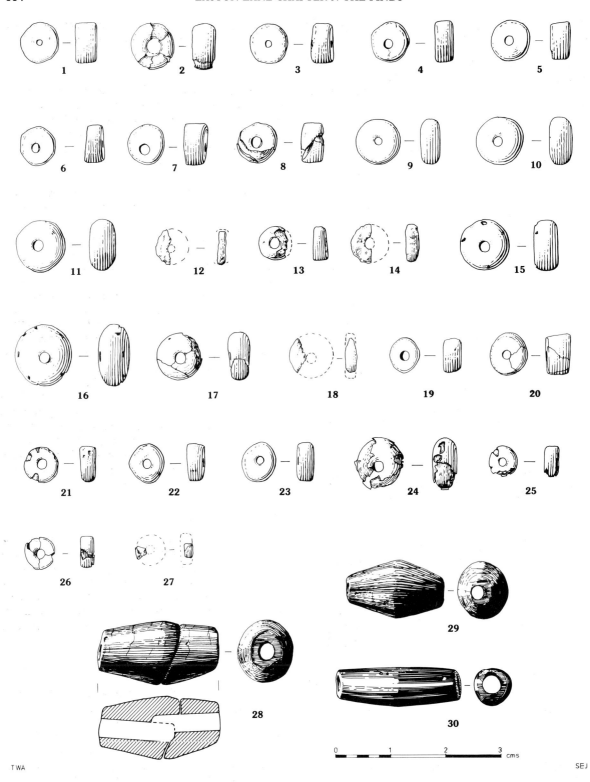

TWA

SEJ

Fig 103.　Easton Lane. Beads of amber (1–27) and of jet/shale (28–30).

Beads of white coral or fossil sponge (Fig 104)

Five beads were recovered from features scattered across the site, however all of them could be dated by association to the Early or Middle Bronze Age. No other general correlation could be made.

1.   White coral or fossil sponge bead, irregular sphere with surface scratches and indentations, c 13mm diameter. Blunt-ended perforation stops just short of opposing face, circular but no rilling marks visible, 4mm diameter. SF 49 in Phase 2, Late Neolithic, pit 851 (cuts pit 80), Area B.

2.   White coral or fossil sponge bead, small irregular sphere with surface indentations, diameter 6.2mm. Single perforation, c 2mm diameter, pecked through from one side. SF 144 in Phase 4, Middle Bronze Age, post-hole 1768 associated with MS 4010, Area D.

3.   White coral or fossil sponge bead, irregular notched sphere, 10.9mm diameter. Opposing pair of incomplete perforations, c 4.8mm diameter. SF 151 in Phase 4, Middle Bronze Age, post-hole 2992 associated with CS 4009, Area D.

4.   White coral or fossil sponge bead, irregular sphere, 13.4mm diameter with crudely pecked opposing pair of incomplete perforations, c 3.8mm diameter. SF 293 in ditch 4744, a recut of Phase 4, Middle Bronze Age, ditch 972, Area A.

5.   White coral or fossil sponge bead, small irregular sphere c 3.5mm diameter with three perforation holes: one opposing pair and one linked at right-angles. Perforation diameters 1.2mm. SF 131 in unphased post-hole 1770, Area D.

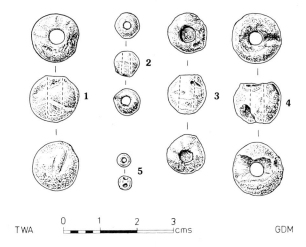

TWA   0   1   2   3 cms   GDM

Fig 104. Easton Lane. Beads of coral.

Metal Working (based on a report from P Wilthew)

The material sent for examination comprised over 100 samples of slag, ironstone, burnt clay, burnt stone and charcoal. Despite the large number of samples the total weight of material was less than 1kg.

The following phases were represented: Phase 2– Late Neolithic; Phases 4 and 5 – Middle and Late Bronze Age; Phases 6 to 8 – Early, Early Middle, and Middle Iron Age; Phase 9 – Late Iron Age/Early Roman; Phase 10 – Medieval.

Each sample is identified in the archive, and the results are discussed by phase below.

Phase 2

The samples from this phase included examples of iron slag, fuel ash slag, ironstone and burnt clay. Fuel ash slag is produced by a reaction between ash and silica-rich material such as sand or clay. It is often associated with metalworking but can be formed in any sufficiently hot fire and could, for example, be produced during a cremation. There is no evidence that the fuel ash slag, or the burnt clay, from this phase was of any technological significance.

Ironstone is a natural mineral which can be used as ore in iron smelting. However there was no evidence that the ironstone found in this phase, or in any of the later phases, had been collected for this purpose. It had not been roasted or prepared in any way and was almost certainly all natural geological material.

Iron slag is produced during both iron smelting and iron smithing, but the samples from this phase, from pit 80, were too small to enable the process which produced them to be identified with certainty. It is highly probable, however, that they were all iron smithing slag, the slag which collects in a blacksmith's hearth. Although a similar fayalite slag is produced during copper smelting there was no evidence for such activity on the site and the slag was virtually certainly intrusive material from the Iron Age or later. The feature also contained a few sherds of intrusive Medieval pottery.

Phases 4 and 5

The majority of the samples were from these phases, but they were almost all fuel ash slag. A few examples of ironstone and burnt stone and one piece of charcoal were also present, but there was no evidence that any of the material had any technological significance. The comments about fuel ash slag and ironstone made above also apply to the material from these phases.

Phases 6–10

The iron slag from these phases was almost certainly iron smithing slag, although the individual samples were too small to be identified with complete confidence. There is no reason to assume that the iron slag from these phases is intrusive, but as small quantities of iron smithing slag are found on most occupation sites of the Iron Age or later date, the presence of such a small quantity does not enable any conclusions to be drawn concerning the likely scale of ironworking activity on or near the site.

There was no positive evidence for iron smelting on the site and the ironstone from these phases was almost certainly naturally occurring geological material.

Although some of the fuel ash slag and burnt stone may have been associated with blacksmithing, it was of no direct technological significance.

Antler and bone objects

Antler

Four antler spatulae were recovered from the fill of inhumation 2752 in Phase 2, Late Neolithic, pit 1017 in Area B (Fig 96.1–2, Fig 97.3–4). They are discussed in detail in the flint report, above 101.

Other pieces of worked antler are a red deer brow tine, bevelled at proximal end and worked at distal end into a point, length 217mm, maximum diameter 29mm, SF 33 in Phase 2, Late Neolithic, pit 80 in Area B; and a sawn-off tine point with cut marks at base and signs of wear at point, length 160mm, maximum diameter 19mm, SF 329 in Phase 10, Medieval, pit 5461 in Area F. Neither is illustrated.

Worked Bone (Fig 105)

The awl from Phase 2, Late Neolithic, inhumation 2752 is described in the flint report, above 103.

1. Gouge made from a small mammal long bone, split longitudinally, one end worked into a point, the other perforated. Length 59mm, diameter of perforation 2.5mm. SF 306 in Phase 3, Early Bronze Age, pit 6053 in Area Mc.

2. Awl made from a small long bone (species unknown), one end intact, the other shaved down to a point. Length 45mm, maximum width 13mm, 3mm thick. SF 307 in Phase 3, Early Bronze Age, pit 6053 in Area Mc.

3. Spindle-whorl, well-smoothed domed surfaces with raised lips around central perforation of 4mm diameter. Maximum diameter 36mm, height 15mm. SF 23 in Phase 8, Middle Iron Age, pit 316 in Area A.

4. Long bone with one end scraped down to form a point. Possible gouge. Length 110mm. SF 813 in Phase 8, Middle Iron Age, pit 238 in Area A.

5. Long bone with one end broken and missing, the other scraped down to form a point, the tip of which is missing. Possible gouge. Length 116mm. SF 326 in Phase 8, Middle Iron Age, pit 4560 in Area A.

6. Thin rectangular bone plaque, diagonal scored decoration on one face, two small iron rivets, probably part of a small handle. Length 39mm, width 8mm, 1mm thick. SF 278 in Phase 10, Late Saxon, pit 654 in Area F.

Worked Shell

Not illustrated. One irregular fragment of oyster shell with a single perforation 2mm in diameter. Fragment 31mm by 25mm. SF 225 in Phase 10 ditch 634 in Area F.

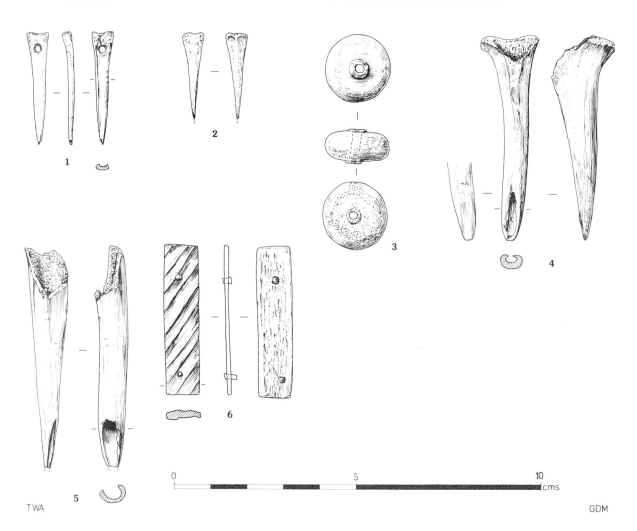

TWA   GDM

Fig 105.   Easton Lane. Worked bone objects.

Chapter 4

The Environmental Evidence

Soil Variability at Easton Lane, by P F Fisher

Introduction

This report presents data collected from the extensive open-area excavations at Easton Lane, near Winchester. No buried soils survived, except possibly in ditch fill sequences, and so the tentative conclusions are based on the interrelationship of two main lines of evidence: the distribution of contemporary soil types, and the nature and distribution of archaeological and periglacial feature fills. Supplementary data include land use records, and landforms.

The report is divided into two sections. The first analyses the modern soils at the site, and discusses these with respect to general soil variability on the chalk, whereas the second is a discussion of the nature of the archaeological feature fills. A discussion concludes the report.

Setting

The site is located on a hill with Upper Chalk outcropping beneath a thin blanket covering of periglacial deposits, Coombe Rock. The upper surface of the Coombe Rock is characterised by linear stripes filled by silty clay marly material. These are also of periglacial origin (Ellis 1981). The swathe of land threatened by motorway construction crossed the hill on a line approximately north to south, and so hillslopes with both northerly and southerly aspect were investigated. The two fields on the hill were wholly arable. Site specific documentary evidence dating back to the Tythe Map of 1838 and including Ordnance Survey maps of 1874, 1932 and 1958, show firstly that the fields had been primarily in arable use since at least 1838, but more interestingly, that subsidiary field boundaries had existed within the present large fields, but never in the same position on any two maps. Thus lynchets within the modern fields resulting from recent ploughing up to boundaries now grubbed out were not to be expected.

Modern Soils

There are three primary soil types formed on the chalk of southern England: rendzinas, calcareous brown earths and argillic brown earths. No evidence was found at this site for clay enriched material which might have been derived from an argillic horizon, and so only the first two have been identified here.

The rendzina soil profile is characterised by two principal horizons, A and C, with an intervening but discontinuous Bw. A typical profile description is as follows (terminology after Hodgson 1974).

Profile 1 (Fig 106)
Ap   Brown (10YR 4.5/3) very calcareous silt loam; medium and fine angular and subangular blocky; small and medium chalk fragments with medium and small flints; abrupt and smooth on:
Bw   Brown (7.5YR 4/4) very calcareous silt loam; fine angular blocky; small chalk fragments; abrupt and smooth on:
C   Coombe Rock; very calcareous silty clay loam; extremely abundant rounded medium and small chalk fragments.

Overall the Ap horizon was always between 29 and 21cm thick (except where the slope angle became large, 6–10%, when the depth was reduced to 17cm), always the same colour (+-1 chroma or value), stoniness, structure, etc. Thus all properties were irrespective of aspect (Fig 106), and so, as might be expected, the properties of the rendzina profiles seemed to have been primarily related to homogenisation by ploughing.

There were two types of calcareous brown earth profiles at the site. The first is described thus:

Profile 12 (Fig 106)
Ap   Brown (10YR 4/3) very calcareous silt loam; fine and medium angular and subangular blocky soil structure; small and medium chalk fragments and medium flint; abrupt and wavy on:
Bw   Yellowish brown (8.75YR 5/6) very calcareous gritty silt loam; medium and fine angular blocky; medium flint and small chalk; clear and smooth on:
C   Coombe Rock, as above.

This profile is typical of all locations where contemporary and immediately past ploughing might have resulted in the accumulation of material: against contemporary field boundaries to the north and

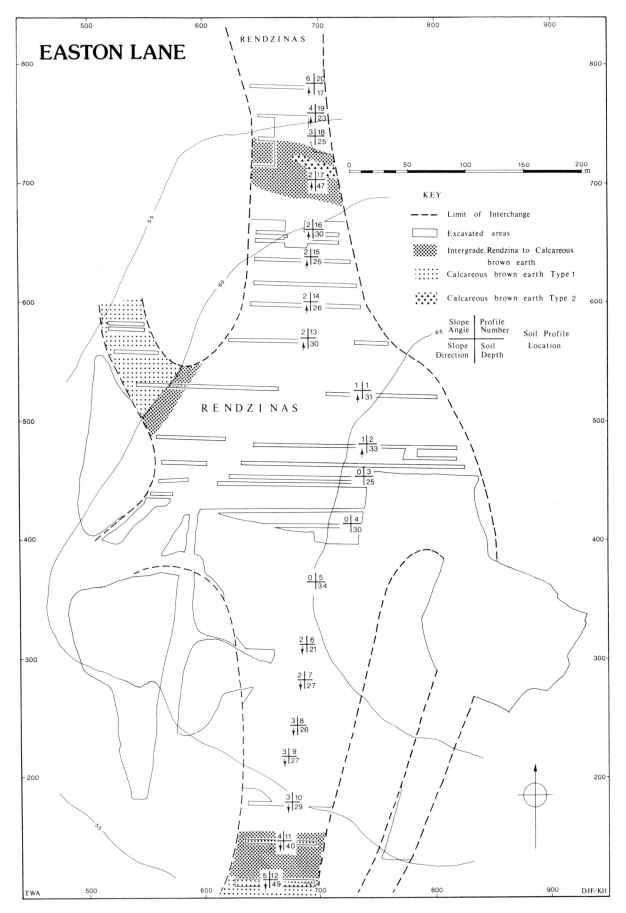

Fig 106.   Easton Lane. Soil survey plan.

northwest of the area, and in the valley bottom to the south (Fig 106). In other words, the soil profile was the product of the accumulation of soil material as the result of accelerated soil erosion due to ploughing.

The soil profile of the second type of calcareous brown earth is:

Profile 17 (Fig 106)

Ap   Brown (10YR 4/3) calcareous silt loam; fine and medium angular and subangular blocky; medium and fine flint, ocasional fine chalk; clear and smooth on:

Bw   Strong brown (7.5YR 5/6) calcareous silty clay loam; fine angular clay blocky; coarse and medium flint, occasional very small chalk; gradual and wavy on:

C   Coombe Rock, as above.

In two important respects this profile is different from those listed above:

i) For the first time the soil is not very calcareous, and chalk fragments are not the dominant stone type, rather flint is;

ii) There is a slight textural difference between the Ap and Bw horizons, implying an increased clay component in the latter, but possibly a reduction in disseminated carbonates.

This profile again represents an accumulation of soil material, but, most significantly, there was no apparent reason in the contemporary or immediately past landscape for such an accumulation (no permanent field boundary since at least 1838). There are several explanations which may however explain this occurrence.

a) It could have been a positive lynchet of a long deserted field system, but if so, why was it not a chalky, calcareous deposit, as might be expected by analogy with lynchets elsewhere (Fowler and Evans 1967)?

b) This may have been the only location where the soil approximated its thickness, pre-human interference (Bell 1982, Limbrey 1978). Why, however, should it have had such a limited occurrence, and why was it not on the hilltop, rather than on the northern flank of the hill (Fig 106)?

c) Most soil material on the chalk is either Late Devensian loess (Catt 1978), or derived from degraded Tertiary bedrock. Differential deposition or preservation of these may account for the soil observed. However, in the first case wind direction would need to have been from the south to cause drifting on the northern hillside, but this is inconsistent with the presumed North Sea origin of the loess (Catt 1978). In the second, erosion, either natural or accelerated, must have been differential, that is greater on the south side, but, again, this is inconsistent with the usual interrelationship of assymetric hillslopes and deposits as observed by Ollier and Thomasson (1957).

In summary, the contemporary soils at Easton Lane were largely as might be predicted for the chalklands. Rendzinas occur on the hilltop and sides, and calcareous brown earths are present in the valley bottom and at contemporary erosion breaks such as field boundaries. A swathe across the northern part of the site, however, had a calcareous brown earth profile in an anomalous location.

Feature Fills

On the whole, the secondary fills of archaeological features at the site had colours similar to those of the rendzina Ap and Bw horizons (brown 10YR 4.5/3 to dark brown 7.5YR 4/4) although lighter colours such as dark brown (7.5YR 5/4) were not uncommon. The fills were generally carbonate and chalk rich; even an apparently stoneless layer contained plentiful chalk grits. The textures were generally silt dominated as is typical of many chalkland soils. These secondary fills are probably due to accumulation by sheet wash and soil creep. Beneath the secondary fills, there are usually extremely chalky primary fills (up to 90% chalk fragments), created by direct disintegration of the chalk rock or Coombe Rock walls of the feature (Limbrey 1975). These generalisations applied to all the archaeological features to the south of the site, in Areas A, B, C, D and E, irrespective of the age of the features.

In Areas F and G, however, the fills were different. The working hollows associated with structure 3918 in Area G contained definable primary and secondary fills, but in the former, chalk fragments often appeared to be less dominant than might be expected, and the latter were chalk free and uniformly approximately brown (7.5YR 5/4). The fills of the variously dated Late Saxon, Medieval and Bronze Age features in Area F, also contained little or no chalk, dark colours (yellowish red, 6.25YR 5/6), and only slightly increased chalk content in the primary fills, over the secondary.

In natural features, both treehole and periglacial stripes, the two-way split of fills between the southern areas and Areas F and G was repeated. Treeholes of all ages were plentiful, and always contained highly calcareous, chalk-rich fills, often with vertical stratification (chalk pinnacles) and irregular outlines. Features of an apparently similar origin were numerous in Areas F and G, but here, although the shapes remained irregular, chalk was often rare or absent from the fill which again had a generally darker appearance. Periglacial stripes in Areas F and G were again brown (7.5YR 7/4) with at least plentiful chalk grits.

As with soil types, several working hypotheses can be defined to explain the spatial variation in feature fills:

i) Chalk-free soil material, deeper than elsewhere, would account for the darker, chalk-free secondary feature fills of the northern areas, but not for the chalkless state of primary fills and treeholes;

ii) A local decalcifying soil regime may account for both the chalk free secondary and primary fills, but the rate of decalcification required in such an explanation is in excess of the generally accepted rate, but not beyond that suggested on other archaeological evidence (Fisher 1983).

Discussion

The site as a whole can be divided into two areas. One includes most of the areas covered by the rendzina and Type I calcareous brown earth soil profiles. Here feature fills were largely calcareous, chalky and exactly as might be expected by analogy with other chalkand sites. In contrast, the feature fills in Areas F and G were anomalous, containing little chalk, and had generally darker colours. Either by coincidence or for similar reasons, Area F was directly associated with the occurrence of Type II calcareous brown earth, and Area G was the nearest other excavated location. Feature fill variations were irrespective of age, that is, features of all ages in each area had similar fills. The difference in properties of feature fills must either have been due to differing depositional or post-depositional conditions in the two areas. An explanation based on soil acidification, after deposition of the feature fills, however, is consistent with the observed sediment properties.

The Human Bones, by Janet D Henderson and Alison Cameron

Introduction

The human bone from this site was examined and recorded in the first instance at the University of Bradford by Alison Cameron. Further examination, in particular of the paleopathogical evidence, was undertaken at the Ancient Monuments Laboratory by the first-named author. The report was also substantially written in the Laboratory.

Observations were made for demography (age and sex), anthropology (metrical and morphological variables) and pathology (including dental and skeletal pathology and stature). The results for each individual are given in the microfiche catalogue (19–38), together with details of the methods (or references) used in each case and tables of the anthropological results.

Bone Preservation

A total of ten cremation and 19 inhumation samples were examined. The cremation samples were all small and in three cases (Cremations 4683 and 6099, and layer 1334 in post-hole 169) it was not even possible to state positively that the bone was human and not animal. Among the inhumations, bone preservation was variable, with five recorded as being poorly preserved, three moderately-well preserved and eight in good condition. Although this might be taken to indicate a bias towards good preservation overall, it should be noted that half of the well-preserved skeletons were only partially represented. There was no apparent difference in bone preservation by period.

Demography

The results for sex, age and stature for the inhumations and for sex, age and sample weight for the cremations are given in Tables 16 and 17. There is very little that can be said about these results owing to the extremely small sample sizes both of inhumed and cremated bone. For the latter, the situation is reflected in the sample weights. The average cremation has been cited as weighing 1.6kg and weights of up to 3.6kg have been recorded (Evans 1963). As with bone preservation, there were no obvious differences by period. With so much data missing it was not possible to assess whether there had been any variations between cremated and inhumed individuals.

Anthropology

In all cases the sample sizes were too small for any analysis to be justifiable. A complete record of the individual results is given in the catalogue (see microfiche).

Dental Pathology

Various categories of dental pathology were observed, including: ante-mortem tooth loss, caries, abscesses, periodontal disease, calculus and enamel hypoplasia. Only one individual had ante-mortem tooth loss (Burial 2752), unusually, perhaps, of all the maxillary incisors. Five had carious lesions (Burials 4978, 5263 and 5264 and pit deposits 1017 and 5027) and on three of them (4978, 5027 and 5264) more than one tooth had been affected. Only one individual had an abscess (5027) and in this case there were two. It was suggested that both of these were associated with caries. There was evidence for periodontal disease on six individuals, for calculus on seven and enamel hypoplasia on eight. Owing to the separation of these individuals by period (hence small sample sizes) it was not thought worthwhile to do more than make a record of, for example, the location and size of caries by tooth.

Skeletal Pathology

Comment on the frequency of any particular class of skeletal pathology could not be justified owing to the small sample sizes. However, it may be noted that, as might be expected, changes linked to joint disease were the most common, followed by trauma and infection. Evidence for joint disease was generally confined to changes which may be associated with ageing changes in the skeleton. Thus, in the seven individuals affected (Burials 2752, 3058, 3695, 4978 and 5264, ditch deposit 354 and pit deposit 5027), all showed degeneration of the vertebral column and in none of them was there any indication of a more specific arthropathy. Bony response to infection was noted in two individuals (Burials 1035 and 4978). In neither of them could it be described as other than non-specific. Two individuals had fractured bones: 5027 (skull) and 5264 (vertebra). Cause was not apparent in either case. Other pathology of note was seen on 2752 (an unusually-shaped first right proximal phalanx of the foot) and 4978 (spondylolithesis affecting the fourth and fifth lumbar vertebrae, see microfiche).

Table 16. Results for sex, age and stature – the inhumations.

Feature	Sex	Age (in years)	Stature Metric (Imperial)
Late Neolithic			
Layer 1049 in pit 1017, Area B	–	Adult	–
Burial 2752 in pit 1017, Area B	Male	35–45	–
Early Bronze Age			
Burial 595, Area F	?Female	Old Adult	–
Layer 597 in pit 596, Area F	–	Adult	–
Early/Middle Bronze Age			
Burial 1708, Area D	–	16–20	–
Burial 3058, Area D	Female	35–45	–
Middle Bronze Age			
Burial 3695, Area D	Female	25–35	–
Iron Age			
Burial in layer 354 ditch 176, Area A	Female	Adult	–
Deposit in layer 354 ditch 176, Area A	?Male	Adult	–
Burial 1035 in ditch 990, Area A	–	1–3	–
Layer 1327 in post-hole 907, Area A	–	Adult	–
Layer 2192 in pit 409, Area A	–	Adult	–
Burial 4978 in ditch 1810, Area D	Male	35–45	1.62 m +/– .0327 (*c* 5′4″)
Layer 5027 in pit 4983, Area A	Female	35–45	–
Late Iron Age/Early Roman			
Burial 5263 in pit 5107, Area H	?Male	Old Adult	–
Burial 5264 in pit 5103, Area H	?Female	35–45	–
Layer 5337 in ditch 5295, Area H	–	Birth +/–	–
Burial 5424A in pit 5338, Area H	Female	17–25	1.64 m +/– .0366 (*c* 5′5″)
Burial 5424B in pit 5338, Area H	–	Birth +/–	–

Table 17. Results for sex, age and weight – the cremations.

Feature	Sex	Age (in years)	Weight in g
Early Bronze Age			
Cremation 507, Area F	–	–	81
Cremation 598, Area F	–	–	33
Early/Middle Bronze Age			
Cremation 1700, Area D	–	Adult	149
Cremation 1705, Area D	?Male	Adult (?young)	3,129
Cremation 1729, Area D	–	–	34
Cremation 1735, Area D	–	–	55
Cremation 1744, Area D	–	–	84
Middle Bronze Age			
Cremation 4683, Area A	–	–	–
Cremation 6099, Area Bc	–	–	–
Iron Age			
Layer 1334 in post-hole 169, Area A	–	–	–

The Animal Bones, by J M Maltby

Introduction

The animal bones were identified using the modern comparative reference collections at the Faunal Remains Unit, University of Southampton. All the bones from phased deposits were computer-recorded and the individual records are stored at the Unit. Copies of summary archives of the data have been placed with the excavator and at the Faunal Remains Unit.

Normal excavation produced 4,089 animal bone fragments from phased deposits. In addition, over 1,800 fragments were derived from water-sieved samples (Table 18).

Although the history of the site could be divided into ten broad chronological phases, the nature of the dating evidence meant that not all the bones could be assigned to a single phase and many could only be dated to within two or more phases. The bones were therefore initially subdivided into 18 groups on the basis of the phasing evidence (Table 18).

Table 18. Animal bone fragments recovered from Easton Lane.

Phase	Unsieved	Sieved	Total
1	–	–	–
2	99	34	133
2–3	202	106	308
2–4	17	5	22
2/10	158	10	168
3	73	51	124
4	74	220	294
5	131	60	191
4–7	37	–	37
5	48	37	85
5–6	22	–	22
6	38	24	62
6–7	70	–	70
7	254	100	354
7–8	674	890	1,564
8	216	249	465
9	444	3	447
10	1,532	★	1,532
Total	4,089	1,789	5,878

Key to Phases

1 Neolithic
2 Late Neolithic
3 Early Bronze Age
4 Middle Bronze Age
5 Late Bronze Age
6 Early Iron Age
7 Early Middle Iron Age
8 Middle Iron Age
9 Late Iron Age/ Early Romano–British
10 Medieval

★ bones from sieved samples not computer-recorded.

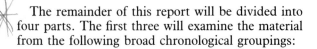

The remainder of this report will be divided into four parts. The first three will examine the material from the following broad chronological groupings:

a) Neolithic and Bronze Age contexts (Phases 1–5);
b) Iron Age and Romano-British contexts (Phases 6–9);
c) Medieval contexts (Phase 10).

In each case there will be a detailed, context-based analysis, paying particular attention to variability of species and element representation caused by preservation conditions, disposal strategies and retrieval methods. The concluding section will examine the evidence for changes in the exploitation of animals in the light of the evidence obtained from these excavations and the earlier excavations at Winnall Down (Fasham 1985). This will incorporate ageing, butchery and metrical data and will attempt to place the results in a broader regional framework, particularly with regard to the Iron Age and Romano-British material.

Animal bones from Neolithic and Bronze Age contexts

Although the excavations produced evidence for the use of the area at various times in the Neolithic and Bronze Age periods, the faunal evidence from contexts of this date was disappointing. No bones were recovered from Phase 1, Neolithic, features and only 860 fragments were obtained by normal retrieval methods from other Neolithic and Bronze Age contexts. These were supplemented by 523 fragments recovered from sieved samples, but most of those consisted of small pieces of bone unidentifiable to species (Table 20).

Phase 2. Late Neolithic
Seven features produced 133 fragments including 34 from sieved samples (Table 18). A sample of 72 fragments was obtained using normal recovery techniques from five pits (80, 852, 3256, 4775 and 6091). Twenty-seven fragments were found in ditch 511. The bones were poorly preserved and badly fragmented. Eighty-six of the 99 unsieved bones displayed erosion and 83 were unidentifiable to species (Table 19). Nine of the ten cattle fragments were recovered from pit 80 context 512 and consisted mainly of carpals, tarsals and phalanges. These bones were not eroded and the three carpals and two tarsals each formed articulated groups. The good preservation of these bones suggests either that they were more recent intrusions or that they were buried more quickly and deeply than the remainder of the bones from these deposits. Pit 3256 context 3257 and pit 4775 context 4792 were the only layers in which sheep/goat bones were identified. Pig bones were found in pit 80 context 512 and pit 3256 context 3257. A tooth of a red deer (Cervus elaphus) was identified in pit 80 context 82.

Twenty of the fragments recovered from sieved samples were from pit 6091 context 6092 and included two bones of an unidentified rodent and an

Table 19. Animal bones in Neolithic and Bronze Age features (unsieved).

Species	2	2–3	2–4	2/10	3	4	4–5	4–7	5	5–6
Cattle	10	24	5	16	14	13	18	4	4	5
Sheep/Goat	3	5	–	32!	22★	5	13	1	5	6
Pig	2	19	1	5	6	2	5	–	–	1
Horse	–	–	1	5	–	1	8	4	5	2
Dog	–	–	–	31★	–	–	–	–	–	–
Red Deer	1	12	–	1	2	2	–	–	–	–
Unid Large Mammal	47	62	6	21	13	26	28	21	15	5
Sheep-sized Mammal	15	27	1	16	10	13	10	3	9	1
Unid Mammal	21	53	3	8	4	12	8	4	5	2
Unid Bird	–	–	–	–	–	–	–	–	1	–
Pine Marten	–	–	–	–	2	–	–	–	–	–
Mouse species	–	–	–	–	–	–	38★	–	–	–
Unid rodent	–	–	–	–	–	–	3	–	–	–
Frog	–	–	–	–	–	–	–	–	3	–
Toad	–	–	–	–	–	–	–	–	1	–
Unid Corvid	–	–	–	23★	–	–	–	–	–	–
TOTAL	99	202	17	158	71	74	131	37	48	22

! includes 8 fragments identified to sheep
★ includes articulated bones

Table 20. Animal bones in Neolithic and Bronze Age features (sieved).

Species	2	2–3	2–4	2/10	3	4	4–5	5
Cattle	–	1	–	–	–	1	–	2
Sheep/Goat	–	2	–	–	3	2	3	–
Pig	–	4	–	–	–	–	–	1
Red Deer	1	–	–	–	–	–	–	–
Unid Large Mammal	2	2	–	–	2	2	6	4
Sheep-sized Mammal	6	14	1	–	17	15	9	1
Unid Mammal	22	56	4	9	26	158	41	22
Unid Bird	–	1	–	–	–	1	–	–
Pine Marten	–	–	–	–	–	1	–	–
Water Vole	–	–	–	–	–	1	–	–
Short-tailed Vole	–	–	–	–	–	–	–	1
Mouse species	–	1	–	–	1	3	–	–
Unid Rodent	2	4	–	1	1	32	–	1
Mole (intrusive?)	–	–	–	–	–	1	–	–
Frog	–	9	–	–	–	–	–	1
Toad	–	7	–	–	–	–	–	–
Frog/Toad	1	5	–	–	1	–	1	4
Fish	–	–	–	–	–	3	–	–
TOTAL	34	106	5	10	51	220	60	37

amphibian bone (Table 20). Other samples that produced animal bones were from pits 80, 852 and 3256. A sample from post-hole 3829 produced three fragments. Only one further fragment was identifiable to species – a worked antler tine of a red deer in pit 80 context 869.

Phase 2–3. Late Neolithic – Early Bronze Age
Apart from three fragments recovered from a sieved sample from pit 6085, all the bones in this group came from layers in pits 1017 and 5456. Two hundred and two fragments were recovered from normal excavation, 70% of which were unidentifiable to species. Most of the bones deposited in pit 1017 were from the upper fills. The top two layers, 1018 and 1019, produced 61 and 43 of the fragments respectively. The high proportion of bones located near the ground surface therefore explains the high percentage of heavily eroded bones in the sample. Few bones of the major food species were recovered in the lower fills, where preservation would have been better. Bones of cattle, sheep/goat, pig and red deer were identified (Table 19). The majority of fragments, particularly in the upper layers, were loose teeth – sturdy elements that can withstand poor preservation conditions better than other parts of the skeleton (see tables in microfiche). The red deer fragments consisted of antler spatulae and an antler, shed with bez and trez worn down probably naturally, all from layer 1049 associated with burial 2752. Amphibian bones were recovered from the sieved samples in context 1049 (Table 20). They were probably the remains of pitfall victims. Bones of the short-tailed vole (*Microtus agrestis*) were also found in samples taken for molluscs in this layer. Pit 5456 supplied 58 fragments from normal recovery and 52 from sieved samples; these included a tibia of an aurochs (*Bos primigenius*) from context 5458. The same layer produced five antler fragments of red deer.

Phase 2–4. Late Neolithic – Middle Bronze Age
Only 22 fragments were recovered from ditch 1054, whose fills contained a mixture of Late Neolithic and Bronze Age pottery. The seven identifiable fragments did include the earliest evidence for horse (a tooth in context 3204). Bones of cattle and pig were also identified.

Phase 2–10. Late Neolithic – Medieval (mixed, not securely dated deposits)
This group consisted of material from pit 5461 in Area F and pit group 653 in Area G. In both cases the bone came from layers insecurely dated; in pit group 653 the associated pottery ranged from Neolithic to Medieval; and pit 5461 cut the Late Saxon structure in Area F but was thought to contain earlier material. Given its uncertain origins, the information gained from the animal bone assemblages is of very limited value to the specialist but it was hoped that the dating of the features would be assisted. One hundred and sixty-eight fragments were recovered including 10 from sieved samples (Tables 19–20). One hundred and seven of these were found in pit 5461 and included 23 bones from an immature corvid skeleton and 31 bones from an immature dog (see table in microfiche). These bones belonged to a stocky animal and its dimensions

would suggest that it was likely to have been of Medieval origin. Indeed, most of the remaining material in this pit, which included 27 of the sheep/goat bones and all five of the pig fragments, possessed characteristics more likely to be encountered in the Medieval period than in the Neolithic. The majority of the identifiable bones from pit group 653 belonged to cattle but the sample was too small to investigate in more detail.

Phase 3. Early Bronze Age
Eight dated features produced 124 fragments, 51 from sieved samples. Most of the bones were obtained from pit 6053 (43 fragments from normal recovery, and 20 from sieved samples). The other features (cremations 507, 598 and 1705; pits 1498 and 4924; post-holes 3721 and 6055; and ditch 1310) each produced only a handful of fragments. Twenty-one of the 23 identified sheep/goat fragments, including three from sieved samples, were from pit 6053 and included 15 bones from the skeleton of a juvenile animal (see table in microfiche). The same post-hole produced two bones of a pine marten (*Martes martes*) and four fragments each identified to cattle and pig. In the other features the bones of cattle and pig were identified more frequently than those of sheep/goat. The cattle bones were of a size comparable with domestic stock. Two worked bone fragments, both from pit 6053, could be identified to species. They were a bone needle from a sheep/goat metatarsus and an awl made from a pig fibula. The pit also contained a red deer ulna fragment. This was the only post-cranial element of this species identified in any of the phases.

Generally, the bones were poorly preserved and 79% of the bones recovered from normal excavation were eroded. Once again, the sample was too small to determine clear trends in animal exploitation at this time.

Phase 4. Middle Bronze Age
Two hundred and twenty of the 294 fragments in this phase were obtained from sieved samples, mainly from post-holes that formed a number of structures of this date. Most of these consisted of small fragments unidentifiable to species (Table 20). Sieving produced only three fragments identifiable to the major domestic species and most of the identifiable bones belonged to small mammals. Water vole (*Arvicola terrestris*), mouse (*Apodemus* sp) and pine marten (*Martes martes*) were identified. Most of the rodent bones were associated with the cremation burial in 1735. The mole (*Talpa europea*) bone in post-hole 5389 may have been a more recent intrusion. Sieving did produce evidence of fish. Three fragments were recovered in post-holes 5416, 5453 and 5583, all in Area D. Unfortunately they consisted of small fragments and were not further identifiable.

Only 74 fragments were recovered from normal excavation procedures and 70% were unidentifiable and nearly every bone was eroded, often severely. Poor preservation is to be expected in shallow features of this sort. Fourteen bones (twelve from

sieved samples) were charred. Bones of cattle, sheep/goat, pig and a horse tooth were identified. Two antler fragments of red deer were also recovered.

Phase 4–5. Middle – Late Bronze Age
Of the 191 recorded fragments, 60 were from sieved samples. All but twelve of the fragments obtained from normal recovery were found in various ditches, mainly in Area A (972, 990, 1493, 1810, 1929, 2663 and 3765). Sixty-two fragments from ditch 1810 included 38 bones of a mouse skeleton. Of the other ditch sections, only 990, 972 and 3765 produced more than ten fragments. Pits 3740 and 3743 and three post-holes from CS 2341 produced a handful of bones. In general, the preservation of bones in these features was slightly better than in earlier phases and 62% were recorded as eroded. The proportion of unidentified fragments decreased to 51%.

Cattle and sheep/goat fragments were the most commonly identified species but there were also eight fragments of horse, perhaps indicating that this species was being exploited more frequently from this time.

Forty of the sieved fragments were from samples taken from various post-holes from CS 2341. As usual most of this material could not be identified. Three sheep/goat fragments and one amphibian bone were the only ones that could be assigned to species.

Phase 4–7. Middle Bronze Age – Early/Middle Iron Age
This group was derived from three ditches, 176, 729 and 4847 a recut of 972, all of which contained pottery of various phases within their fills. Only 37 fragments of bone were recorded from them and nine were identifiable to species (cattle, sheep/goat and horse). Of the fragments, 32 were found in ditch 176 and most of these may have been of Iron Age origin. Nearly all the bones were eroded.

Phase 5. Late Bronze Age
The 85 recorded fragments from this phase included 37 from sieved samples taken mainly from post-holes that formed structure 2159. Bones retrieved during normal excavation were obtained from the post-holes of structure 2159, post-hole 2309 and ditches 3200, 3274 and 3692. Only 14 fragments of the major species were identified, including five of horse. However, the two horse phalanges in 3200 (3201) belonged to large animals and these may have been more recent intrusions into the deposits. Cattle and sheep/goat fragments were also identified; 29 of the fragments were eroded.

The sieved samples produced the only identified fragment of pig from this phase, as well as fragments of cattle, short-tailed vole (*Microtus agrestis*) and amphibian bones, but 27 of the fragments could not be identified (Table 20).

Phase 5–6. Late Bronze Age – Early Iron Age
Twenty-two fragments from ditch 928 were recorded. Eleven of these were eroded and a few fragments of cattle, sheep/goat, pig and horse were identified (Table 19).

Animal bones from Iron Age and Romano-British contexts

The Iron Age and early Romano-British faunal assemblages (Phases 6–9) also produced relatively small samples compared to some contemporary sites in Hampshire. However, their main value lies in the fact that they can be directly compared with the more substantial assemblages obtained from the Winnall Down excavations.

Phase 6. Early Iron Age

This phase was contemporary with the Phase 3 deposits at Winnall Down. Four pits, 342, 1147, 2154 and 4577, produced 62 fragments including 24 (all unidentifiable) from sieved samples. Cattle, sheep/goat, horse and dog were identified (Table 21). Eighteen fragments were eroded.

Table 21. Animal Bones in Iron Age and Romano-British Features (Unsieved).

Species	Phase					
	6	6–7	7	7–8	8	9
Cattle	8	7	44	72	45	120
Sheep/Goat	7	12	56★	160★	50	68
Pig	–	5	3	19	8	14
Horse	3	9	26	19★	16	30
Dog	1	–	–	1	7	3
Unid Large Mammal	7	8	54	60	26	172
Sheep-sized Mammal	6	12	56	148	41	19
Unid Mammal	6	11	14	33	11	18
Pine Marten	–	–	–	82★	–	–
Weasel	–	–	–	23★	–	–
Water Vole	–	1	–	–	1	–
Short-tailed Vole	–	–	–	2	2	–
Mouse species	–	1	–	2	–	–
Unid Rodent	–	4	–	14	–	–
Frog	–	–	–	17	2	–
Toad	–	–	–	6	7	–
Frog/Toad	–	–	1	15	–	–
Common Buzzard	–	–	–	1	–	–
TOTAL	38	70	254	674	216	444
Sheep	–	–	3	35	3	–
Goat	–	–	9★	–	–	–

★ includes articulated bones

Phase 6–7. Early Iron Age – Early Middle Iron Age

Seventy fragments were recorded from gully 237 CS 2408, three post-holes of CS 2404 and ditches 971 and 1011. Most of this sample was obtained from 237 (49 fragments). In this phase 60% of the bones were eroded. Fragments of sheep/goat, horse, cattle and pig were identified in that order of frequency (Table 21). The horse fragments included four lower incisors (probably of the same mandible) in post-hole 117. Loose teeth were the most commonly recorded identifiable elements, reflecting the relatively poor preservation of the sample (see tables in microfiche).

Phase 7. Early Middle Iron Age

These features from Area A to the east and northeast of the Winnall Down excavations produced pottery that was earlier in date than the material from Phase 4 at Winnall Down. Animal bones were obtained from seven pits, 329, 407, 409, 496, 707, 982 and 1391, and from post-holes and gullies of structures 2404, 2406, 5602 and 5634. The 354 recorded fragments included 100 from sieved samples (Table 18).

Two hundred and sixteen of the fragments recovered from normal excavation procedures were obtained from the pits. Pit 496 produced 87 fragments including 17 of horse, 14 of cattle and 13 of sheep/goat. In this pit, horse, cattle and unidentified large mammal contributed 34 of the 41 fragments in the topmost layer, 1188. In contrast, layer 1053, towards the bottom of the pit, included only 12 such fragments whereas sheep/goat and sheep-sized fragments provided 22 of the 41 fragments in that layer. This may reflect variable preservation conditions for bones in different parts of the pit, although both contexts were similar, resulting in the under-representation of the more fragile sheep/goat and sheep-sized bones in the upper layer. There were nine ivoried and one eroded bone in layer 1053 compared to 23 eroded bones in layer 1188. The presence of ivoried bone usually indicates good preservation. It is also possible that the contrast reflects the differential disposal of carcasses of large and sheep-sized mammals. There were marked contrasts in the distribution of cattle and horse bones and those of sheep/goat and pig at Winnall Down (Maltby 1985, 137).

Pit 329 produced only 17 bones, but 15 of these belonged to cattle and included the remains of four substantially complete skulls in layer 1012. One skull bore chop marks, made when both its horn cores were removed. Although these skulls were well preserved, the absence of many of the teeth from the maxillae perhaps indicates that they were not buried immediately after slaughter and butchery. Their deposition may nevertheless have had some ritual significance.

In the small samples from other pits, sheep/goat fragments were usually the most commonly identified. From all the pits, 42 cattle, 40 sheep/goat, 25 horse but only two pig fragments were identified leaving 49% of the assemblage as unidentifiable.

Only 38 bones from normal recovery came from structures. These included nine bones of goat, probably from the same animal in post-hole 4573 CS 5602. Although goat bones were rarely encountered from the Winnall Down excavation, both the Early and Middle Iron Age phases there produced evidence for its presence in small numbers.

From all contexts, 123 (48%) fragments were eroded, 16 were ivoried and 22 showed evidence of canid gnawing. This relatively high incidence of gnawing indicates that many of the bones were accessible to scavengers before burial in these features.

The sieved samples included 70 fragments from MS 2406. The only identifiable fragments consisted of a sheep/goat tooth fragment, a fragment of horse ilium and two bones of a frog/toad. In addition, post-hole 420 layer 2142 produced a vertebra of a small fish of indeterminate but probably freshwater species. Another unidentifiable fish vertebra was found in post-hole 4604 layer 4605, and a tooth, possibly of a pike (*Esox lucius*) was retrieved from post-hole 4581 layer 4582. Therefore, although sieving did not produce much in the way of identifiable material, it did show that fish may have been occasionally exploited.

Phase 7–8. Early Middle Iron Age – Middle Iron Age
This group of features produced the largest sample from any of the prehistoric phases, 1,564 fragments. This total was inflated by the presence of large numbers of small mammal and amphibian bones amongst the sieved sample (Table 22).

Table 22. Animal bones in Iron Age and Romano-British features (sieved).

Species	Phase				
	6	7	7–8	8	9
Cattle	–	–	–	2	–
Sheep/Goat	–	1	15	15	–
Pig	–	–	3	–	–
Horse	–	1	–	–	–
Unid Large Mammal	–	–	3	3	–
Sheep-sized Mammal	–	4	55	59	–
Unid Mammal	24	86	230	94	3
Pine Marten	–	–	2	–	–
Water Vole	–	–	54	–	–
Short-tailed Vole	–	–	393	6	–
Mouse Species	–	–	2	1	–
Common Shrew	–	–	2	–	–
Unid Rodent	–	3	24	60	–
Frog	–	–	10	3	–
Toad	–	–	10	–	–
Frog/Toad	–	2	85	6	–
Fish	–	3	2	–	–
TOTAL	24	100	890	249	3
Sheep	–	–	1	–	–

Six hundred and forty-one of the 674 fragments obtained by normal retrieval methods came from eight pits, 238, 316, 317, 4560, 4567, 4622, 4886 and 4993 and one ditch, 350. Three pits produced over 100 fragments.

Sixty-five of the 260 fragments in pit 4567 were small mammal and amphibian bones from layer 4724. These included 23 bones of a weasel (*Mustela nivalis*). These animals were probably pitfall victims. Layer 4580 included the ulna of a buzzard (*Buteo buteo*). Amongst the domestic species, fragments of sheep/goat, 63, were consistently found in greater numbers than cattle, 20, throughout the pit. Indeed, ten of the cattle fragments consisted of the bones of the lower hindlimb of one animal in layer 4881 (see

table in microfiche). Six pig fragments and one fragment each of horse and dog completed the list of identified bones. The bias towards sheep/goat in this pit is also reflected amongst the unidentifiable material, of which 77 fragments were assigned to the sheep-sized category compared to only 13 large mammal fragments.

Pit 4560 produced 118 fragments. Although sheep/goat fragments, 35, were again the best represented, cattle, 25, and horse, 13, formed a higher proportion of the assemblage than in most of the pits excavated at Easton Lane or at Winnall Down (Maltby 1985, 103). Six of the horse bones from layer 4561 consisted of the metatarsals and three tarsals of the ankle joint affected by spavin. Pig, represented by six fragments, was the only other species identified. The skeleton of a pine marten in layer 741 accounted for 82 of the 113 fragments in pit 317. This pit also produced a large number of small mammal bones amongst the sieved samples (see below) but contained only seven fragments, six sheep/goat and one pig, identifiable to the major food species.

From all the pits, excluding articulated bones, sheep/goat provided 63% of the identifiable fragments of the major food species, cattle 24%, pig 9%, and horse 5%. Such figures indicate that sheep/goat fragments were better represented overall than in the Early and Middle Iron Age pits at Winnall Down. However, this sample was relatively small and the results reflect, mainly, the unusually high proportion of sheep/goat fragments in the one pit, 4567.

The 38 fragments recovered by normal retrieval methods from the structures included some 13 limb bones of the partial skeleton of an adult sheep in post-hole 4632 (see table in microfiche). Five fragments were recovered from ditch 350.

The preservation of the bones in these features was better than in any of the previous phases, since more of the bones were buried more deeply in pits. Excluding small mammal and amphibian bones, only 24% of the bones were eroded, whereas 27% were ivoried. Gnawing was recorded on 13% of the bones, indicating that much of the sample was the subject of secondary deposition and many bones must have been destroyed entirely. This was reflected mainly in the sheep/goat sample, which was biased towards denser fragments such as loose teeth and shaft fragments of tibia and radius (see table in microfiche). The smaller and more fragile bones of sheep/goat were more susceptible to destruction by scavengers than those of cattle, particularly since more of them belonged to immature animals. Fifty-seven per cent of the cattle major limb bones (scapula, humerus, radius, femur, tibia and metapodia) possessed articular surfaces, compared to only 33% of the sheep/goat limb bones (excluding bones from partial skeletons).

The sieved bones included 591 fragments from samples in pit 317. Layer 731 included the death assemblage of at least 14 short-tailed voles and layer 732 contained the skeletons of at least eight more, plus at least three water-voles. It is possible that this pit remained open for some time while these pitfall victims accumulated. Pit 316 produced 62 bones from sieved samples, mostly of frog and toad from layer 751. The 128 sieved fragments recorded from post-hole 4632 may all have been associated with the partial sheep skeleton discussed above. Sieving also produced bones of pine marten (probably from the skeleton discussed above), mouse and common shrew (*Sorex araneus*). Two fish bones were recorded. Post-hole 1193 contained a vertebra probably of a freshwater species (*cf* Cyprinidae), and a fragment of an indeterminate species was found in a sample from pit 4622.

Phase 8. Middle Iron Age

The 465 fragments were from features contemporary with Phase 4 at Winnall Down. Only 216 fragments were obtained from normal retrieval. One fragment (a sheep/goat tooth) came from ditch 975, the remainder from seven pits, 17, 1100, 4620, 4921, 4928, 4951 and 4983. The density of bones in these pits was generally low compared to those from Winnall Down. The two largest samples produced more cattle than sheep/goat fragments (pit 17 – 79 fragments; pit 4921 – 43 fragments). Overall, amongst the bones identified to the major food species, sheep/goat provided 42% of the 119 fragments, cattle 38%, pig 7% and horse 13%. This compares with figures of 52% sheep/goat, 19% cattle, 10% pig and 9% horse from Phase 4 pits at Winnall Down. The pits at Easton Lane, therefore, contained a higher proportion of large mammal fragments than the much larger samples from Winnall Down. Since both samples seem to have been relatively well preserved, the differences in species representation cannot be explained by factors of differential preservation. Seventeen percent of the fragments from these excavations were eroded, compared to 15% from the pits at Winnall Down. The discrepancy may simply be due to the fact that the small sample from Easton Lane produced unreliable figures. It is also possible, however, that a greater proportion of the large mammal carcasses may have been butchered away from the main focus of the settlement at that time, resulting in the better representation of cattle and horse bones in the fills of the pits in this peripheral area. The 34 fragments with evidence of gnawing may indicate that most of this material was probably of secondary deposition. Exceptions to this may have been the complete horse femora and tibia found in pit 17. Twenty-four per cent of the bones were ivoried.

Sieving produced 249 fragments with 15 fragments of sheep/goat and two of cattle being the only major food species identified. These results imply that sheep/goat bones were more likely to be overlooked during normal excavation, particularly their smaller bones such as the carpals, small teeth and phalanges (see table in microfiche). As usual, however, most of the identifiable bones from the samples belonged to small mammals and amphibians. There were no large concentrations of such species, but pit 4983 produced 47 bones of such pitfall victims.

Phase 9. Late Iron Age / Early Romano-British

Eleven features from Area H produced 447 fragments, all but three of them from unsieved samples. The ditch sections which produced animal bones, 5007, 5039, 5042, 5293, 5295, 5302 and 5623, belonged to the southern part of the series of enclosures investigated in the Winnall Down excavations (Fasham 1985, 31–7). All the material therefore is contemporary with the bones from Phases 5 and 6 of those excavations (Maltby 1985, 107–112).

A total of 387 fragments was recovered from the ditches. The largest sample was obtained from ditch 5293 (151 fragments). The other sections each produced less than 100 fragments. Only 57 fragments were recovered from the pits dated to this phase, 5327, 5347, 5349 and 5361. Of these, 44 were from pit 5347.

The cattle assemblage included 14 ribs and vertebrae of the same animal in ditch 5295 and three articulating cervical vertebrae in ditch 5293. In addition, cattle and other large mammal fragments were well represented in most features. Ditch 5293 produced the majority of sheep/goat fragments (37) but they were not well represented elsewhere. This may have been due to the slightly better preservation of bones in that feature. Overall, 61% of the bones were eroded which compares closely with the Winnall Down Phase 6 ditches, where 62% were eroded. Only two bones were ivoried and 26 were gnawed. The sample was therefore less well preserved than the earlier Iron Age phases. Horse fragments again outnumbered those of pigs. Only three dog bones were identified. No goat or domestic fowl bones were recorded.

Table 23 compares the percentages of fragments of the major food species represented at Easton Lane with those from the Phase 6 ditches at Winnall Down (Maltby 1985, 109). In the much smaller sample from Easton Lane, cattle fragments were 4% higher and sheep/goat 4% lower than at Winnall Down. In both samples, however, cattle fragments outnumbered those of sheep/goat. The sample from the pits at Easton Lane was too small to be of much value.

Table 23. Relative percentages of major food species at Easton Lane Phase 9 and Winnall Down Phase 6.

	Cattle	Horse	Sheep/ Goat	Pig	Total Fragments
Easton Lane Ditches	47.0	12.4	33.5	7.0	185
Winnall Down Ditches	43.0	12.8	37.6	6.7	1,439
Total Ditches	43.4	12.7	37.1	6.7	1,624
Easton Lane Pits	(57.6)	(21.2)	(18.2)	(3.0)	33
Winnall Down Pits	27.2	10.0	56.0	6.8	191
Total Pits	31.7	11.6	50.4	6.3	224
Total Easton Lane	48.6	13.8	31.2	6.4	218
Total Winnall Down*	41.2	11.3	41.2	6.4	2,018
Combined Total	41.9	11.5	40.2	6.4	2,236

* also includes bones from scoops, hollows and quarries. Totals exclude articulated bones.

The decrease in the proportion of sheep/goat fragments in Phase 9 may be misleading since the poorer preservation of bones may have biased the sample in favour of cattle. Twenty-three bones (34%) of the sheep/goat sample consisted of loose teeth and the sample was more heavily biased towards sturdy fragments such as these, the mandible and tibia.

Animal bones from Medieval contexts

Phase 10. Late Saxon and Medieval

Normal excavation methods produced 1,532 fragments from these deposits. The majority of these belonged to skeletons of various species in several of the pits (Table 24). The largest accumulation was found in pit 5265, which produced 605 bones from eight largely complete sheep skeletons, mostly of adult ewes, but there was also a partial skeleton of an immature male. In addition, at least four foetal or newborn lambs were represented by 32 bones. Although it was not possible to separate all the bones of the skeletons, it is clear that these were buried together without skinning or butchery.

Table 24. Species represented in Medieval contexts (unsieved).

Species	5265	537	600	634	654	5103	Other	Total
Cattle	–	151*	3	20	2	–	9	185
Sheep/Goat	643*	–	35	98	39*	71*	38	924
Pig	–	–	1	5	2	–	5	13
Horse	–	–	74*	10*	1	–	1	86
Dog	–	–	–	1	2	–	–	3
Unid Large Mammal	–	–	12	37	5	–	27	81
Sheep-sized Mammal	–	–	21	91	38	–	30	180
Unid Mammal	1	–	5	17	4	–	6	33
Unid Bird	–	–	–	–	–	–	1	1
Frog	–	–	–	–	1	–	–	1
Fish	–	–	–	–	–	–	1	1
Domestic Fowl	–	–	–	–	7*	–	–	7
Corvid species	–	–	–	–	17*	–	–	17
TOTAL	644	151	151	279	118	71	118	1,532
Sheep	637*	–	2	4	9*	71*	3	726

* includes articulated bones.

The reason for their burial remains something of a mystery. Probably these were animals that died of natural causes, either through disease or during severe weather conditions. No evidence of disease was found on the bones apart from the usual dental pathology associated with older sheep. The presence of the foetal or newborn lambs suggests that the disaster occurred during the winter or early spring. The age and sex of the animals suggests that this was part of a flock composed mainly of breeding ewes.

Measurements were taken where possible and these revealed that the skeletons belonged to small sheep of a restricted size range. Estimates of withers heights (see table in microfiche) showed that the lengths of the metapodia consistently gave higher estimates than those from the upper limb bones when Teichert's (1975) conversion factors were applied. The results suggested that the sheep may have had withers heights of between 50–55cm. These sizes and other measurements are typical of Medieval sheep in the area. They were generally slightly smaller than the sheep represented in the Iron Age and Romano-British levels at Easton Lane and Winnall Down. The immature skeleton did, however, belong to a larger male animal.

Pit 5103 produced 71 bones of a much larger sheep. This gave estimated withers heights of 61–65cm. Four bones from the forelimb of a lamb were recovered from pit 654. See microfiche for the list of articulated bones recovered from these skeletons.

Pit 537 produced 151 bones of a cattle burial, probably of an adult steer (see table in microfiche). Three of the cervical and two of the thoracic vertebrae had pathological deformations of their articular surfaces. Pit 600 contained 74 bones of a horse, mostly consisting of vertebrae and ribs and displaying severe pathology of several thoracic and lumbar vertebrae. Several vertebrae had developed exostoses and had fused together. Although this condition is commonly found on thoracic vertebrae of older wild and domestic horses, the presence of such pathology on the lumbar vertebrae was more probably caused by being ridden. Pit 634 included eight bones from the ribs and vertebral column of another adult horse. Pit 654 produced three partial bird skeletons. Layer 3378 contained at least 17 bones of two young birds of the crow family (Corvidae) and layer 694 contained seven bones of a young domestic fowl.

The fact that the Medieval assemblages were dominated by bones of burials is indicative of the practice of burying only those carcasses not destined for consumption. To leave these to rot may have been considered a health hazard or could have attracted scavengers. Waste from carcass processing and cooking may have been less of a problem and the bones associated with these processes may have been left on the surface to rot or have been scattered on the fields. At any rate, disarticulated bones from Medieval contexts were not found in great numbers.

Sieving produced little new information from the Medieval deposits, apart from the recovery of several fish bones in pit 654. These were examined by Jennie Coy. Some of the bones appear to have been chewed and the material may have come from a cess deposit. Common eel (*Anguilla anguilla*) was represented by at least four vertebrae, and two vertebrae of herring (*Clupea harengus*) were identified. Bones of freshwater species included five inferior pharyngeals of small dace or chub (*Leuciscus sp*) and a premaxillary, possibly of a perch (*cf Perca fluviatilis*).

Discussion

The Easton Lane animal bone assemblage was quite small, but its study provides an opportunity to reassess the conclusions obtained from the Winnall Down excavations in the light of this evidence and data from other recent excavations in the area.

Species Representation

The samples from the Neolithic and Bronze Age deposits were too small to derive many conclusions. Tentatively, we can suggest that pigs were exploited relatively more frequently in these periods than in the Iron Age. This tends to support the evidence obtained from the land mollusca, which indicate that there was more woodland in the area during the Neolithic and Early Bronze Age. This was cleared to produce open, dry grassland by the Middle Bronze Age, by which time the proportion of pig bones in the assemblage had decreased. No red deer bones were identified in deposits later than Middle Bronze Age date. However, since all but two of their fragments consisted of antler, they may have been rarely exploited for meat even in the earlier periods. It is, of course, possible that the carcasses of hunted animals were butchered at the kill site and their bones not brought to this site. There is no firm evidence that horses were exploited until the Middle Bronze Age. One aurochs bone was found in a Late Neolithic context.

The analysis of the Iron Age and Romano-British samples at Winnall Down demonstrated that changes in species representation were often determined by context variability. Generally, although sheep and cattle were the dominant species exploited, their relative importance was difficult to gauge because of these variations. The Easton Lane samples produced further evidence of such contextual variability.

Given the differential preservation of sheep/goat and cattle bones, a better reflection of their comparative abundance may be obtained by comparison of only those bones which survive well in both species. The analysis of the Owslebury samples (Maltby nd1) indicated that comparisons of the number of tibia fragments may provide a better guide to their relative abundance than counts of all their identified fragments. Tibia fragments are usually abundant in sheep/goat samples. Although articular surfaces are often destroyed by scavengers, their shaft fragments are quite dense and survive reasonably well.

Table 25 shows the number of cattle and sheep/goat tibia fragments recorded in the Iron Age and Romano-British deposits at Easton Lane and Winnall Down. Sheep/goat usually provided 66–71% of the total fragments, although there were still notable contextual variations between the Early Iron Age pits and other contemporary features at Winnall Down. The small sample from the Phase 9 deposits from Easton Lane contained a high percentage of sheep/goat, but this had relatively little effect on the overall total when it was added to the contemporary Phase 6 assemblage from Winnall Down. The results show that at least twice as many sheep as cattle were

Table 25. Cattle and sheep/goat tibia fragments in Iron Age and Romano-British deposits at Easton Lane and Winnall Down.

Site	Cattle	Sheep/ Goat	%Sheep/ Goat
Winnall Down Phase 3 Pits	9	31	78
Other	26	35	57
Total	35	67	66
Easton Lane Phase 6	–	1	–
Easton Lane Phase 6–7	1	3	–
Easton Lane Phase 7	4	7	–
Easton Lane Phase 7–8	8	27	71
Easton Lane Phase 8	3	3	–
Winnall Down Phase 4	58	112	66
Winnall Down Phase 6	38	80	68
Easton Lane Phase 9	2	14	–
Total Late Iron Age/ RB	40	94	70

Totals exclude bones from articulated groups and sieved samples.

represented in the deposits throughout these phases. This figure reflects the number of carcasses, not the relative number of live animals kept. The figures are still subject to some bias resulting from differential preservation, fragmentation and disposal strategies. They may, however, indicate little change in the relative abundance of these species during these phases.

By the Iron Age, pigs appear to have formed a relatively insignificant part of the diet of the inhabitants of these settlements. Table 26 compares the number of sheep/goat and pig fragments only from Easton Lane and Winnall Down. In general the Easton Lane samples produced relatively fewer pig fragments than the Winnall Down excavations and

Table 26. Sheep/goat and pig fragments in Iron Age and Romano-British deposits at Easton Lane and Winnall Down.

Site	Sheep/ Goat	Pig	%Pig
Winnall Down Phase 3 Pits	314	61	16
Ditch	105	31	23
Other	170	31	15
Total	589	123	17
Easton Lane Phase 6	7	–	–
Easton Lane Phase 6–7	12	5	–
Easton Lane Phase 7	47	3	(6)
Easton Lane Phase 7–8	147	19	11
Easton Lane Phase 8	50	8	(14)
Winnall Down Phase 4	1307	259	17
Winnall Down Phase 6	831	129	13
Easton Lane Phase 9	68	14	17
Total Late Iron Age/ RB	899	143	14

Totals exclude bones from articulated groups and sieved samples.

generallly they formed less than 20% of the assemblage. These were lower figures than those obtained from contemporary deposits from the Micheldever Wood Banjo enclosure (Coy nd) and from Owslebury (Maltby nd1). The low percentage of pig in the early Romano-British period is very interesting in the light of results obtained from the town of Winchester. The relatively small early Romano-British sample from excavations on the Staple Gardens site produced a figure of 42% pig fragments when identical calculations were made (Maltby nd 2). The results from this and other sites in Winchester suggest that pork may have been a more important element in the diet there than at Winnall Down, where the meat diet may have continued along the lines established during the Iron Age.

Horse was well represented at Easton Lane and Winnall Down, compared to other Iron Age sites in the area. Horse fragments outnumbered those of pig in many of the Iron Age contexts. Comparing the number of cattle and horse fragments only (Table 27), horse contributed at least 17% of the fragments in the various phases at the two sites. They were particularly well represented in the Easton Lane Iron

Table 27. Cattle and horse fragments in Iron Age and Romano–British deposits at Easton Lane and Winnall Down.

Site	Cattle	Horse	%Horse
Winnall Down Phase 3 Total	699	165	19
Easton Lane Phase 6	8	3	–
Easton Lane Phase 6–7	7	9	–
Easton Lane Phase 7	44	26	(37)
Easton Lane Phase 7–8	62	13	(17)
Easton Lane Phase 8	45	16	(26)
Winnall Down Phase 4	838	244	23
Winnall Down Phase 6	831	227	21
Easton Lane Phase 9	120	30	20
Total Late Iron Age/ RB	951	257	21

Totals exclude bones from articulated groups and sieved samples.

Age deposits. Similar calculations from Owslebury produced figures usually of 10–20% horse in both the Iron Age and Romano-British deposits (Maltby nd1). Consequently, the exploitation of horse may have been more important for the inhabitants associated with this settlement complex. Again, there is a marked contrast with this percentage of horse obtained from the Late Iron Age and Romano-British deposits at Easton Lane (20–21%) with the urban assemblages from Winchester, where most samples produced less than 10% horse and this figure often fell below 5%. The greater importance of cattle as a producer of meat probably accounts for this discrepancy. The demands for beef from the population at Winchester acted as a stimulus for the importation of more cattle to the town. The inhabitants of the Roman town may also have had a preference for beef, whereas the inhabitants of estab-

lished rural settlements like Winnall Down and Owslebury may have continued to exploit horses for their meat as well as for their transport qualities.

The excavations at Easton Lane lent support to the suggestion that domestic fowl were not kept during the Iron Age at this settlement complex. Indeed, the only domestic fowl bones encountered were of Medieval date. Although most of the sheep/goat bones that could be identified to a particular species belonged to sheep, the partial skeleton of a goat was recovered from an Early/Middle Iron Age post-hole. Goat bones were also found in small numbers at Winnall Down in Iron Age contexts and rather more frequently in some Middle Iron Age features at Owslebury (Maltby nd 1). Although there was abundant evidence of their scavenging, dogs were poorly represented in the Easton Lane deposits. The sieving programme did provide evidence that fish were occasionally exploited during the Iron Age.

Unfortunately, the small samples from Easton Lane produced comparatively little ageing evidence to add to the results from Winnall Down. Only eight cattle mandibles bore tooth eruption evidence. Both specimens from Phase 8 had fully erupted tooth rows and belonged to animals probably over five years old. The two mandibles from Phases 7–8 belonged to younger cattle. In one case the second molar had not erupted; in the other the fourth permanent premolar was not in wear. Two of the Phase 9 mandibles had fully erupted toothrows while two others belonged to immature cattle. The evidence from Winnall Down suggested that the usual practice was to keep cattle until maturity and these results do not significantly alter that impression.

Nineteen sheep/goat mandibles from Iron Age and Romano-British deposits provided tooth eruption data. Most of the specimens from Phases 7–8 and 8 either had fully erupted toothrows, three cases, or belonged to lambs which only had the deciduous premolars and first molar in wear, six examples. There was also one mandible of a foetal or newborn lamb. This pattern fits the one observed in the Phase 4 deposits at Winnall Down, where most of the sheep mandibles from the pits belonged either to animals under a year old or to relatively old animals (Maltby 1985, 106). The lack of mandibles belonging to sheep killed at the prime age for meat production is a feature of most of the Iron Age samples examined from Hampshire chalkland sites, including Danebury (Grant 1984). Meat production may have been more important at Owslebury and Micheldever Wood, where mandibles of sheep culled at this age were found rather more frequently (Maltby nd1). Three of the six mandibles from the Phase 9 deposits were at that stage of development (M2 in wear, M3 not in wear); the others had completed their tooth eruption sequence.

Three pig mandibles of Iron Age date bore tooth eruption data. Two (one from Phase 7–8, one from Phase 8) had the third molar in early wear and were probably over two years of age. All four ageable specimens from Phase 9 belonged to younger animals. None of them possessed fully erupted second molars and one only had the deciduous premolars in wear. This would have belonged to a pig under six months old.

Apart from the Medieval sheep skeletons already discussed, metrical data from Easton Lane was limited by the fragmentary nature of much of the material. All the measurements from the Iron Age phases fell within the ranges of those obtained from Winnall Down, confirming that all the domestic stock were of comparatively small types. There was no evidence for the presence of much larger stock prior to the Romano-British period. Even then most of the measurements were no larger than those obtained from Iron Age contexts.

Analysis of butchery data continued to demonstrate that most of the carcass processing in the Iron Age was performed with implements which produced fine knife cuts on the bones. These included the ulna of a dog in pit 17, which had cuts made during disarticulation of the elbow joint. Several horse bones also bore cutmarks confirming that their carcasses were often butchered for meat. A cattle scapula from a Phase 9, Late Iron Age/Early Roman, context had had its lateral spine chopped off during removal of the flesh. Such distinctive butchery was also encountered at Owslebury, mainly in deposits of Romano-British date (Maltby nd1). However, the butchery techniques at both these sites were in marked contrast to those introduced to Winchester at this time. There, cattle carcasses in particular were subjected to much more intensive butchery, usually employing cleavers. This resulted in quite different patterns of butchery marks and fragmentation. This is yet another example of how the faunal remains from Romano-British urban and rural settlements display significant differences from each other. It is only by the comparison of samples on a regional basis that such variability can be monitored and a better understanding of animal exploitation achieved.

The Carbonised Plant Remains, by W J Carruthers

Soil samples of 8–10 litres were subjected to on-site manual flotation with the flots being collected in a sieve of mesh 250 microns. The results are summarised in Table 28. An appendix in microfiche contains the list of samples examined for plant remains.

Identification

Many of the flots contained fibrous roots and modern seeds, and the small amount of carbonised grain recovered from these flots was often badly eroded. It is possible that some of these samples may have been contaminated with modern carbonised seeds but no anachronistic taxa were recorded.

Wheat
Almost all of the identifiable glume bases recovered were spelt (*Triticum spelta* L). Only one glume base

could be definitely identified as belonging to emmer (*Triticum dicoccum* Schübl) on the basis of the presence of both primary and secondary veins and the absence of distinct intermediate veins. However, it is possible that some of the indeterminate glume bases were emmer, since in many cases, insufficient amounts were preserved to be able to distinguish between emmer and the rather similar glume bases of the terminal spikelets of spelt. Measurements of the glume base widths (Fig 107) showed that as many as 14% fall below the width range obtained by Helbaek (1953) for spelt from Fifield Bavant. A small percentage of these may be emmer glume bases, but there are also likely to be several terminal spikelets of spelt amongst them which could not be identified as such due to the state of preservation.

The few caryopses of wheat recovered can only tentatively be identified to species level, as grain morphology alone is not a sufficient basis for identification.

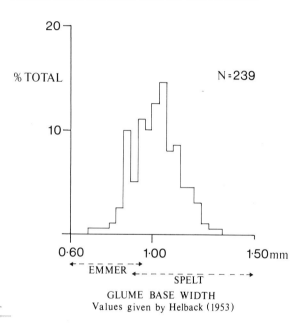

Fig 107.   Easton Lane. Glume base widths.

Barley
Most of the caryopses were identifiable as hulled barley, since in many cases adhering fragments of lemma were visible and the grains were angular. Where twisted grains or rachis were present it was possible to be certain that six-rowed hulled barley (*Hordeum vulgare* L emend) was represented. The single bevelled lemma base and fairly long rachis internodes are characteristic of the lax variety of barley, but neither of these characters are completely reliable and Jones (1978) suggests that the division into genetically distinct lax and dense eared forms may not yet have occurred by the Iron Age.

Oats
The absence of any oat lemma bases from the samples makes it impossible to determine whether the few oats recovered were of a wild or cultivated species.

Table 28. Plant remains from Easton Lane.

FEATURES			Pit 5456	Four pits	Two graves	Eight phs	Three pits	Pit 4928	Pit 4983	Seven pits	Total 27
Number of samples examined			4	19	2	8	4	12	11	12	72
Number of samples containing plant remains			1	15	1	5	3	11	8	0	44
Area			F/G	Mc	D	D,H	D,B	A	A	A	
CEREALS/GRASSES											
Triticum dicoccum Schübl.	(emmer glume bases)		–	–	–	–	–	1	–	–	
T spelta L	(spelt glume bases)		–	–	–	–	–	144	3	–	
	(spelt spikelet forks)		–	–	–	–	–	9	–	–	
T cf *spelta*	(spelt grains)		–	–	–	–	–	5	–	–	
Triticum sp	(wheat grains)		–	–	–	–	–	3	5	–	
	(wheat glume bases)		–	1	–	–	–	253	29	–	
	(wheat spikelet forks)		–	–	–	–	–	26	3	–	
	(wheat rachis internodes)		–	–	–	–	–	6	–	–	
Hordeum vulgare L emend	(hulled 6–row barley grains, straight)		–	3	–	–	–	–	–	–	
	(hulled 6–row barley grains, twisted)		–	–	–	–	2	–	–	–	
	(hulled 6–row barley, lemma base)		–	–	–	–	–	1	–	–	
	(hulled 6–row barley, rachis internodes)		–	–	–	–	–	5	–	–	
Hordeum sp	(barley grains)		–	–	–	–	1	–	–	–	
	(barley rachis internodes)		–	–	–	–	–	25	–	–	
Avena sp	(oat grains)		–	–	–	–	–	3	–	–	
Indeterminate grains			2	29	1	2	10	82	46	–	
Indeterminate rachis internodes			–	–	–	–	–	3	–	–	
Straw nodes			–	–	–	7	–	–	2	–	
Bromus sect Bromus	(chess)		–	–	–	–	–	41	–	–	
Gramineae gen et sp indet			–	–	–	–	–	48	1	–	
Gramineae gen et sp indet	(culm frags and culm bases)		–	–	–	–	–	10	–	–	
OTHER TAXA											
Pteridium aquilinum (L) Kuhn	(bracken)	WSHGa	–	–	–	–	–	4	–	–	
Ranunculus acris L	(meadow buttercup)	Gd	–	–	–	–	–	2	–	–	
Silene cf *vulgaris* (Moench) Garke	(bladder campion)	DA	–	–	–	–	–	2	–	–	
Stellaria media (L) Vill	(chickweed)	DA	–	–	–	–	–	–	1	–	
Atriplex patula L / *hastata* L	(orache)	DA	–	–	–	–	–	3	–	–	
Chenopodium album L	(fat hen)	DA	–	–	–	–	–	1	–	–	
C cf *polyspermum* L	(all–seed)	DA	–	–	–	–	–	–	1	–	
Medicago lupulina L	(black medick)	DG	–	–	–	–	–	11	2	–	
Vicia sp/ *Lathyrus* sp	(vetch)	WSHDG	–	–	–	–	–	–	3	–	
Polygonum aviculare agg	(knotgrass)	DA	–	–	–	–	–	3	–	–	
Rumex cf *crispus* L	(curled dock)	DAG	–	–	–	–	1	8	5	–	
Rumex sp	(dock)		–	–	–	–	–	1	–	–	
Corylus avellana L	(hazel nut shell frags)	WS	–	262	–	–	–	–	–	–	
Lithospermum arvense L	(corn gromwell)	A	–	–	–	1	–	1	1	–	
Galium aparine L	(cleavers)	DA	–	–	–	–	1	40	1	–	
Valerianella dentata (L) Poll	(lamb's lettuce)	DA	–	–	–	–	–	1	1	–	

Table 28, continued. Plant remains from Easton Lane.

FEATURES			Pit 5456	Four pits	Two graves	Eight phs	Three pits	Pit 4928	Pit 4983	Seven pits	Total 27
Anthemis cotula L	(stinking mayweed)	DAd, h	–	–	–	–	–	7	–	–	
Chrysanthemum leucanthemum L	(ox–eye daisy)	G	–	–	–	–	–	1	–	–	
Eleocharis subg Palustres	(spike rush)	M	–	–	–	–	–	4	–	–	
Carex sp	(sedge)	MG	–	–	–	–	–	12	–	–	
TOTAL			2	295	1	10	15	766	104	0	

HABITAT TYPES:

A = arable	D = cultivated/disturbed land	G = grassland
H = heath	M = marsh, pond margins *etc.*	S = scrub/hedgerows
W = woodland	a = preference for acidic soils	d = damp soils h = heavy soils

Discussion

Of the 72 samples examined only 44 produced carbonised plant remains, and of these, only the samples from two Middle Iron Age pits contained enough material to merit a detailed discussion. Plant remains from the Late Neolithic/Early Bronze Age and Bronze Age periods are grouped into these broad divisions, as little environmental information could be extracted from the small number of samples examined.

Phases 2 and 3. Neolithic and Bronze Age

The Late Neolithic/Early Bronze Age pits in Area Mc were notable only in the uniformity of the plant remains recovered. Almost all of the samples examined contained a number of small fragments of carbonised hazel nut shell and a few eroded cereals. The total number of nuts represented is probably only about 20, but the ubiquitous nature of the fragments suggests their probable use as a food source.

Samples from the Bronze Age pits, post-holes and graves produced a few poorly preserved cereals with hulled six-row barley being the only recognisable species. A few common weeds of arable and disturbed land were also present.

Phase 8. Middle Iron Age

The wider range of carbonised plant remains recovered from two Middle Iron Age pits was of more value in providing economic information, particularly as a comparison could be made with material from the previosly excavated site at Winnall Down (Monk and Fasham 1980, Fasham 1985). The pits lie to the northwest of the site excavated in 1976/7 and may be associated with its Phase 4, Middle Iron Age, period of occupation.

The assemblages from the two beehive-shaped pits were similar to each other in character, although pit 4928 contained greater quantities of material than pit 4983. In both pits most of the plant remains were recovered from the primary pit fills. They consisted principally of the chaff components of spelt and barley, and seeds of a variety of weed species. Relatively few cereal grains were recovered, the ratio being 1:6.85 grain to chaff fragments and 1:1.87 grain to weed seeds for the primary pit fill of 4928. These high ratios suggest that the assemblage represents primary crop-processing debris.

Similar assemblages were recovered by Monk (1985) from Middle Iron Age pits at the adjacent Winnall Down site, although in some pits the grain to weed seed ratios indicated the presence of stored grains as opposed to crop processing debris. Further evidence for the use of pits for grain storage was provided by Jones (1984) as the result of a detailed examination of a carbonised deposit from Danebury. The extent of caryopsis germination at different levels in the deposit followed the proposed pattern given by Reynolds (1967, 1974) for cereals stored in pits. It is possible that pits found to contain debris had also previously functioned as grain storage pits, but that they had not been subjected to sterilisation by fire (as described by Reynolds 1974) prior to being used for the disposal of rubbish. Thus, any uncarbonised grain remaining at the base of the pit would have left no archaeological record.

The concentration of crop processing debris in the primary fills of pits of this type and this period suggests that the presence of this material is not merely due to the casual deposition of domestic refuse. It might be explained by the quote from Pliny given by Monk (1985) concerning the storage of grain in pits: 'and before all things care is taken to make them in dry soils and then to floor them with chaff'. Perhaps, as Monk (1985) suggests, these remains are the result of burning such a pit lining. Further ethnographic and historical evidence from Europe and beyond shows that straw was often used to line and seal grain storage pits (Fenton 1983).

From Hillman's (1981) model, based on ethnographic parallels, the carbonised assemblages in the two pits most resemble burnt waste from stage 12 of the processing, that is, from the third sieving using a mesh size similar to that of the grain, which removes small weed seeds and heavy chaff fragments such as glume bases and rachis segments. This waste would seem to have been less suitable than straw for lining pits, but perhaps the straw was valued for other uses, such as for thatching, bedding or fodder.

The Weed Flora

Most of the weed species represented are typical weeds of arable or disturbed land. Pit 4928 also contained a number of seeds of grasses, grassland weeds, the marshland plant spike rush (*Eleocharis* subg Palustres) and sedges (*Carex* sp), many of which colonise marshy ground. This may indicate the use of wetter land bordering the River Itchen some 800m away for grazing or hay making. Waste bedding or animal dung may have been burnt and deposited as refuse in the pit. Alternatively, the seeds may have been harvested with the crop from damp field margins. The arable weed, stinking mayweed (*Anthemis cotula* L), prefers heavier, damp soils (Kay 1971) and on lighter soils it is usually replaced by scentless mayweed (*Tripleurospermum maritimum* ssp *inodorum*). Examination of the weed flora of the Winnall Down pits, and Easton Lane pit 4928 showed that, in pits where there was a predominance of barley, of the two species it was almost always scentless mayweed that was present, whereas predominantly wheat pits usually contained stinking mayweed. This apparent relationship may be due to the fact that barley is better suited to growing on a free-draining calcareous soil like that on which the site is located, whilst wheat grows better on heavier soils and may have been cultivated on the heavier alluvial soils in the river valley. Pit 4928 contained predominantly wheat chaff and, of the two species, only stinking mayweed was present.

Other differences in the weed floras of wheat-dominated and barley-dominated pits can be seen. Chess (*Bromus* sect *Bromus*) is said to be a common weed of spelt and was found to occur in much greater numbers in pits containing predominantly wheat. However, it would also appear to have been a weed of barley on this site, as Monk (1985) recovered a number of chess caryopses from an otherwise relatively clean deposit of barley. Cleavers (*Galium aparine* L) was also particularly abundant in wheat-dominated pits, as it was in pit 4928, and this is probably due to its association with winter-sown crops.

Other weed species of note are lamb's lettuce (*Valerianella dentata* L Poll) and all-seed (*Chenopodium* cf *polyspermum* L). Jones (1978) noted that, together with stinking mayweed, their occurrence in Iron Age samples at Abingdon was interesting, since Godwin (1975) had considered them to be probable Roman introductions. All three species occurred in pit 4928, and lamb's lettuce and stinking mayweed were recovered from the Winnall Down samples.

A fragment of carbonised bracken (*Pteridium aquilinum* L Kuhn) frond was recovered from pit 4928. Bracken is characteristically a plant of light, acid soils which frequently colonises areas of recently cleared woodland. The local calcareous soils may not have provided favourable conditions for growth but it is currently found on nearby areas of clay-with-flints and may have been collected for use as bedding.

The presence of grass culm bases and roots may be due to the pulling up of grasses for fodder and bedding, the weeding of crops, or uprooting along with the crop during harvesting.

One notable difference between the weed floras of the two sites is the small number of leguminous seeds in these pits when compared with the large numbers recovered from some of the Winnall Down pits. In addition, no cultivated legumes were found in the two pits.

The precise relationship of the two Middle Iron Age pits with the Winnall Down settlement is uncertain, but similarities in the carbonised plant assemblages are apparent. Although the majority of the pits examined by Monk (1985) showed a predominance of barley over wheat, the situation was said to be reversed in the area of the Middle Iron Age circular buildings to the west of the site. The two pits examined here were positioned to the northwest of the circular buildings and showed a predominance of wheat over barley. Whether the relationship between wheat-dominated and barley-dominated pits represents spatial or temporal differences in the site is uncertain.

The assemblages are generally typical of the period. By the Middle Iron Age, the cultivation of spelt predominated and emmer was only of secondary importance in Wessex (Green 1981). The dominance of wheat over barley may have varied more from site to site, being more closely related to soil suitability and specialisation of use. It is uncertain whether the few oat caryopses recovered from these pits and the pits examined by Monk (1985) represent a minor crop or weed contamination.

Land Snails, by M J Allen

Samples were analysed for mollusca from ditch and pit sections which have allowed an almost complete site environment to be reconstructed. This data, when reviewed with Mason's (1982, 1985) mollusc work at both Winnall Down and Easton Down and Waton's (1982) palynological evidence from Winnall Moor provide a basis for evaluating the landscape history of the Easton Lane site and its environs.

Table 29. List of samples.

Features	Samples	Phases	Feature type
1017	451–444	2	Pit
1017	125, 123–119	3	Pit
1810B	520–526	4–5	Ditch
176A	68–73	4–7	Ditch
990A	509–510	6	Ditch
971	2121	6	Ditch

Methodology

The methods of mollusc analysis employed followed Evans (1972, 40–45): soil being soaked and disaggregated in water and hydrogen peroxide (H_2O_2) and washed through a nest of sieves of 5.6mm, 2mm, 1mm and 0.5mm mesh aperture. Mollusca were extracted, identified and quantified using a x10 to x30 stereobinocular microscope. The residues were then weighed and the fraction calculated as a percentage of the initial sample weight.

The nomenclature for the mollusca follows Walden (1976) and the sediment descriptions provided by the excavator were augmented by the author's quantitative descriptions which follow Hodgson (1974), appendix in microfiche. The tripartite classification of ditch sediment (primary, secondary and tertiary) is that outlined by Evans (1972, 321–328) and Limbrey (1975, 290–300).

The results of mollusc analyses are shown in Table 30 and graphically as histograms of relative abundance (Figs 108 and 109) in which each species is plotted as a percentage of the total individuals, excluding the burrowing, and thus palaeoecologically insignificant, species *Cecilioides acicula*, which is recorded as a percentage over and above the rest of the assemblage. The sieved fractions mentioned above were grouped into particles larger than 5.6mm, those between 5.6mm and 0.5mm and those smaller than 0.5mm. These data provide a crude index to the extent of weathering and the rate of sedimentation, and thus enable some evaluation of the suitability of conditions to mollusc life at the time.

The Mollusca

Phase 2. Late Neolithic, Pit 1017

The pit, which was in excess of 2m deep and c 3m in diameter, contained at its base, a fine calcareous mud which was overlain by a coarse vacuous rubbly primary fill above which was burial 2752 (Fig 16). The tertiary deposits sealing the burial were much finer and were probably ploughwash.

Mollusca from pits are not, generally, ideal for palaeoenvironmental reconstruction because they may include faunas which enjoyed the shady pit micro-habitat or which had eroded from ancient soils through which the pit was cut (Thomas 1977a, Shackley 1976). These deposits, however, seem quite unmixed and molluscan preservation uniform within each context.

The basal deposit reflects the pre-pit environment and contained high mollusc numbers, 437. The shade-loving assemblage was dominated by *Carychium tridentatum*, associated with high proportions of the predatory Zonitids, *Punctum pygmaeum* and the rupestral species *Acanthinula aculeata*. *Trichia hispida* also occurred in comparatively high numbers. The high mollusc numbers and large number of taxa present in the basal fill indicate a brief episode of stability. Although the pit microenvironment is partially reflected in the mollusc assemblage, *Carychium tridentatum*, *Discus rotundatus* and the predatory Zonitids indicate leaf litter and suggest the presence of a broadleafed deciduous woodland. Furthermore, the presence of *Ena montana*, today a species of old woodland, is surprisingly common in Neolithic and Bronze Age woodland where much human interference was clearly already present (Kerney 1968). This might account for both *Trichia hispida* which, although rare in woodland, does occur in such in the pre-henge environment at Durrington Walls (Evans 1971), and *Vallonia costata* which occurs in open woodland. The overlying layer

displays a similar assemblage, but a significant increase in *Pomatias elegans* might reflect clearance.

The coarse rubbly primary fills contained very few molluscs, probably due to the rapid weathering and infilling of this unit.

The finer secondary fill at c 1.38–1.48m contained an assemblage dominated by *Trichia hispida*, but otherwise not dissimilar from the basal fills. The absence of many rupestral species and the reduction in *Carychium tridentatum* indicate both a reduction in shade and leaf litter.

A sequential series of samples through the tertiary fills shows a gradual increase in open conditions. The overall decrease in shade-loving species (Fig 108) is not due to an actual reduction in these species, but to an increase in open country species and individuals such as *Pupilla muscorum*, *Vallonia costata* and *Helicella itala*. Two factors contribute to this trend: firstly, the increasing effect of the open country habitat on the fauna; and secondly, the reduction of the shady pit micro-habitat by infilling. The uppermost context contained a very open country assemblage dominated by *Pupilla muscorum*, Vallonia and Helicellids and contained the Introduced Helicellids *Candidula intersecta* and *Cernuella virgata*, indicating the onset of Kerney's (1977) mollusc biozone 'f', that is, the Medieval period. The open country conditions that prevailed from at least the Middle Bronze Age (see below) are slightly obscured and retarded by the pit micro-habitat affording shade.

Phases 4–7. Middle Bronze Age – Early Middle Iron Age ditches 1810B and 176A (Fig 109)

Two ditch sections and the primary fills of two further ditches were analysed (Allen 1985). The ditches, although constructed in the Middle and Late Bronze Ages, were visible and perhaps still partially open in the Early Middle Iron Age.

None of the coarse, basal fills displayed any evidence of a troglophile mollusc fauna, characterised by *Oxychilus*, *Vitrea* and *Discus*, typical of rock-rubble habitats (Evans and Jones 1973). Nor was any evidence for Evan's (1972, 331) 'Punctum group' (*Punctum pygmaeum*, *Euconulus fulvus*, *Nesovitrea hammonis* and *Vitrina pellucida*) typical of early stages of ditch colonisation by plants, recognised. All the assemblages show very little ecological variation up profile and all represent a typical very open dry grassland dominated throughout by *Helicella itala*, *Vallonia excentrica*, *Pupilla muscorum* and *Trichia hispida* (Fig 109). The assemblage is a fairly specialised one, being consistent with field boundary ditch and colluvial deposits recorded at the Bishopstone lynchet (Thomas 1977b), valley fills at Kiln Coombe, Itford and Chalton (Bell 1983), and field boundary ditches at Cuckoo Bottom (Allen and Fennemore 1984) and Wharram Percy (Allen 1984), which are all interpreted as resulting from arable and pastural regimes. These land snail assemblages represent continuous, stable, dry open downland and suggest that limited short-grazed grassland episodes were interrupted by arable activity.

Table 30. The mollusc data.

FEATURE	1017													1017
CONTEXT	3231	2798	2763	2763	2763	2763	2763	3233	1042	1019	1019	1019	1018	1018
Sample	451	450	449	448	447	446	445	444	125	123	122	121	120	119
Weight	2000g	2000g	2000g	2000g	2000g	2000g	2000g	2000g	2000g	1000g	1000g	1000g	1000g	1000g
Pomatias elegans (Müller)	10	5	1	+	1	+	+	12	8	7	9	6	2	4
Carychium cf *minimum* (Müller)	5	1	–	–	–	–	–	–	–	–	–	–	–	–
Carychium tridenatum (Risso)	131	18	–	–	–	–	1	9	40	24	22	12	1	–
Carychium spp	25	9	–	–	–	–	–	–	13	9	7	14	–	1
Cochlicopa lubrica (Müller)	3	–	–	–	–	–	–	–	1	2	–	1	–	–
Cochlicopa lubricella (Porro)	1	–	–	–	–	–	–	–	–	–	–	–	–	–
Cochlicopa spp	15	2	–	–	–	–	–	–	1	3	2	1	1	1
Vertigo pygmaea (Draparnaud)	10	–	–	–	–	–	–	1	–	–	–	–	–	–
Vertigo antivertigo (Draparnaud)	–	–	–	–	–	–	–	1	–	1	–	–	–	–
Vertigo spp	16	3	+	–	–	–	–	–	–	–	–	–	–	–
Pupilla muscorum (Linnaeus)	1	1	–	–	–	–	–	1	–	5	5	12	14	22
Vallonia costata (Müller)	10	2	–	–	–	2	–	2	4	6	10	17	21	27
Vallonia pulchella (Müller)	–	–	–	–	–	–	–	–	–	–	–	–	–	–
Vallonia excentrica Sterki	–	–	–	–	–	–	–	–	–	–	1	3	9	10
Vallonia spp	1	–	–	–	–	1	–	–	–	–	–	–	–	6
Acanthinula aculeata (Müller)	26	8	–	–	–	–	–	–	5	2	2	–	1	–
Ena montana (Draparnaud)	1	1	–	–	–	–	–	–	–	–	–	1	–	–
Ena obscura (Müller)	1	–	–	–	–	–	–	–	2	–	–	1	–	–
Punctum pygmaeum (Draparnaud)	26	10	–	–	–	–	–	1	4	1	1	1	–	–
Discus rotandatus (Müller)	13	5	–	–	–	1	–	18	13	9	3	1	1	–
Vitrina pellucida (Müller)	2	–	–	–	–	–	–	–	–	1	–	–	–	–
Vitrea contracta (Westerlund)	15	2	–	–	–	–	–	2	12	7	3	3	–	1
Vitrea crystallina (Müller)	10	1	–	–	–	–	–	–	–	–	–	–	–	–
Vitrea spp	1	–	–	–	–	2	–	–	–	–	–	–	–	–
Nesovitrea hammonia (Ström)	2	–	–	–	–	–	–	–	–	–	–	–	–	–
Aegopinella pura (Alder)	25	1	–	–	–	–	–	4	11	3	–	5	–	1
Aegopinella nitidula (Draparnaud)	16	9	–	–	–	–	–	5	20	13	–	11	–	–
Oxychilus cellarius (Müller)	–	1	–	+	–	–	–	–	6	3	–	5	–	1
Limacidae	–	1	–	–	–	–	1	–	1	–	–	–	1	–
Ceilioides acicula (Müller)	–	–	–	–	–	–	1	3	41	67	51	96	153	151
Cochlodina laminata (Montagu)	1	–	–	–	–	–	–	–	1	–	–	1	–	–
Clausilia bidentata (Ström)	4	–	–	–	–	–	–	–	1	–	–	1	–	–
Candidula intersecta (Poriet)	–	–	–	–	–	–	–	–	–	–	2	7	9	13
Candidula gigaxii (Pfeiffer)	–	–	–	–	–	–	–	–	–	–	–	–	–	–
Cernuella virgata (da Costa)	–	–	–	–	–	–	–	–	–	–	1	1	1	1
Helicella itala (Linnaeus)	–	–	–	–	–	–	–	–	1	8	3	7	–	–
Helicidae	–	–	–	–	–	–	–	–	–	–	–	–	–	16
Trichia striolata (C Pfeiffer)	4	–	–	–	–	–	–	2	3	1	–	–	–	–
Trichia hispida (Linnaeus)	60	4	–	–	+	1	4	60	21	4	4	9	3	1
Arianta arbustorum (Linnaeus)	1	+	–	–	–	–	–	–	+	+	–	–	+	–
Helicigona lapicida (Linnaeus)	+	–	–	–	–	–	–	–	+	–	–	–	–	–
Capaea/Arianta spp	1	1	–	+	+	–	–	4	1	1	1	1	+	–
MOLLUSCA TOTAL	437	85	1	+	1	4	8	123	168	111	75	121	64	105
MOLLUSCA TAXA	25	19	1	–	1	3	4	15	18	19	15	21	11	13

+ = non-apical fragment

Totals exclude *Ceiliodes acicula* (Müller).

Table 30, continued. The mollusc data.

FEATURE	176A					176A	1810B				1810B	990A	990A	971
CONTEXT	808	427	427	411	352	352	1825	1824	1823	1822	1822	2120	2120	2121
Sample	68	69	70	71	72	73	520	521	522	523	524	509	510	517
Weight	1000g	1000g	1000g	1000g	1035g	1150g	1000g	1000g	1000g	1000g	1200g	1000g	1000g	1000g
Pomatias elegans (Müller)	6	1	+	4	+	+	1	4	1	1	4	+	+	1
Carychium cf minimum (Müller)	–	–	–	–	–	–	–	–	–	–	–	–	–	–
Carychium tridenatum (Risso)	–	–	–	–	–	–	–	–	–	–	–	–	–	–
Carychium spp	–	–	–	–	–	–	–	–	–	–	–	–	–	–
Cochlicopa lubrica (Müller)	–	1	2	–	2	1	1	1	1	–	–	–	–	–
Cochlicopa lubricella (Porro)	–	–	–	–	–	–	–	–	–	–	–	–	–	–
Cochlicopa spp	4	1	–	1	1	1	–	1	–	–	3	–	–	–
Vertigo pygmaea (Draparnaud)	2	1	–	1	–	1	–	–	–	–	–	–	–	–
Vertigo antivertigo (Draparnaud)	–	–	–	–	–	–	–	–	–	–	–	–	–	–
Vertigo spp	–	–	–	–	–	–	–	–	–	–	–	–	–	–
Pupilla muscorum (Linnaeus)	15	9	10	52	29	41	–	5	7	1	19	9	2	15
Vallonia costata (Müller)	11	1	–	7	–	3	–	7	1	–	4	–	–	15
Vallonia pulchella (Müller)	3	3	3	11	3	6	–	2	1	–	2	–	–	–
Vallonia excentrica Sterki	23	13	6	45	52	37	–	9	8	–	26	1	3	32
Vallonia spp	–	–	–	–	–	–	–	–	–	–	–	–	–	–
Acanthinula aculeata (Müller)	–	–	–	–	–	–	–	–	–	–	1	–	–	–
Ena montana (Draparnaud)	–	–	–	–	–	–	–	–	–	–	–	–	–	–
Ena obscura (Müller)	–	–	–	–	–	–	–	–	–	–	1	–	–	–
Punctum pygmaeum (Draparnaud)	–	–	–	–	–	–	–	–	–	–	–	–	–	–
Discus rotandatus (Müller)	–	–	–	–	–	–	–	2	–	–	–	–	–	–
Vitrina pellucida (Müller)	–	–	–	–	–	–	–	–	–	–	–	–	–	–
Vitrea contracta (Westerlund)	–	–	–	–	–	–	–	–	–	–	–	2	–	–
Vitrea crystallina (Müller)	–	–	–	–	–	–	–	–	–	–	–	–	–	–
Vitrea spp	–	–	–	–	–	–	–	–	–	–	–	–	–	–
Nesovitrea hammonia (Ström)	–	–	–	–	–	–	–	–	–	–	–	–	–	–
Aegopinella pura (Alder)	–	–	–	–	–	–	–	–	–	–	–	–	–	–
Aegopinella nitidula (Draparnaud)	–	–	–	–	–	–	–	1	–	–	–	–	–	–
Oxychilus cellarius (Müller)	–	–	–	–	–	–	–	–	–	–	–	–	–	–
Limacidae	–	–	2	–	–	2	–	–	–	–	1	–	–	1
Ceilioides acicula (Müller)	22	45	56	101	40	178	–	81	24	8	99	61	25	85
Cochlodina laminata (Montagu)	–	–	–	–	–	–	–	–	–	–	1	–	–	–
Clausilia bidentata (Ström)	–	–	–	–	–	–	–	–	–	–	–	–	–	–
Candidula intersecta (Poriet)	–	–	–	6	3	13	–	–	–	3	3	–	–	–
Candidula gigaxii (Pfeiffer)	–	–	–	–	–	–	–	–	–	–	1	–	–	–
Cernuella virgata (da Costa)	–	–	–	3	–	3	–	–	–	–	5	–	–	–
Helicella itala (Linnaeus)	17	2	7	11	23	10	5	34	6	5	13	3	3	4
Helicidae	–	–	–	–	–	–	–	–	–	–	–	–	–	–
Trichia striolata (C Pfeiffer)	–	–	–	–	1	2	–	1	–	–	–	–	–	–
Trichia hispida (Linnaeus)	5	5	8	12	23	3	–	4	–	1	3	1	+	7
Arianta arbustorum (Linnaeus)	–	–	–	–	–	–	–	–	–	–	–	–	–	–
Helicigona lapicida (Linnaeus)	–	–	–	–	–	–	–	–	–	–	–	–	–	–
Capaea/Arianta spp	1	+	1	1	1	–	+	3	–	–	1	1	–	–
MOLLUSCA TOTAL	87	37	39	154	138	123	7	74	25	11	88	17	8	75
MOLLUSCA TAXA	10	9	8	12	9	12	3	12	7	5	16	6	3	6

+ = non-apical fragment
Totals exclude *Ceiliodes acicula* (Müller).

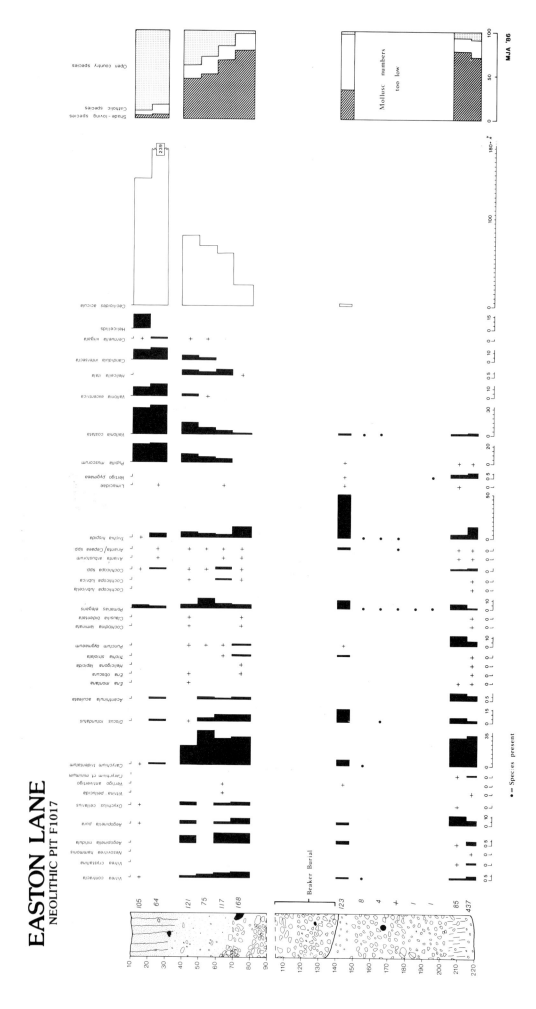

Fig 108. Easton Lane. Histogram of relative mollusc abundance, Neolithic pit F1017.

EASTON LANE

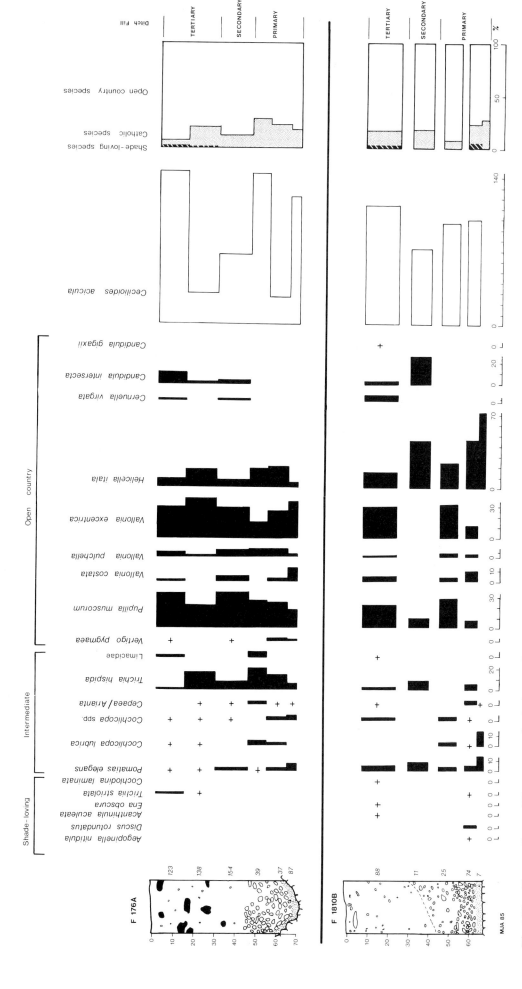

Fig 109.   Easton Lane. Histogram of relative mollusc abundance, ditches 176 and 1810.

Phases 8–10. Middle Iron Age – Medieval (tertiary fills of 1017, 1810B, and 176A)

The tertiary deposits of all these features produced a restricted taxa, almost exclusively of open country preference, and, with the exception of the Introduced Helicellids, undifferentiatable from the assemblages recovered from the Middle Bronze Age and later fills. Thus the open downland suggested above can be seen as present in the Medieval period.

Conclusion

In the later Neolithic contexts analysed, environmental interpretation is made more complex by the pit micro-habitat contributing to the molluscan faunas. However, it is clear that a deciduous woodland was probably cleared for the pit, though there is no evidence that this clearance was long standing. Shady conditions prevailed soon after construction of the pit. Although there is no environmental evidence for the Early Bronze Age, it is clear that the Middle Bronze Age linear ditches were cut into a well established, pre-existing, open downland environment. It is therefore likely that the secondary woodland/shrubland was extensively cleared in the Early Bronze Age. The arable and short grazed pastural grassland agronomy suggested by the mollu-

scan evidence is attested by Maltby's faunal analysis and Monk's plant remains. Open downland prevailed throughout later prehistory and the Medieval period until very recent times.

Table 31. Summary of environmental conclusions.

Phase	Period	Environment	Activity
1.	Neolithic	–	–
2.	Late Neolithic	Deciduous woodland Regeneration Open woodland	Limited clearance
3.	Early Bronze Age	Open woodland?	Extensive clearance?
4.	Middle Bronze Age	Open downland	Arable and Pastural activities
5.	Late Bronze Age	↓	↓
6.	Early Iron Age	↓	↓
7.	Early Middle Iron Age	↓	↓
8.	Middle Iron Age	↓	↓
9.	Late Iron Age/ Early Roman	↓	↓
10.	Late Saxon and Medieval	↓	↓

Chapter 5

Discussion

The Sampling Programme

The excavation of the Easton Lane site was an exercise designed to see whether an area which appeared to contain almost no archaeological features was really as sterile as it seemed. The programme was designed to enable the project to expand if archaeological features were encountered. The sampling fraction of 10% was chosen on economic grounds. A 10% sample could be examined within the budget while leaving sufficient resources to excavate small additional areas. A system of parallel transects, randomly selected from within zones of comparable width, was the most convenient sampling system to use (Figs 2 and 4). The width of the transects was determined by the width of the machine used; the transects could be easily selected and located on the ground. The 33 transects revealed 363 features; eight transects contained no archaeological features. The features by type were: 223 post-holes, 35 natural features, 32 ditches, 28 pits, 14 gullies, 14 scoops, nine stake-holes, three slots, two floors, one quarry, one burial and one hollow.

A computer-based analysis of the data from the transects was undertaken after the excavation was completed to see if comparison could be made between a computed prediction of the distribution of archaeological features by data and feature type and the final archaeological record as excavated, thereby confirming objectively the intuitive process by which the excavation was expanded from the sample.

However, the high variation in the data, including transects with no features and large numbers of features in tight clusters, militated for a more discriminating test, or a larger sample than was practically available, both in terms of cost of sample size and robustness of statistical test . A stratified random sample of 10% can be seen as a practical response and it has been suggested that a simple visual plot of results is perhaps more useful than further statistical tests (Samels 1986).

The Phase Sequence

Attempting to establish a reasonable chronological sequence which related sensibly to the archaeological features has proved a worrying experience. The archaeological features were generally widely scattered, there was no stratigraphy, there was no scope for topsoil investigation above known feature groups (feature groups were only located by machine-excavated transects), and there were remarkably few finds from the post-hole groups. All of these factors were unhelpful. Once plotted, the distribution of diagnostic pottery proved to be the most useful tool in establishing a phased sequence. As at Winnall Down, Medieval pottery occurred in most feature groups, but prehistoric and Roman pottery of all types produced relatively discrete groups. Exceptions included the fills of many of the ditches, which showed long sequences of activity. Indeed, the upper fills contained molluscs of Medieval date, as did feature group 653 with associated CS 3918. A more secure date for that feature would have been most helpful. The distributions of pottery have been displayed throughout this report, as they form the entire basis of the chronological sequence for Easton Lane.

The excavations of Winnall Down in 1976/7 and Easton Lane in 1982/3 have produced an episodic account of settlement, ceremonial and agricultural activites from the middle of the fourth millennium BC until the Norman Conquest and a little after.

The phasing of the two sites is summarized in Table 32.

Table 32. Phase sequences for Easton Lane and Winnall Down.

Description	Phase Easton Lane	Winnall Down
Neolithic	1	1
Late Neolithic	2	No Phase
Early Bronze Age	3	No Phase
Middle Bronze Age	4	2a
Late Bronze Age (post Deverel-Rimbury)	5	2b
Early Iron Age	6	3
Early Middle Iron Age	7	No Phase
Middle Iron Age	8	4
Late Iron Age	9	5
Early Roman	↓	6
Late Saxon and	10	–
Medieval	↓	7

Neolithic. Easton Lane Phase 1, Winnall Down Phase 1

The lack of earlier Neolithic sites, apart from long barrows (RCHM 1979), is a well-known aspect of the archaeology of Hampshire. The Winnall Down excavation revealed a ring ditch of 16.5m external diameter. Red deer antlers in the bottom of the ditch produced radiocarbon dates which, when calibrated, fall in the middle of the fourth millennium BC (Fasham 1982). Features like this remain enigmatic but may have ceremonial connections. Hampshire may not be quite so devoid of earlier activity as the existing archaeological record shows. It has been argued that the demand for agricultural land in the Iron Age and Roman period may have led to the disappearance of monuments of standing stones (Fasham 1980) and that the absence of causewayed camps, henges or 'ritual' sites in Hampshire may be deceptive (Schadla-Hall 1977, 17). Renfrew has suggested that the large Neolithic monuments of Wessex required a high degree of central organisation (Renfrew 1973), and Barker and Webley (1978) have argued for organised land-use over large areas. An organised landscape has been suggested for Sussex (Drewett 1978). Hampshire seems, therefore, to be a part of a different social organisation to the rest of Wessex and Sussex, unless, of course, it is at the centre and the causewayed enclosures and henges are all peripheral. This is most unlikely.

The chances of discovering occupation sites of Neolithic date are slim. Extensive field survey in the environs of Stonehenge (Richards forthcoming) has demonstrated just how elusive these sites are on the dry chalkland of southern England. Surface collections of lithic material have revealed concentrations of broadly Neolithic (rather than Late Neolithic) date, but sample excavations have revealed few, if any, contemporary subsurface features. Shennan (1985) has rightly pointed out that the substantial surface scatters collected by G W Willis in the early twentieth century in the Basingstoke area, with their numerous diagnostic flint implements, may represent permanent settlements. So far, none of those surface scatters has been re-examined in the field or subjected to any form of sample excavation. In considering the thin covering of surface flint of Neolithic and Bronze Age date in eastern Hampshire, Shennan (1985, 70) considers the possibility that this might be a reflection of the way archaeological evidence for mobile occupation accumulates.

About a millennium before the ring ditch at Winnall Down was dug, there was a major episode of clearance in the Itchen Valley at the nearby site of Winnall Moors (Waton 1982). To confirm this unusually early clearance horizon, a further sequence of radiocarbon dates is being processed.

The Easton Lane excavation provided further glimpses of Neolithic activity. It is possible that the distribution of ceramic material at the north of Area B, around pit 1017 and ditch 1054, reflects a localized activity area of Neolithic date.

Late Neolithic. Easton Lane Phase 2, Winnall Down no phase

The dating of CS 3918 is, and will remain, problematic and probably impossible to resolve. The excavation and recording of the structure was rigorous and thus the location, both horizontally and vertically, of the pottery is reasonably secure. The Neolithic pottery is described as 'mainly fresh and unworn' (Ellison pers com) and this may indicate that the pottery is contemporary with the infilling of the hollow in which the structure was built. The worked flint from this area is not out of place in a Late Neolithic context, and broadly contemporary with pit 5456, 50m to the north. There were a few undated post-holes to the east but a geophysical survey revealed no other features comparable to feature group 653 which contained CS 3918. Magnetic anomalies recorded in the adjacent area were revealed to be patches of clay-with-flints when the topsoil was stripped. CS 3918, with its ringbeam and principal rafter construction, is of a structural type common in the later Bronze Age in Sussex (Drewett 1979; Burstow and Holleyman 1957) and Dorset (Woodward forthcoming). The post-ring provided internal roof support while the outer boundary of the house would have coincided with the lip of the depression. The position of pit 3802 on the line of the post-ring seems to substantiate this. Since this was a building with no contemporary surviving structures it is not possible to speculate on social organisation. The southeast facing entrance would have provided reasonable light, and a number of craft activites could have been undertaken within its shelter, such as those suggested for Hut 3 in compound 4 at Black Patch, Sussex (Drewett 1979, 9–10).

The major difference between this house and most of the Bronze Age examples is that, in the latter, the entrances face downhill whereas CS 3918, in order to maximise the light from the southeast, has an entrance facing upslope. The 'back to front' arrangement may acount for the isolation of the structure, as the period of use may have been quite short, assuming the unsuitability of the aspect was soon discovered. The south-facing slopes a few hundred metres to the south were settled in the Bronze Age.

Evidence for flint-working was present in pit 5456, which was cut by the Late Saxon enclosure. The flint was knapping-waste from a flake industry using both prepared and unprepared cores. The badly preserved pieces of red deer antlers which were in pit 5456 may have been present for making into antler tools or for use in flint-working.

Another small trace of occupation activity was provided by the four small pits in Area Mc. The flintwork from them may represent domestic refuse.

The cone-shaped pits in Area B are an addition to the corpus of 'unusual' Late Neolithic features in Hampshire. The burial in pit 1017 can be classed with those of male burials normally accompanied by Beakers but which also include aceramic inhumations. Despite the absence of a Beaker from

Easton Lane, a number of similarities exist which suggest that the burial may be placed with the Primary and Developed Southern Beakers. The six Green Low arrowheads and the four antler spatulae both have regular associations with these Beaker groups

Additional grave goods, although less diagnostic, do not contradict these ceramic associations. Their occurrence and association with antler spatulae have been used (Smith and Simpson 1966) to interpret these burials as those of craftsmen with their 'tool kits'. The possibility that spatulae are pressure flakers reduces the likelihood that 'tool kits' can be associated with a specific (leather) trade, and suggests that they represent general-purpose tools. Awls of both metal and bone, scrapers, knives and flint flakes, which feature under Clarke's (1970, 203) 'exotic' Primary Southern Beaker equipment, are all common in graves of this type (Smith and Simpson 1966, Table 1). The bone awl from Green Low, also a Primary Southern Beaker grave, was found on the pelvis, a similar position to that of the Easton Lane grave. The scraper from pit 1017 was recorded with finds from the disturbed grave fill but its proximity to the burial increases the probability that it formed part of the original deposit. The knife and flint flakes were clearly selected, and formed a deliberate part of the burial.

Negative evidence also suggests possible connections with Primary and Developed Southern Beakers. Clarke (1970, 204) notes that, despite the strong connections with archery, there is an absence of stone bracers and of bronze daggers from Primary Southern Beaker graves in particular.

The Easton Lane burial rite can also be paralleled among some Primary Southern Beakers. This Beaker group includes sporadic use of deep shafts (Clarke 1970, 202) between three and six feet deep. The Acklam Wold inhumation lay in a chalk shaft six feet deep (Mortimer 1905, 91–2).

Pit 1017 was excavated in a small local clearance, a situation similar to the contemporary feature, a possible stone alignment on Burntwood and Bridget's Farm (Fasham 1979). One km north of Easton Lane, the Bronze Age ring ditch in Easton Down cut through an earlier, probably Late Neolithic, feature. The mollusca indicated that the feature had been set in open, grazed downland. Woodland regenerates, but by the time the Middle Bronze Age ditch system was formed, open grassland was well established. However, clearance will be localized and woodland must still have been a most important element of both the landscape and daily activites. Regenerated woodland was present at Bridget's Farm 4km to the north in the first millennium BC (Fasham 1979).

The cone-shaped pits 80 and 1017 were 36m apart. Five small pits formed an arc which is tangential to a straight line between pits 80 and 1017. The five pits had decalcified fills and contained the following finds: an antler and a Medieval sherd in pit 372; and a Beaker or Early Bronze Age sherd and another Medieval sherd in pit 368.

The burial of an arrow-maker or archer in pit 1017 and the arrangement of the arc of pits with pit 80 hints at an area of special importance; an area perhaps indicated in an almost monumental fashion. If that is the case, the special area does not seem to have been separated by a physical barrier or a great distance from more ordinary areas.

The cluster of pits in Area Mc, with their more everyday contexts, were only 125–150m to the south-west.

The non-long barrow, ceremonial aspects of the Neolithic in Hampshire remain obscure. Even if at Easton Lane a small ceremonial area has been recorded, and even if the holes at Burntwood Farm really had contained stones (Fasham 1979), the Neolithic of Hampshire is still different to neighbouring areas.

Early Bronze Age. Easton Lane Phase 3, Winnall Down no phase

The distribution of Early Bronze Age pottery across the site suggests activity over a wide area. In certain areas continuity with later phases is suggested by residual Early Bronze Age pottery occurring in Middle Bronze Age and later ditches, such as 1054 and 3765.

The two cemeteries, one to the north in Area F and the other in the south in Area D, provide the most interest; both are mixed cremation and inhumation groups.

The northern cemetery, disturbed by Late Saxon and Medieval activity, comprised at least two cremations and one inhumation. One cremation, with a bronze awl, was in an inverted Collared urn, and the second cremation may also have been in an urn. The former cremation was partly destroyed by the digging of Medieval pit 600 in which there were fragments of a different Collared urn. Inhumation 595 was in a shallow grave and the deepest cremation pit was only 0.25m in depth. The shallowness of these burial features, if not a consequence of soil erosion, is perhaps an indication that the burials were in an unditched barrow. The cremations contained very little human bone and, although it can be argued that 507 with its urn was a burial, the 33g of cremated human bone in 598 may represent the *ad hoc* disposal of the pyre remains.

There is no evidence to suggest that the southern cemetery was originally in a barrow. It was of triangular shape with the two inhumations forming the base line and the double Biconical urn cremation the apex. There was one other inurned cremation. During excavation, three other pits with burnt material and burnt flints were recorded as cremations and are so described in Chapter 2. In these three features there were 34g, 55g and 84g only of burnt human bone compared to the 3,129g from the double biconical urn and 149g from the other inurned cremation. It is conceivable that the three holes were filled with the residues and rubbish from funeral pyres and are not, in any sense, cremations of specific individuals. The mixed burial rites are commonplace in barrow groups, but cemeteries remote from barrows are unusual. The two cemeteries are unusual in containing both inhumations and cremation burials but lacking a barrow or a ditch or any substantial marker. Perhaps they are isolated forerunners of the later Bronze Age urnfield cemeteries. The Kimpton cemetery involved the use of slabbed pots (Dacre and Ellison 1981). The size of the two Easton Lane burial grounds seem to relate to the possible internal social grouping suggested by Ellison (1981).

Middle Bronze Age. Easton Lane Phase 4, Winnall Down Phase 2

The rectilinear ditch system was laid out in this phase, intersecting at the south with a long east-west lynchet which defines the south side of the complex in Area D. The physical evidence for the ditches was slight and only ditch 1810 was substantial enough to be visible on aerial photographs. The arrangement is analogous with the contemporary sites at Fengate (Pryor 1980). The Wessex linear ditch system was a cause for interest half a century ago when it was related to ranching (Hawkes 1939). In the late 1960s and the 1970s, Bowen demonstrated that the linear ditch system was far more extensive than originally perceived (1975a, 1975b, 1978) and, with Evans and Race, turned to investigate the environment of some of these remarkable land boundaries (Bowen et al 1978). The emergence in the Wessex region of the early components of the linear ditch system as a response to social stress in the Middle Bronze Age has been suggested by Bradley (1980). At Easton Lane, the system seems to be planned but is not related to existing landscape features such as barrows. The relationship between the ditches and the vestigial traces of ancient fields visible on aerial photography is not clear. The only possible relationship was in Area D, where a linear ditch and a very long lynchet intersected. There was, however, no stratigraphic relationship. Subjectively, the lynchet seemed to be earlier, but this was not demonstrable.

Although the ditches seem to have been formed in an open downland, the proportion of pig bone perhaps suggests that there were still copses and patches of woodland. Indeed, there were many features at the south of Area B that can only be described as natural, but which may have been tree holes. The presence of fish bones in a post-hole in Area D suggests that the natural resources of the River Itchen were exploited. It would be surprising if herds were not taken to the river. The linear ditch system initially stopped (or started) at the southern edge of the activities in Area D. The ditch system seems to have been later than both the Bronze Age cemeteries but contemporary with the later activities of fences, rectangular buildings and circular structures in Area D. Elsewhere, the relationship between the Bronze Age structures and the ditches is not clear.

Easton Lane perhaps provides an insight into an infra-structure of the system which will only be fully revealed when large areas are available for investigation.

The contemporary occupation extends over an area of 15 hectares (37 acres). This includes the pits with Globular urns and saddle querns discovered under the Winnall Industrial Estate, whose position is shown on Figure 1 (Hawkes 1969) and excludes CS 3918, which is regarded as Late Neolithic. The structures lie between the 60m and 65m contours in a broad band on the south side of the slight ridge which ran across the site.

This may just be an example of an early form of settlement with dispersed houses, a settlement type which might account for the apparently isolated chance finds at Chalton (Cunliffe 1970) or West Meon (Lewis and Walker 1977). Parts of the settlement can be considered as groups and reveal similar characteristics to the enclosed sites of Itford Hill (Burstow and Holleyman 1957), Black Patch (Drewett 1979), whose internal organisation might be similar, and to Down Farm which also has similar structure types (Bradley pers com). It has been suggested that the enclosed sites in Wessex were perhaps used for centralized food storage (Barrett and Bradley 1980). An alternative explanation to the agricultural base for the settlement is that the site was also part of a far-reaching exchange network.

The majority of the Middle Bronze Age post-built structures fulfil the criteria for 'axial-line symmetry' suggested by Guilbert, and so demonstrate the 'design-conciousness' of their builders (Guilbert 1983). CS 5636 in Area H has a post-hole, 5244, at its central point, and by running a line through the entrance in such a way that it cuts post-holes 5244 and 5586, a reasonably symmetrical arrangement becomes apparent. In fact, the resultant pattern allows us to postulate a missing post-hole mid-way between post-holes 5248 and 5271, with a considerable degree of confidence (Guilbert's example of P17 from Moel y Gaer, 1983). Given our acceptance of the hypothesis that the outer walls of these structures lay beyond the post-hole rings, a number of well-built, substantial structures were present during this phase. Fleming (1979, 117–118) makes an interesting comparison between the living space within prehistoric 'hut-circles' on Dartmoor with that within the upper halves, or living-quarters, of Medieval long-houses, in order to re-evaluate their status. The average covered area of structures at Easton Lane during the Middle Bronze Age (see Table 33) compares well with that of Medieval long-houses, and as Fleming suggests, byres could be assumed to exist as seperate buildings, perhaps represented here as those clusters of post-holes which had less easily definable, or regularly-spaced, ground plans. Some, such as MS 5650, were regular in plan but apparently incomplete, while others, such as MS 5657, were discrete groups of post-holes without readily discernible structural plans. These irregular structures are regarded therefore as being animal pens, some possible roofed, although direct evidence for their function is lacking.

Ellison (1978) proposed that the later settlement at Itford Hill in Sussex could be seen as incorporating a standard range of domestic and auxiliary units of structures. Drewett's interpretation of compound 4 at Black Patch (Drewett 1979) proposes a structural hierarchy involving five huts. The interpretation uses several classes of information which include a comparison of size and degree of terracing for each structure, distributions of artefacts and the relationship of the huts to the fenced areas and ponds. This level of information was not available at Easton Lane but it should be noted that the structural groups in areas B, D and H were of comparative size and complexity to the post-hole ground plans of the compounds at Black Patch. If the terrace contours and the ponds on the established plan of compound 4 are disregarded, then the remaining features are circular structures (huts 1, 2 and 3) and a number of fence lines and irregular groups of post-holes (see Fig 110). This highlights the problem of interpretation and even recognition of auxiliary structures. Hut 5 in compound 4 would be extremely difficult to pick out without the boundaries of its terrace, although it is perhaps the same class of structure as MS 5654 or 5657 from Easton Lane. Around and inside many of the circular structures at Easton Lane are recognisable, paired post-holes, which presumably represent contemporary activity, though not necessarily structural features. It would therefore seem more informative to illustrate and consider post-hole clusters and groups of clusters *in toto* than to over-concentrate on the more easily recognisable symmetrical post-hole rings.

Finally, it should be noted that in Reynold's (1983) report on the reconstruction of the Pimperne house (a large, 12.5m diameter, Iron Age structure), he points out that, given a topsoil depth of some 0.30m, none of the posts or stakes used would penetrate significantly into the underlying chalk, so it could be assumed that many of our apparently vestigial traces of round-houses represent the tip of the iceberg and that most were probably surrounded by auxiliary structures of slighter construction which left little or no trace in the bedrock.

Although it is not possible to prove that all the structures in this phase were exactly contemporary, and indeed structures 2373 and 2375 could not have been, it is possible to consider some of the structures as forming discrete groups. The best example of this occurs in Area H where a circular structure, 5636, formed a small self-contained group with RS 5637 and MS 5652, potentially a house with attached fence, animal pens (MS 5652) and a four-post structure (RS 5637, granary ?). In Area B, the sizeable circular structure 2341 could well have controlled the nearby possible animal pens MS 5654 and MS 5657.

Again, in Area D, the closeness of structures 4008, 4009, 5653 and 4010 suggests that their physical relationship mirrored a social relationship. MS 4010 was a major structure of unusual form and would certainly have provided the focal point of this group, while structures 4008 and 4009 (if they were used as houses) could have housed dependants tied by blood or social links. Structure 5653 was less well represented on the ground and may have provided auxiliary,

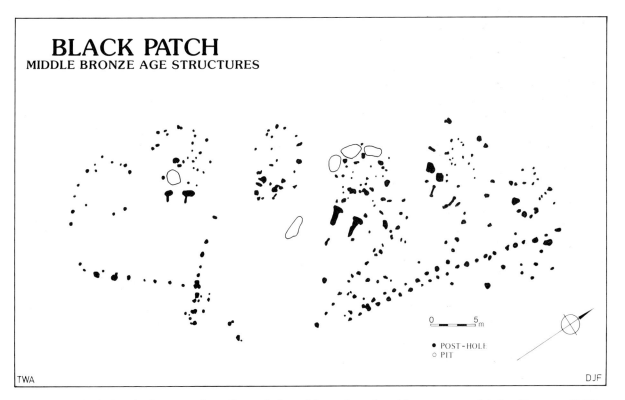

BLACK PATCH
MIDDLE BRONZE AGE STRUCTURES

0 ____ 5 m

• POST-HOLE
○ PIT

TWA   DJF

Fig 110.   Black Patch, Sussex: plan of post-holes with earthwork evidence removed (after Drewett 1979).

covered working space. A joint family group could be postulated if all these structures were contemporary. However, structure 4010 represents a distinct deviation from the accepted norm for Middle Bronze Age houses and so could indicate a similar unusual social group, or activity in the area. Structure 4010 was a round-ended, rectangular building with symmetry about its short axis. The rounded ends and lack of symmetry about the long axis could suggest that it was not a variation on a long house but an early experiment in semi-detached residences of two circular houses.

The only other broadly contemporary structure in Wessex, which is of a comparable form, was excavated at Down Farm, Dorset (Bradley and Green pers com). It was about twice as long as the Easton Lane example and seems to have more in common with European types. However, a rectangular building 17m by 6m excavated in 1967 at Nijnsel in Holland had one rounded end and a complex arrangement of internal posts (Beex and Hulst 1968). The excavators regarded the structure as a long house in the true sense with a living area and a byre under one continuous roof. A French example of a rectangular post-built structure with one rounded end was recently excavated at Bucy-le-Long in Picardy by Mlle Pommepuy. The ground plan was 17.5m by 5m and showed symmetry about its short axis (Fig 111). The rounded end was considered to be a strengthening device to counteract the effects of the prevailing wind (Massy 1983, 231–61).

Various combinations of structure groups can be proposed for Area D, none of which are mutually exclusive (Fig 53).

Combination 3 repeats several similarities with the enclosure at Down Farm where a pair of circular buildings were replaced and enclosed within a fenced and partly ditched area, within which a sequence of circular and rectangular buildings is proposed (Bradley and Green pers com). Combination 3 has the rectangular building facing west into a yard in which stands circular structure 4009. A fence line ran north and south from the rectangular building to enclose a quarter of a circle against either fence lines or lynchets at the south and ditch 1810 in the west. Circular structures 4008 and 5653 were outside that enclosure. Within the enclosure were a range of two- and four-post structures and another fence. This could be regarded as a single domestic unit, similar to those proposed by Ellison (1978), developing adjacent to the slightly earlier cemetery.

Combination 1 was an arrangement of three arcs of

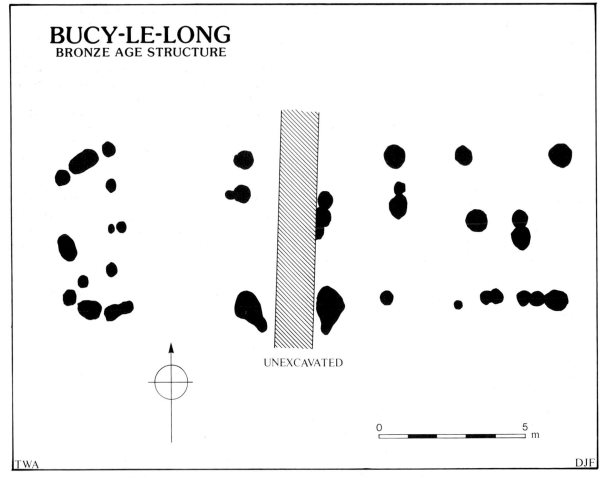

Fig 111.   Bucy-le-Long, France: simplified plan of Bronze Age structure, for comparison with MS 4010 in Area D (after Massy 1983, Fig 1, 232).

posts again delimiting the quadrant defined by ditch 1810 and fence/lynchet in the south. Possible entrances in the inner arc were lined up with a funnel entrance through its outer arc leading to the south of the cemetery. This arrangement obviously hints at a ceremonial function. Associated with it could have been circular structures 4008 and 5653.

The possible combinations of structures makes interpretation of Area D difficult. The cemetery seems to be slightly earlier than the structures and so a possible ceremonial arrangement of structures may have come first, to be supported by more domestic considerations, although, of course, a ceremonial function may have continued right through. Equally, domestic function may have been contemporary with the cemetery.

Structure 2159 stood apart from the rest of the Bronze Age structures both in form and location. It occurred in a corner of the Middle Bronze Age ditch system and consisted of an oval of sixteen large, closely-spaced post-holes. It was similar to Buurman's temporary crop storage structures (Buurman 1979, Fig 1, type e) and its position in a field corner is perhaps apposite. The smaller, similar but later structures B and C at Winnall Down (Fasham 1985, 13 and 127) were also suggested as grain storage facilities akin to the Scottish byre (Dunbar 1932; Monk and Fasham 1980). Unfortunately further evidence of cereal crop processing or storage was not recovered and so the parallel cannot be pursued further.

CS 3918 at the north of the site has been reported as Late Neolithic. If, however, it was contemporary with the Middle Bronze Age occupation its awkward isolation on the north-facing slope may represent a social element, perhaps a punishment or isolation because of disease, physical or mental.

The relationship of structures to ditches was complex. There was only one physical relationship, where the post-hole ring from CS 4009 could have intersected Ditch 1810 in Area D. The apparent absence of post-holes from the upper fill of the ditch does not necessarily mean that the structure predated the ditch as it could have been built between recuts of the ditch. The structures were on the hillside and related to the contours, while the ditch systems strike against the contours, and thus it may be that the structures are earlier. However, ditch 1810 originally stopped on the southern limit of Area D and indicates a contemporaneity with one phase of activity in that area. If the structures in Areas B, C and E are taken as one group and Area D as another group then the Middle Bronze Age structures can be seen as moderate-sized units comparable with both Itford Hill (Burstow and Holleyman 1957) and Black Patch (Drewett 1979), and called small farmsteads (Group A sites) by Ellison (1981). At Black Patch the settlement units, of which the excavated site is but one, were scattered over an area but linked to one another within the contemporary field system by tracks. At Rowden in Dorset the huts were not grouped as in the Sussex examples but were isolated, even if linked by lynchet tracks (Woodward forthcoming). The Easton Lane structures do not appear to have been integrated into the field system. They may actually represent nothing more than the mobility of a single family unit moving from one location to another over a number of years or centuries.

The Middle Bronze Age occupation, when the pits from Winnall Industrial Estate are included (Hawkes 1969), does extend over a large area and, in terms of size, falls into Ellison's Group B (Ellison 1981) of large defended enclosures. Easton Lane is large but undefended. The size of the site, rather than the display of its defensive (or delimiting) boundary may be more important. In her discussion of settlement and regional exchange, Ellison has examined the relationship between the small (Group A) and large (Group B) sites and the regional distribution of pottery and metalwork (Ellison 1980). The Easton Lane site lies close to the theoretical junction of three of the large distribution centres at Ram's Hill, Martin Down and Highdown Hill; between the distribution of Type I and Type II globular urns; on the edge of the distributions of Wessex everyday ware; not far from the junction of Rowlands' hoard clusters 1 and 2 (Rowlands 1976); and in the centre of the distribution of Class 4 palstaves (Figs 112 and 113). Rowlands (1976) argued for the development of bronze working industries on the south coast and there is a cluster of various bronze types in the general area of the Solent and the Itchen valley. Assuming that the settlement is not a small mobile farmstead, then its size and location suggests that, in the Middle Bronze Age, the settlement at Easton Lane may have been an important element in the distribution networks of Wessex. The site is in a commanding position above the River Itchen and could easily have controlled trade into the hinterland. The area around Winchester is a preferred location during the Iron Age which included both the hillfort at St Catherine's Hill (Hawkes et al 1930) and the extensive enclosure under Winchester, and during the Roman period with the establishment of a possible fort (Biddle 1984) and a town. There is no reason why earlier in prehistory the trading and communication advantages of the Winchester gap should not have been recognised.

Late Bronze Age. Easton Lane Phase 5, Winnall Down Phase 2b

The ditch systems continued in use, with the ditches being recut or replaced. On the Easton Lane part of the site no structures can definitely be placed in the Late Bronze Age. On Winnall Down there was the small cluster of four houses, almost certainly not contemporary, and a fence associated with post-Deverel-Rimbury pottery. The settlement could have been continued by further buildings in the unexcavated area immediately west of Winnall Down which remains archaeologically intact.

The later Bronze Age settlement seems to have been more restricted than its Middle Bronze Age predecessor. It was set amongst field ditch systems

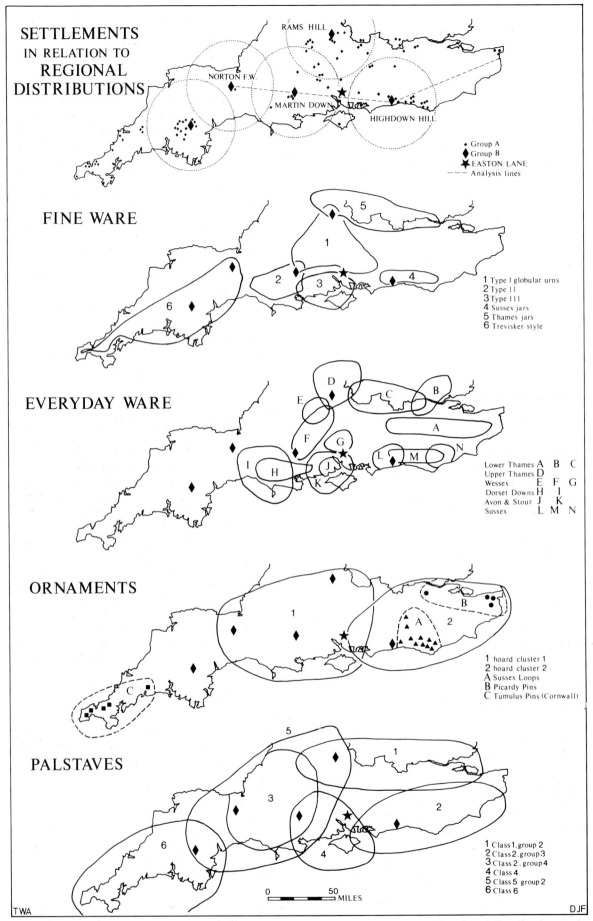

Fig 112.   Easton Lane and its relationship to other Bronze Age settlements, and regional distributions (after Ellison 1980, Fig 2).

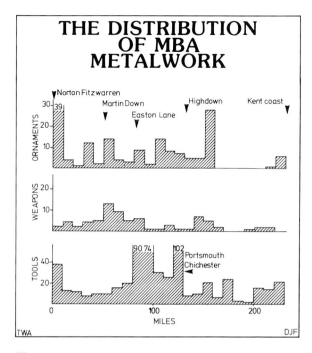

Fig 113. Easton Lane and the distribution of Bronze Age metalwork along the analysis line of Fig 112 (after Ellison 1980 and with the addition of finds made since, notably Hughes and Champion 1982)

which were still in use and, although the evidence for structures was confined to one area, this does not mean that the related activity was so reduced.

At Easton Lane there was a period early in the last millennium BC for which there is no evidence, or for which the evidence, mainly pottery, has still not been identified.

At Old Down Farm, Andover, there was an occupation during the 'earliest' Iron Age (Davies 1981), and on Easton Down there seems to be activity of this period (Fasham 1982). Elsewhere in Wessex, particularly in Wiltshire, this earliest Iron Age phase is well represented, perhaps most interestingly at the midden side of Potterne (Gingell forthcoming).

Early Iron Age. Easton Lane Phase 6, Winnall Down Phase 3

Although Early Iron Age pottery was recovered from Easton Lane, mainly in Area A, no further structures were added to the Winnall Down results. For the first time in at least a millennium of activity, the principle settlement was enclosed by a bank and ditch. The internal area of the enclosure was 0.4 hectares which, it has been argued, was divided into separate areas for living, weaving, grain storage and perhaps bone working. In the enclosure there was one gully-built circular structure, seven post-built circular buildings and various auxiliary structures. The whole enclosure formed a relatively self-contained unit, although it is possible that the enclosure ditch and bank were breached in the northwest corner during this period.

Early Middle Iron Age. Easton Lane Phase 7, Winnall Down no phase

There was always doubt about the continuity of activity at Winnall Down from the Early Iron Age to the Middle Iron Age. The pattern of discontinuity was not fully explored in the Winnall Down report. The discovery of Iron Age occupation features associated with early vegetable-tempered (Fabric B3) saucepans fills a gap in the occupation sequence known from Winnall Down. The Early Middle Iron Age occupation recorded at Easton Lane to the west and northwest of the Winnall Down enclosure was defined by the existence of the Middle-Late Bronze Age ditch systems, with ditches 176, 729 and 1810 in the west, ditch 1493 in the north and ditch 3692 in the south. Ditch 928 divided the excavated part of this settlement into northern and southern elements. The zone of occupation may extend into the unexcavated land west of Winnall Down.

The Early Middle Iron Age occupation included nineteen gully and post-built circular structures. In the southern area, south of ditch 928, there was insufficient space between ditch 1810 and the east of the excavations to observe any east-west spatial patterning of features. A possible north-south arrangement could be identified. CS 5602 in the southwest corner may have been a discrete element with an auxiliary structure, 5632, attached. Circular structure 5634 might have been a focal point for circular structures 5633 and 5638 and four-post structures 2158 and 5659. It is possible that these structures were all to the west of a north-south path. The northern part showed clear evidence for internal organisation. The structures were grouped on either side of a central north-south path or road which probably entered this part of the site between fences LS 5645 and LS 5646. The north of the area was defined by ditch 1493, and the evidence suggests that there was an open space, or certainly no gully-built houses, in a six metre wide band south of the ditch. To the east of the path, structure 2408 appeared as a principle building with the miscellaneous structure 2410 perhaps being used as animal pens. The semi-circular gully structures 2160 and 5622 were probably successive. They seem to work best as shelters for working in or behind. A similar pattern of principle building, 2404, with ancillary stuctures was present west of the path and along ditch 176. In this group are a series of short, straight post arrangements. There was a range of structures west of ditch 176 which may be contemporary.

Four of the structures assigned to the Early Middle Iron Age, 5634, 2404, 2288 and 2408, were of standard form, with penannular gullies in varying degrees of completeness. Within these, concentric rings of post-holes were apparent, although it was not always possible to suggest definite internal plans. The indications were that the internal rings were quite slight, thereby making it less likely that a first floor could have been supported on a horizontal plate surmounting the post-ring. Perhaps this reflected a desire to minimise on timber use in an area of open downland (see Allen, above 134).

Given that the size and extent of the inner post-rings is unclear, it is difficult to assess the position of the outer wall. The question arises with penannular gullies as to whether they were foundation trenches or drainage gullies. Certainly Pryor has cogently argued that the gully around Structure 1, Newark Road subsite, Area IV (Pryor 1980), functioned as an eavesdrip drain which fed into a drove ditch, thereby making it likely that the outer wall occurred somewhere between the gully and the internal post-ring. On the other hand, in Phase 4 of Winnall Down (Fasham 1985), post-settings were recorded within the penannular hut gullies, as they were in CS 2408 at Easton Lane. The reconstruction of the Conderton house allowed Reynolds (1983) to observe that the predicted drip gully below the eave did not occur, indeed the sheltered area encouraged the growth of grass which in turn protected the ground. It would seem likely therefore that, where gullies relate to drainage, they are deliberately created rather than the effect of erosion. At Easton Lane it is difficult to see how the penannular gullies could have worked as drains, and so they have been considered as foundation trenches or perhaps as prepared ground for stake emplacement, although direct evidence for post-settings within gullies occurred only with the gully around CS 2408.

A number of secondary structures were recorded amongst the gully-built structures, eg 4019, 4020, 2410, 5633 and 2406. These were initially recognised merely as discrete clusters of post-holes. In some it was possible to suggest the presence of a post-ring, eg 5633, 4019 and 4020, and therefore that the structures could have been roofed. In others, eg 2406 and 5656, only recurrent patterns of post-hole arcs were discernible, and roofed structures could not be posited. This type of arc was also recognised within gully-built structures 2404 and 2408, and MS 2410 and MS 4019. Four-post structures and four-post lines were also recognised.

From this it will be seen that a variety of different structures, which presumably fulfilled a variety of different functions, coexisted. In the absence of anything other than minimal recovery of artefacts specific to structures, it is difficult to speculate further as to the functional division of buildings. However, the general arrangement of the structures would seem to suggest that the four main gully-built structures represent living space for four family-sized units. Structures 5622 and 5602 may represent accomodation for dependant relative groups while the rest of the structures provided additional working and storage space. The overall layout of the structures would suggest that most were contemporary. The division into northern and southern areas by the enigmatic curved ditch 928 may represent a change of status rather than one of time, and indeed both groups retain the same alignment on the old Bronze Age ditch line.

The settlement in this period was as organised as in both the earlier enclosed phase and the later, perhaps larger, open settlement period to the east. However, only eight pits were of this phase and no environmental data are available from them. When the scarceness of the pits is compared with the numerous Middle Iron Age pits, it is apparent that either further pits must remain undiscovered or that a different form of storage served the settlement during this phase. Possibly the small ovoid post-hole groups discovered both inside and outside the main structures were the result of a form of above ground storage.

Middle Iron Age. Easton Lane Phase 8, Winnall Down Phase 4

The Middle Iron Age activity was restricted to sixteen pits among and on the eastern fringe of the Early Middle Iron Age settlement, but west of the contemporary settlement at Winnall Down. The Middle Iron Age settlement excavated in 1976–7 was very clearly defined. A group of about 70 pits were in a broad band running north-south. West of the pits were circular gully and post-built structures, some perhaps with pits in them, and two or three pits to the west of the huts. The Easton Lane pits had one distinct difference from the Middle Iron Age pits in the east of the settlement. Maltby (1985, 105) suggested in his report on Winnall Down that the animal bone evidence for pit 6595, the most western pit excavated in 1976–7, contained the butchery waste of large mammals. A similar phenomenon has been observed on Easton Lane and Maltby has suggested that large mammal carcasses may have been butchered on the periphery of the site away from the main settlement focus.

Horse remains are an important element in the animal bone assemblages. Fish was still exploited and the seed evidence suggests that the wetter land of the Itchen valley may have been exploited for grazing or hay-making. Bracken may have been exploited for bedding; it was certainly used in the 'banjo' enclosure in Micheldever Wood (Fasham 1987) but care has to be taken to prevent bracken-poisoning of livestock (Evans 1976).

The Iron Age sequence has revealed a picture of settlement mobility moving from an enclosed settlement adjacent to its Late Bronze Age predecessor, to the edge of a ditch system laid out in the Bronze Age and presumably still visible, and then back as an open (without a ditch or bank) settlement on the site of the earlier enclosure. The west side of the enclosure having been levelled to enable houses to be built across the ditch, the east side must have remained visible, as it was incorporated into the conquest period and later enclosure system.

Late Iron Age – Early Roman. Easton Lane Phase 9, Winnall Down Phases 5 and 6.

The complete plan of the small, first century AD enclosure has not been revealed. The eastern portions of enclosures D and E lay astride the excavation area, as did the presumed continuation of the track along the eastern side of the system. The southern additions to the sequence did not seem to be as complex as the northern enclosures and related to enclosure stages II and III of Winnall Down with, on the excavated evidence, little subsequent refinement of the system. The right-angled, two-sided post-built structure, MS 5630, in Enclosure E has been assigned to this phase and is the most convincing, if incomplete, structure of the first century AD. The burial of five individuals suggested to be of this date lay on the west edge of the enclosures.

Late Saxon and Medieval. Easton Lane Phase 10, Winnall Down Phase 7

One of the underlying themes behind the design of the project was the prospect of locating an Anglo-Saxon settlement of perhaps sixth–eighth century AD on the gentle ridge along which Easton Lane ran. There was no such settlement. There was, however, the Late Saxon complex in Area F. The ditched enclosure was 40m by 16.5m with an entrance to the east. It has always been interpreted as an enclosure although it could, of course, have been a building. However, its overall dimensions and lack of post or plank settings, either within the ditch or cut into the surrounding chalk, suggest otherwise. Dimensions such as 12.5m by 6.7m for S13 from Portchester (Cunliffe 1976, 34–39) or ranges of about 17m by 6m for the larger eleventh–twelfth century structures at Brighton Hill South, Basingstoke (Fasham and Keevil forthcoming), are common for post-in-slot construction buildings, while the post-pit forms present at Cheddar (Rahtz 1979) were only slightly larger (c 17m by 8.5m for west halls I-III). Even structures of great social importance such as the Middle Saxon timber hall at Northampton (Williams 1985) measured only 29.7m by 8.6m and hall A3 from Yeavering (Hope-Taylor 1977) 30m by 9.9m. In both cases these were main halls with subsidiary annexes, not single constructions.

General Considerations

In the report on the 1976–7 excavations of Winnall Down it was noted that the site was part of a complex of contiguous settlements, fields and tracks spread over 600 hectares of the Hampshire countryside (Fasham 1985, 134). In 1982/3 a further ten hectares of that landscape was investigated, and produced important evidence for an additional phase to the Iron Age, a phase of activity that was missing from the Winnall Down excavations. Greater chronological depth was given to the whole landscape, especially for various activities in the second millennium BC.

The known sequence in this landscape started in the middle of the fourth millennium BC with construction of the interrupted ring ditch, which remains an unusual phenomenon in the archaeology of Hampshire in this period. Activity restarted about 2000 BC with the inhumation in the pit, the possible arc of pits immediately south and the hints elsewhere

in the excavated area of domestic activity, or at least of flint-working.

The precise nature, form and intensity of activity during the second millennium BC is not clear. The site investigations record several areas of activity represented by huts and other structures, cemeteries and field boundaries, but the evidence is not sufficient to claim a continuity of activity in the second millennium BC. The excavation has examined ten hectares out of a prehistoric landscape of 600 hectares and, if settlement generally was mobile during the Bronze Age, then it is unlikely that a relatively small excavation would or could produce evidence for continuous activity during that period. It is more likely that the excavation has recorded some elements of that mobility as and when the focus of activity extended into the areas under investigation. However interpreted, as several elements of a small mobile family unit or as a larger trading complex, the precise evidence for Bronze Age activity is valid and will always be a subject for reinterpretation. The chalkland of southern England in the Bronze Age seems to have supported a series of homesteads in fields with occasional larger sites and defended enclosures, supplanted by the linear ditch systems indicative of a different agricultural regime but not necessarily disturbing the patterns of settlement.

Four houses associated with post-Deverel-Rimbury pottery were recorded in the Winnall Down excavation but the next evidence for occupation was the furrowed bowls in the ditch of the D-shaped enclosure. Once again settlement had moved out of the area of the investigation, although within the broader landscape, there is evidence from Easton Down (Fasham 1982) for activity in this period. From the introduction of furrowed bowls to the end of the first century AD, with the possible exception of the time of the earliest saucepans, a continuous sequence of occupation has been recorded and there is clear structural patterning and shifts in focal centres of the occupation. It has been necessary to impose crude chronological divisions in what might be gradual shifts from the enclosed settlement to the open settlement to the west and open settlement back on the site of the enclosure. Perhaps settlement mobility should be perceived as a continuous movement rather than episodic phases. The episodic nature of this movement may account for the changing relative frequencies of pottery types in primary positions in features or residual material.

The relationship of the second Winnall enclosure, assuming it to be Iron Age, has not been considered, but as with the earlier phases, only a part of the Iron Age landscape has been investigated.

There seems to be a hiatus at the end of the first century BC when pottery of that period was present but not in primary positions in features and thus there seem to be no substantial features. By the conquest, however, the features and the pottery are present in abundance. The enclosures are devoid of really convincing contemporary structures and it is hard to understand the nature of the activities, but the ditches of the enclosure system are filled with pottery. The pentagonal cropmark enclosure with an internal rectangular feature about 400m east of the excavations may be a Romano-British temple, but other components of the Roman landscape, including the settlement foci, are not obvious.

The Late Saxon enclosure on the north of the site was a surprising discovery and was presumably used for agricultural purposes.

In the Winnall Down report attempts were made to guess population size from a combination of floor areas of huts and grain storage capacity. The data from the Easton Lane excavations are insufficient to extend that exercise, but it is worth just considering the floor area of the structures (Table 33). The principle structure through all the settlement stages was the circular house; a simple post-ring initially, but eventually incorporating a foundation gully of some form. Most of the Bronze Age circular structures were of relatively elegant and well-designed forms with fairly regular spacing of posts and elements of symmetry, although some showed considerable lack of co-ordination. There was only the one terraced structure and, despite all efforts and arguments, its date remains uncertain. The emergence of the gully form of foundation seems to occur, as an experiment, in the Early Iron Age and is subsequently developed later in the Iron Age. At Little Waltham the gully-built structures dated to *c* mid-third to late-second centuries BC (Drury 1978). Even when allowing for the outer walls of post-ring structures being outside the post-hole ring, the size of the average structure per period increases smoothly through time, as Table 33 shows.

Table 33. Winnall Down and Easton Lane structure sizes.

Period	Average structure size (expressed as covered area in m²)
Middle Bronze Age	33
Late Bronze Age	59
Early Iron Age	71
Early Middle Iron Age	106
Middle Iron Age	98

In considering the Iron Age houses in a little more detail, if we take five structures, 2288, 2404, 2408, 5602 and 5634, as the maximum number of houses likely to have been standing at any one time during the Early Middle Iron Age, the resulting combined surface area, taking the outer house walls to rest on the penannular gullies, is 624.5m². At Winnall Down, during the Early Iron Age and Middle Iron Age, the maximum number of contemporary houses and combined surface areas were six and 315m² and six and 650m² respectively. This would seem to reflect the expansion from the restricted area of the Early Iron Age enclosure to the open settlements of the Early Middle Iron Age and Middle Iron Age.

Expansion, contraction and movement seem to be the key elements that have been faced in understanding the landscape evidence as revealed by the excavation.

In Conclusion

The project design for the investigation of the fifteen hectares was based on a programme of 10% sampling by transects followed by excavation of extended areas. The first three transects ominously contained no archaeological features, yet an area of ten hectares eventually was cleared of topsoil and archaeological features recorded therein. The value of a sampling strategy, as urged by Cherry, Gamble and Shennan (1978), was demonstrated in this instance. The archaeological results are exciting and much new data have been produced for several periods, both prehistoric and historic. In comparison with Winnall Down, the paucity of artefacts from the site does not allow an extension of the discussions of spatial and functional considerations of features and feature groups.

One of the implicit problems of chalkland archaeology and the study of settlement on the chalk is that of the site-specific approach. It is perfectly understandable as the only record that is preserved is on a site by site basis rather than in terms of areas. The wholesale extraction of gravel in river valleys, particularly the Thames, has long enabled the perception of settlement mobility through time to be developed. At Appleford in Oxfordshire salvage and excavation work over 20 hectares of gravel revealed features relating to the Late Bronze Age, Iron Age and Romano-British periods (Hinchcliffe and Thomas 1980). The excavation at Farmoor showed settlement mobility possibly contemporary and related to seasonal water levels, on the banks of the Thames (Lambrick and Robinson 1979). On the chalk, however, investigation into settlements has usually been site-specific: a site has been selected because of its basic morphology. Hence Little Woodbury was excavated for the Prehistoric Society (Bersu 1940) and Gussage All Saints was selected as a modern version of Little Woodbury (Wainwright 1979). At Old Down Farm there was a long sequence, interrupted in the Roman period and completed with Anglo-Saxon sunken-floored buildings (Davies 1980 and 1981).

One of the objectives of the programme at Brighton Hill South was the examination of the diachronic and spatial relationship of four apparent prehistoric and/or Roman enclosures set in 100 hectares (Fasham and Keevil forthcoming). The relationship proved quite dramatic because, of the three enclosures investigated, two were Iron Age and Roman and one was Medieval. Easton Lane produced the opportunity to investigate a large area of chalk and observe the movements and shifts of settlements and activities. There are times in the last two millennia BC when, even with the large area excavated, there is no evidence for human activity. For instance, what happened between the Late Neolithic and the earlier Bronze Age, between the

Middle and Late Bronze Ages and between the post-Deverel-Rimbury open occupation and the Early Iron Age enclosed site? Social and economic pieces of the detailed picture are still missing, partly because of the paucity of artefactual evidence in the second millennium BC and partly, for the Iron Age at least, because the second enclosure on Winnall Down remains unexcavated (Site 3 on Fig 1). This sentiment about the Iron Age was expressed in the last paragraph of the Winnall Down report. In the final paragraph of this report it is possible to record that the excavation of ten hectares of chalk has added much to the appreciation through time of settlement form and mobility, but also that the area excavated is only a small part of a landscape which has always been evolving and changing.

Chapter 6

The Microfiche and Archive

The Microfiche

A microfiche is included at the back of this volume. It contains interpretative plans of post-hole structures and appendices for the metal-working debris, human bone, animal bone, carbonised plant remains and land snail reports. Detailed contents are provided below.

Contents of Microfiche

The Archive

The context numbers which were assigned to layers, features and structures during excavation and post-excavation were retained in the published report. Archive and publication coding is therefore identical except for structure codes which received a prefix identifying type in the publication:

CS Circular structure
LS Linear structure
MS Miscellaneous structure
RS Rectangular structure.

The finds, field records and the archive are housed at the Hampshire County Museum Service (Accession Number A 1987 14). A copy of the microfiche is with the National Monuments Record.

The archive consists of field records, field drawings, post-excavation drawings and ordered files on the different classes of artefacts and feature types. All these records are on microfiche and are listed below.

References

The abbreviations used are generally those suggested in *Signposts for Archaeological Publication* (CBA 1979). Bold numbers indicate volume or series numbers.

Abercromby, J 1912 *A study of the Bronze Age Pottery of Great Britain and Ireland*, Oxford.

Addyman, P V and Leigh, D 1973 The Anglo-Saxon village at Chalton, Hampshire: second interim report, *Medieval Archaeol* **17** 1–25.

Allen, D 1981 The Excavation of a Beaker Burial Monument at Ravenstone, Buckinghamshire, in 1978, *Archaeol J* **138** 72–117.

Allen, M J 1984 Land snails from Wharram Percy, unpub AM Lab Rep 4203.

———— 1985 Land mollusca of Middle Bronze Age to Early Iron Age contexts from the multiperiod site at Easton Lane, Hampshire, unpub AM Lab Rep 4626.

———— 1986 Land mollusca from the Late Neolithic/Early Bronze Age pit (F 1017) at Easton Lane (W29) Hampshire, 1982–3, unpub AM Lab Rep.

———— 1988 Archaeological and environmental aspects of colluviation in South-east England, in Groenman-van Waateringe and Robinson (eds) *Man-Made Soils*, Brit Archaeol Rep **S410**, Oxford.

Allen, M J and Fennemore, A V 1984 Field boundary ditch, Cuckoo Bottom, Lewes (TQ 393 105), *Sussex Archaeol Collect* **122**.

Annable, F K and Simpson, D D A 1964 *Guide Catalogue of the Neolithic and Bronze Age Collections in Devizes Museum*, Wiltshire Archaeol and Natur Hist Soc.

Anon 1886–7 untitled, *Proc Soc Antiq Scot* **21** 132–3.

ApSimon, A M 1954 Dagger Graves in the Wessex Bronze Age, *Univ London Inst Archaeol Rep 1954* 37–61.

Ashbee, P 1957 The Great Barrow at Bishop's Waltham, Hampshire, *Proc Prehist Soc* **23** 137–166.

Ashbee, P 1978 Amesbury Barrow 51: Excavations 1960, *Wiltshire Archaeol Natur Hist Mag* **70/71** 1–61.

Barker, G and Webley, D 1978 Causewayed Camps and Early Neolithic Communities in Central Southern England, *Proc Prehist Soc* **44** 161–86.

Barrett, J and Bradley, R 1980 Later Bronze Age settlement in South Wessex and Cranborne Chase, in Barrett and Bradley (eds) *Settlement and Society in Later Bronze Age Britain*, Brit Archaeol Rep **83**.

Bateman, T 1848 *Vestiges of the Antiquities of Derbyshire*, London.

Beex, G and Hulst, R S 1968 A Hilversum-Culture settlement near Nijnsel, municipality of St Oedenrode, North Brabant, *Berichten van de Rijksdienst voor het Oudheidkundig Bodermonderzoek* **18**.

Bell, M 1982 The effects of landuse and climate on valley sedimentation, in Harding (ed) *Climatic Change in Later Prehistory* 127–142.

Bell, M G 1983 Valley sediments as evidence of prehistoric land-use on the South Downs, *Proc Prehist Soc* **49**, 118–150.

Bersu, G 1940 Excavations at Little Woodbury, Wiltshire, *Proc Prehist Soc* **6** 30–111.

Biddle, M 1983 The Study of Winchester: Archaeology and History in a British Town, 1961–1983, *Proc Brit Acad* **69** 93–135.

Biddle, M and Emery, V W 1973 *The M3 Extension: An Archaeological Survey*, Winchester.

Bordes, F 1961 *Typologie du Paleolithique Ancien et Moyen*, Bordeaux.

Bowen, H C 1975a Pattern and interpretation: a view of the Wessex landscape from Neolithic to Roman times, in Fowler (ed) *Recent Work in Rural Archaeology*.

———— 1975b Air Photography and the development of the landscape in central parts of Southern England, in Wilson (ed) *Aerial Reconnaissance for Archaeology* 103–18.

———— 1978 'Celtic' fields and 'ranch' boundaries in Wessex, in Limbrey and Evans (eds) *The Effect of Man on the Landscape: the Lowland Zone* 115–22.

Bowen H C, Evans J G, and Race E 1978 An Investigation of the Wessex Linear Ditch System, in Bowen and Fowler (eds) *Early Land Allotment*.

Bradley, R 1980 Subsistence, Exchange and Technology – A Social Framework for the Bronze Age in Southern England *c* 1400–700bc, in Bradley and Barrett (eds) *Settlement and Society in Later Bronze Age Britain*, Brit Archaeol Rep **83**.

Brothwell, D R 1981 *Digging up Bones*, London.

Burleigh R, Longworth I H, and Wainwright G J 1972 Relative and absolute dating of four Late Neolithic Enclosures: an exercise in the interpretation of Radiocarbon Determinations, *Proc Prehist Soc* **38** 389–407.

Burstow, G P and Holleyman, G A 1957 Late Bronze Age Settlement on Itford Hill, *Proc Prehist Soc* **23** 167–212.

Buurman, J 1979 Cereals in circles – Crop processing activities in Bronze Age Bovenkarspel, *Archaeo-Physica* **8** 21–37.

Calkin, J B 1964 The Bournemouth Area in the Middle and Late Bronze Age, with the 'Deverel Rimbury' Problem Reconsidered, *Archaeol J* **CXIX** 1–65.

Catt, J A 1978 The contribution of loess to soils in lowland England, in Limbrey and Evans (eds) *The effect of Man on the Landscape: the Lowland Zone* 12–20.

Cherry J F, Gamble C, and Shennan S 1978 *Sampling in contemporary British archaeology*, Brit Archaeol Rep **50.**

Christie, P M 1967 A Barrow-cemetery in the Second Millenium BC in Wiltshire, England, *Proc Prehist Soc* **33** 336–366.

Clarke, A J 1975 Magnetic Scanning, in Fasham (ed) *M3 Archaeol 1974*, Winchester.

Clarke, D L 1970 *Beaker Pottery of Great Britain and Ireland*, Cambridge.

Clarke D V, Cowie T G, and Foxon A 1985 *Symbols of Power at the Time of Stonehenge*, Edinburgh HMSO.

Collis, J R 1978 *Winchester Excavations: Vol II*, Winchester.

Corney A, Ashbee P, Evison V I, and Brothwell D 1969 A prehistoric and Anglo-Saxon burial ground, Ports Down, Portsmouth, *Proc Hampshire Fld Club Archaeol Soc* **24** 20–41.

Coy, J P nd Animal bones from the Micheldever Banjo, Hampshire, R27, M3 Motorway Rescue Excavations, unpub AM Lab Rep 3288.

Cunliffe, B W 1970 A Bronze Age settlement at Chalton, Hampshire, *Antiq J* **50** 1–13.

———— 1976 *Excavations at Portchester Castle: Vol II Saxon*, London.

———— 1984 *Danebury: an Iron Age hillfort in Hampshire*, Counc Brit Archaeol Res Rep 52.

Dacre, M and Ellison, A B 1981 A Bronze Age Urn Cemetery at Kimpton, Hampshire, *Proc Prehist Soc* **47** 147–204.

Davies, S M 1980 Excavations at Old Down Farm, Andover Part 1: Saxon, *Proc Hampshire Fld Club Archaeol Soc* **36**.

———— 1981 Excavations at Old Down Farm, Andover Part 2: Prehistoric and Roman *Proc Hampshire Fld Club Archaeol Soc* **37**.

DoE 1975 *Principles of Publication in Rescue Archaeology*, London.

Drewett, P L 1978 Neolithic Sussex, in Drewett (ed) *Archaeology in Sussex to AD 1500*.

———— 1979 New evidence for the structure and function of Middle Bronze Age round houses in Sussex, *Archaeol J* **136** 3–11.

Dunbar, D 1932 Corn byres of Caithness, *Proc Soc Antiq Scot* **66** 136–7.

Drury, P J 1978 *Excavations at Little Waltham 1970–71*, Counc Brit Archaeol Res Rep **26**.

———— 1983 *Structural Reconstruction*, Brit Archaeol Rep **110**.

Ellis, S 1981 Patterned ground at Wharram Percy, North Yorkshire; its origin and paleoenvironmental implications, in Neale and Fenley (eds) *The Quaternary in Britain* 98–107.

Ellison, A B 1978 The Bronze Age, in Drewett (ed) *Archaeology in Sussex to AD 1500*.

———— 1980 Settlements and Regional Exchange: a Case Study, in Barrett and Bradley (eds) *Settlement and Society in Later Bronze Age Britain*.

———— 1981 Towards a socioeconomic model for the Middle Bronze Age in southern England, in Hodder, Isaacs and Hammond (eds) *Pattern of the Past: Studies in honour of David Clarke* 413–38, Cambridge.

Evans, J G 1971 Durrington Walls: the pre-henge environment, in Wainwright and Longworth *Durrington Walls: Excavations 1966–1968*, Res Rep Soc Antiq **27**.

———— 1972 *Land Snails in Archaeology*, London.

Evans, J G and Jones, H 1973 Subfossil and modern land-snail faunas from rock rubble habitats, *J Conch* **28** 103–129.

Evans, W C 1976 Bracken thiaminase – Medicated neurotoxic syndromes, *Botanical Journal of the Linnaen Society* **773** 113–131.

Evans, W E D 1963 *The Chemistry of Death*, Charles C Thomas, Illinois.

Fasham, P J 1979 The excavation of a Triple Barrow in Micheldever Wood, Hampshire (MARC 3 Site R4), *Proc Hampshire Fld Club Archaeol Soc* **35** 5–40.

———— 1980 Excavations on Bridgett's and Burntwood Farms, Itchen Valley Parish, Hampshire 1974 (MARC 3 Sites R5 and R6) *Proc Hampshire Fld Club Archaeol Soc* **36** 37–86.

———— 1982 The excavation of four ring-ditches in Central Hampshire, *Proc Hampshire Fld Club Archaeol Soc* **38**, 19–56.

———— 1985 *The Prehistoric Settlement at Winnall Down, Winchester*, Hampshire Fld Club Monograph 2.

———— 1987 *A 'Banjo' enclosure in Micheldever Wood, Hampshire (MARC 3 SITE R27)*, Hampshire Fld Club Monograph **4**.

Fasham, P J and Hawkes, J W 1980 Computerised recording systems and analysis in an archaeological unit: some observations, in Stewart (ed) *Microcomputers in archaeology*, MDA Occ paper **4**.

Fasham, P J and Keevil, G D forthcoming *Excavations at Brighton Hill South, Basingstoke 1983–4*, Hampshire Field Club Monograph.

Fasham, P J and Whinney, R J B forthcoming *Archaeology on the M3*.

Fenton, A 1983 Grain Storage in Pits: Experiment and Fact, in O'Connor and Clarke *From the Stone Age to the 'Forty Five*, Edinburgh.

Fisher, P F 1983 Pedogenesis within the archaeological landscape at South Lodge Camp, Wiltshire, England, *Geoderma* **29** 93–105.

Fleming, A 1971 Territorial Patterns in Bronze Age Wessex, *Proc Prehist Soc* **37.1** 138–167.

———— 1979 'The Dartmoor Reaves: Boundary Patterns and Behaviour Patterns in the Second Millenium bc', in Maxfield (ed) Prehistoric Dartmoor in its context, *Proc Devon Archaeol Soc* **37**.

Forde-Johnston, J 1965 The Dudsbury Barrow and Vessels with Shoulder Grooves in Dorset and Wiltshire, *Proc Dorset Natur Hist Archaeol Soc* **87** 126–141.

Fowler, P J and Evans, J G 1967 Plough-marks, lynchets and early fields, *Antiquity* **41** 289–301.

Gingell, C J forthcoming *The Marlborough Downs*, Wiltshire Archaeol Soc Monograph 1.

Godden, B 1966 List of Bronze Age Pottery in Southampton City Museums, *Hampshire Fld Club Archaeol Soc Newsletter* **1.3** 34–37.

Godwin, H 1975 *History of the British Flora* (2nd ed), Cambridge.

Grant, A 1984 Animal Husbandry, in Cunliffe, *Danebury: an Iron Age Hillfort in Hampshire; Volume 2 The Excavations 1969–1978: The Finds*, Counc Brit Archaeol Res Rep 52 496–548.

Gray, H St G 1966 *The Meare Lake Village*, Vol 3, Taunton Castle, privately printed.

Green, C and Rollo-Smith, S 1984 The Excavation of Eighteen Round Barrows near Shrewton, Wiltshire, *Proc Prehist Soc* **50** 255–318.

Green, F J 1981 Iron Age, Roman and Saxon Crops; the Archaeological evidence from Wessex, in Jones and Dimbleby (eds) *The Environment of Man: the Iron Age to the Anglo-Saxon Period*, Brit Archaeol Rep **87** 129–153.

Green, H S 1976 Neolithic and Bronze Age Flint, Stone and Bonework from Wetton Mill Rock Shelter, in Kelly *The excavation of Wetton Mill Rock Shelter, Manifold Valley, Staffs*, City of Stoke-on-Trent Museum Archaeol Soc Rep **9** 66–74.

———— 1980 *The Flint Arrowheads of the British Isles*, Brit Archaeol Rep 75.

Grinsell, L V 1957 List of Wiltshire barrows in *Victoria County History of Wiltshire* **1** 134–245.

———— 1959 *Dorset Barrows*, Dorset Natur Hist Archaeol Soc, Dorset.

Guilbert, G 1983 Post-ring symmetry in roundhouses at Moel y Gaer and some other sites in prehistoric Britain, in Drury *Structural Reconstruction*.

Hall, D and Woodward, P 1977 Radwell excavations, 1974–75: the Bronze Age ring-ditches, *Beds Arch J* **12** 1–16.

Halpin, C in prep Barrow Hills, Radley, 1983–5.

Harding, P 1986a The Flint Industries, in Gingell *The Marlborough Downs*, Wiltshire Archaeol Soc Monograph 1, forthcoming.

———— 1986b The Flint Industries from Rowden and Cowleaze, in Woodward *The South Dorset Ridgeway: The Pre-Iron Age Landscapes*, forthcoming.

Hawkes, C F C 1939 The Excavations at Quarley Hill 1938, *Proc Hampshire Fld Club Archaeol Soc* **14** 136–94.

Hawkes C F C, Myers J N L and Stevens C G 1930 St Catharine's Hill, Winchester, *Proc Hampshire Fld Club Archaeol Soc* **11**.

Hawkes, S C 1969 Finds from two Middle Bronze Age pits at Winnall, Winchester, Hampshire, *Proc Hampshire Fld Club Archaeol Soc* **26** 5–18.

Helbaek, H 1953 Early Crops in Southern England, *Proc Prehist Soc* **18** 194–233.

Hillman, G 1981 Reconstructing Crop Husbandry Practices from Charred Remains of Crops, in Mercer (ed) *Farming Practice in British Prehistory*.

Hinchliffe, J and Thomas, R 1980 Archaeological Investigations at Appleford, *Oxoniensia* **45** 9–111.

Hodgson, J M (ed) 1974 *The Soil Survey Field Handbook*, Technical Monograph 5, the Soil Survey, Harpenden.

Hope-Taylor, B 1977 *Yeavering: an Anglo-British centre of early Northumbria*.

Hughes, M and Champion, T 1982 A Middle Bronze Age ornament hoard from South Wonston, Hampshire, *Proc Prehist Soc* **46** 487–489.

Jones, M 1978 The Plant Remains, in Parrington *The Excavation of an Iron Age Settlement, Bronze Age ring ditches and Roman features at Ashville Trading Estate, Abingdon (Oxon)*, Oxfordshire Archaeol Unit Rep 1, Counc Brit Archaeol Res Rep 28.

Jones, M 1984 The Plant Remains, in Cunliffe (ed) *Danebury: An Iron Age Hillfort in Hampshire*, Counc Brit Archaeol Res Rep 52 483–495.

Jones, M U and W T 1975 The cropmark sites at Mucking, Essex, England, in Bruce-Mitford (ed) *Recent Archaeological Excavations in Europe 1975* 133–187, London.

Kay, Q O N 1971 Anthemis cotula L, *J Ecol* **59** 623–636.

Kerney, M P 1968 Britain's fauna of land Mollusca and its relation to the Post-glacial thermal optimum, *Symp Zool Soc* **22** 273–291.

Kerney, M P 1977 A proposed zonation scheme for late-glacial and post-glacial deposits using land Mollusca, *J Archaeol Sci* **4** 387–390.

Lambrick, G and Robinson, M 1979 *Iron Age and Roman riverside settlements at Farmoor, Oxfordshire*, Oxfordshire Archaeol Unit Rep **2**, Counc Brit Archaeol Res Rep **32**.

Lanting, J N and van der Waals, J D 1972 British beakers as seen from the continent, *Helinium* **12** 20–46.

Lewis, E R and Walker, G 1977 A Middle Bronze Age Settlement Site at Westbury, West Meon, Hampshire, *Proc Hampshire Fld Club Archaeol Soc* **33** 33–45.

Limbrey, S 1975 *Soil Science and Archaeology*, London.

————— 1978 Changes in quality and distribution of the soils of lowland Britain, in Limbrey and Evans (eds) *The Effect of Man on the Landscape: the Lowland Zone*, 21–27.

Longworth, I H 1984 *Collared Urns of the Bronze Age in Great Britain and Ireland*, Cambridge.

Longworth, I H and Ellison, A B forthcoming *Pottery from Grimes Graves, Norfolk*, BM fascicule, London.

Maltby, J M 1985 The animal bones, in Fasham 1985.

————— nd 1 The animal bones from Owslebury: an Iron Age and Romano-British settlement in Hampshire.

————— nd 2 The animal bones from the Iron Age and Romano-British phases of the Staple Gardens excavation, Winchester.

Mason, C 1982 Land Snails, in Fasham 1982.

Massy, J L 1983 Circonscription de Picardie, *Gallia* **41** 231–261.

Meaney, A L and Hawkes, S C 1970 *Two anglo-Saxon Cemeteries at Winnall, Winchester, Hampshire*, Medieval Archaeol Monograph **4**.

Mercer, R J 1970 Metal arrowheads in the European bronze and early iron ages, *Proc Prehist Soc* **36** 171–213.

Millet, M 1980 *Excavations at Cowdery's Down, Basingstoke*, Basingstoke.

Monk, M A 1985 The Plant Economy, in Fasham 1985.

Monk, M A and Fasham, P J 1980 Carbonised Plant Remains from Two Iron Age Sites in Central Hampshire, *Proc Prehist Soc* **46** 321–344.

Morris, M 1987 St Martin's Close, in Hughes (ed) *Archaeology and Historic Buildings in Hampshire, Annual Report for 1986*, Hampshire County Council Planning Department.

Mortimer, J R 1905 *Forty Years' Researches in British and Saxon Burial Mounds of East Yorkshire*.

Newcomer, M H 1971 Some Quantitative Experiments in Hand-Axe Manufacture, *World Archaeol* **3** 85–94.

————— 1974 Study and Replication of Bone Tools from Ksar Akil, *World Archaeol* **6.2** 138–153.

Newcomer, M H and Karlin, C 1987 Flint Chips from Pincevent, in Sieveking and Newcomer (eds) *The Human Uses of Flint and Chert: Papers from the Fourth International Flint Symposium*, Cambridge.

Ollier, C D and Thomasson, A J 1957 Assymetrical valleys of the Chiltern Hills, *Geogr J* **123** 71–80.

Pearson, G W and Stuiver, M 1986 High Precision Calibration of the Radiocarbon Time Scale, 500–2500 BC, *Radiocarbon* **28** 839–862.

Peacock, D P S and Williams, D F 1986 *Amphorae and the Roman Economy*.

Pitts, M W 1978a On the shape of Waste Flakes as an index of technological change in Lithic Industries, *J Archaeol Sci* **5** 17–37.

————— 1978b Towards an understanding of Flint Industries in Post-Glacial England, *Univ London Inst Archaeol Bull* **15** 179–97.

Pliny 1961 edition *Naturalis Historiae Books XVII–XIX*, Rackham (trans).

Pryor, F 1980 *Excavations at Fengate, Peterborough, England; The Third Report*, Northhamptonshire Archaeol Soc Monograph **1**.

Rahtz, P 1979 *The Saxon and medieval palaces at Cheddar*, Brit Archaeol Rep **65**.

Renfrew, A C 1973 Monuments, mobilisation and social organisation in Neolithic Wessex, in Renfrew (ed) *The Explanation of Culture Change; models in prehistory*.

Reynolds, P J 1967 Experiment in Iron Age Agriculture, *Trans Bristol Gloucestershire Archeaol Soc* **86** 60–73.

————— 1974 Experimental Iron Age Storage Pits: an Interim Report, *Proc Prehist Soc* **40**, 118–131.

————— 1983 Substructure to superstructure, in Drury 1983.

Richards, J C forthcoming *The Stonehenge Environs Project*, HBMC.

RCHM 1979 *Long Barrows in Hampshire and the Isle of Wight*, HMSO.

Rowlands, M J 1976 *The Organisation of Middle Bronze Age Metalworking in Southern Britain*, Oxford.

Russel, A forthcoming An early Beaker grave at Chilbolton, Hampshire, *Proc Prehist Soc*.

Samels, N A nd *Statistical Analysis of sample data from Easton Lane: an Archaeological site*, unpub dissertation, University of Southampton.

Saville, A 1981 *Grimes Graves, Norfolk, Excavations 1971–2 Vol II The Flint Assemblage*, London.

Scaife, R G 1982 Late-Devensian and early Flandrian vegetational changes in southern England, in Bell and Limbrey (eds) *Archaeological Aspects of Woodland Ecology*, Brit Archaeol Rep **S146** 57–74.

Schadla-Hall, R T 1977 *The Winchester District: The Archaeological Potential*, Winchester.

Semenov, S A 1964 *Prehistoric Technology*.

Shackley, M L 1976 The Danebury Project: an experiment in site sediment recording, in Davidson and Shackley (eds) *Geoarchaeology*, London.

Shennan, S J 1985 *Experiments in the Collection and Analysis of Archaeological Survey Data: The East Hampshire Survey*, Sheffield.

Smith, I F 1965 *Windmill Hill and Avebury: Excavations by Alexander Keiller 1925–1939*, Oxford.

Smith, I F and Simpson, D D A 1966 Excavation of a Round Barrow on Overton Hill, North Wiltshire, *Proc Prehist Soc* **32** 122–155.

Stewart, T D 1979 *The Essentials of Forensic Anthropology*, Springfield, Illinois.

Teichert, M 1975 Osteometrische Untersuchungen zur Berechnung der Widerristhohe bei Schafen, in Clason (ed) *Archaeozoological Studies*, 51–69 Amsterdam.

Thomas, K D 1977a 'The mollusca from an Iron Age pit at Winklebury', in Smith, The excavation of Winklebury Camp, Basingstoke, Hampshire, *Proc Prehist Soc* **44** 70–74.

———— 1977b 'A preliminary report of the Mollusca from the lynchet section', in Bell, Excavations at Bishopstone, *Sussex Archaeol Collect* **115**, 258–264.

Thorpe, I J and Richards, C 1984 The decline of Ritual Authority and the Introduction of Beakers into Britain, in Bradley and Gardiner (eds) *Neolithic Studies*, Brit Archaeol Rep **133**, Oxford.

Tomalin, D 1983 *British Biconical Urns: their character and chronology and their relationship with indigenous Early Bronze Age ceramics*, unpub PhD thesis, University of Southampton.

Trotter, M 1970 Estimation of stature from intact long limb bones, in Stewart (ed) *Personal Identification in Mass Disasters* 71–83, Washington National Museum of Natural History.

Wainwright, G J 1979 *Gussage All Saints: An Iron Age Settlement in Dorset*, London.

———— 1979 *Mount Pleasant, Dorset: Excavations 1970–1971*, Res Rep Soc Antiq **37**.

Wainwright, G J and Longworth, I H 1971 *Durrington Walls: Excavations 1966–68*, Res Rep Soc Antiq **27**.

Wainwright, G J and Spratling, M 1973 The Iron age settlement of Gussage All Saints, *Antiquity* **47** 109–130.

Walden, H G 1976 A nomenclature list of the land mollusca of the British Isles, *J Conch* **29** 21–25.

Warne, C 1866 *The Celtic Tumuli of Dorset*, London.

Waton, P V 1982 Man's impact on the Chalklands: some new pollen evidence, in Bell and Limbrey (eds) *Archaeological Aspects of Woodland Ecology*, Brit Archaeol Rep **S146** 75–91.

Williams J H, Shaw M and Denham V 1985 *Middle Saxon Palaces at Northampton*, Northampton Development Corporation Archaeol Monograph **4**.

Willis, G W 1954 Bronze Age Burials round Basingstoke, *Proc Hampshire Fld Club Archaeol Soc* **18** 60.

Wilson, G H nd *Cave Hunting in Peakland, Chesterfield*, privately printed.

Woodward, P J forthcoming *The South Dorset Ridgeway Survey and Excavation 1977–1983: The Pre-Iron Age Landscapes*, Dorset Natur Hist Archaeol Soc Monograph.